Graphic Design

Graphic Design

**Graphic Design**

Graphic Design

Graphic Design

Graphic Design

**Graphic Design**

Graphic Design

Graphic Design

Graphic Design

Graphic Design

Graphic Design

*Russell W Blanchard*

# GRAPHIC
# DESIGN

# GRAPHIC DESIGN

*Russell W. Blanchard*

PRENTICE-HALL, INC., Englewood Cliffs, New Jersey 07632

*Library of Congress Cataloging in Publication Data*

BLANCHARD, RUSSELL W. (date)
  Graphic design.

    1. Graphic arts—United States. 2. Commercial artists
—Vocational guidance—United States. I. Title.
NC998.5.A1B56 1984        741.6′0973        83-24710
ISBN 0-13-363226-1

Editorial/production supervision: Barbara Alexander
Interior, color insert, and cover design: Christine Gehring-Wolf
Page layout: Maria Carella
Art paste up: Jill S. Packer
Manufacturing buyer: Harry P. Baisley

Printed in the United States of America
10  9  8  7  6  5  4  3  2  1

ISBN 0-13-363226-1

Prentice-Hall International, Inc., *London*
Prentice-Hall of Australia Pty. Limited, *Sydney*
Editora Prentice-Hall do Brasil, Ltda., *Rio de Janeiro*
Prentice-Hall Canada Inc., *Toronto*
Prentice-Hall of India Private Limited, *New Delhi*
Prentice-Hall of Japan, Inc., *Tokyo*
Prentice-Hall of Southeast Asia Pte. Ltd., *Singapore*
Whitehall Books Limited, *Wellington, New Zealand*

# CONTENTS

v

# Part III  THE DESIGN PROFESSION

# Part IV  THE MECHANICS OF DESIGNING

# PREFACE

Design is an art form. It is, perhaps, one of the most exciting and interesting of all art forms because it grows from so many experiences and blooms in so many expressions. Seeing design work reproduced through mass media forms is as rewarding for the designer as a successful exhibition is for the painter, sculptor, or other visual artist. Design, in all its forms, is art for human use. It is as close to being "art for the masses" as any art medium will ever be. At its best, it is as intellectually and aesthetically profound as any of the "traditional" fine art forms. At its worst, it is no more badly conceived nor visually ugly than any other art medium. The one great difference between design and its sister art forms, is that its beauty or ugliness is seen and consumed by millions of people everyday. It is not sheltered in the cloistered halls of galleries and museums.

Design is the only constantly regenerative, throw-away art form. It is governed by its own rules, separate from its creative counterparts, and rebuilds not only in reaction to itself, but from the constant human need for change from the status quo. The basic theories and principles of art are no different for applied design than for the fine arts. They are only more specifically employed.

Graphic Design is a major discipline in the art form of design. The variety of guises it assumes makes it one of the most blatantly influential. And Graphic Design is the one discipline that thrives on rapid change. This is a book for the would-be Graphic Designer. It is above all practical, a book of specifics as well as theory, with basic Graphic Design information—skills, tools, procedures—its key focus. It also gives an overview of Graphic Design in all its varied aspects . . . and they are many. This book will give the student a factual presentation of what a career in Graphic Design will be like.

The creative process of design is as varied as the individuals that make up the profession. The theoretical basis for one designer's work may be the very antithesis of another's. Indeed, it might be safe to say that what professional designers have most in common is their lack of agreement on the aesthetic principles of design. If there is a common thread, it is in the professionals' approach to the *practice* of design. Unfortunately, for the student, knowledge of the practice of design is difficult to come by. Like doctors, many designers are reluctant to talk about the everyday aspects of their profession to anyone but their fellow professionals. The general attitude is still pretty much one of letting young designers experience the "ins and outs" of design for themselves. Reasons for this attitude among professionals and educators vary. Some feel the "nitty-gritty" aspects of design might turn off or discourage the young designer. Others believe that the "adjustment period" approach to the business world is a part of the initiation into the ranks of the profession. Many instructors in design schools feel, perhaps rightfully, that four years is too few to mold both "a design aesthetic" in their charges *and* introduce students to the world of professional practice. Ancient animosities between the theoretician and the practitioner also come into play. All professional designers consider it imperative for the beginning designer to be familiar with the working skills of the profession. All design educators are concerned with laying out a theoretical basis for design and the teaching of design thinking. Too few individuals at either end of the design spectrum place much importance upon having a general understanding of the *nature* of the *design business* or the *process* of *design development* in the "real" world.

What many teachers and designers fail to realize is that today's students *want very much* to understand that process, and to know what the different branches of the design field have to offer them as individuals. Today, students are not so much concerned with just getting a design job as they are with getting into an area that is compatible with their values and goals; one that will carry them along the path they want to travel. There is no question that experience is a good basis for judging one's interest and potential, but it is not the only basis worth consideration. There is no reason why the design *student* should not have as much right, opportunity, and encouragement to consider *in advance,* areas of his field that interest him. Law, business, medicine, and many other professional curriculums offer this.

Ultimately, this book is a travelogue, a Baedecker of Graphic Design, that presents a sampling of its best (and the worst) aspects for the young designer who will one day be going out, portfolio in hand, to beat down the doors of the design establishment.

## *What Is Graphic Design?*

What areas of design fall into the all-too-vague category of "Graphic"? What makes the Graphic Designer different from the Industrial Designer, the Interior Designer, or the Exhibit or Environmental Designer?

Actually, there is some argument over what "Graphic" Design is, or is not. Webster defines *graphic arts* as "the fine and applied arts of representation, decoration, and writing or printing on flat surfaces together with the techniques and crafts associated with them,"

and defines *designer* as someone who "devises something for a specific function or end," who "makes a drawing, pattern or sketch according to plan," and *design* itself—in part—as "a mental project or scheme in which means to an end are laid down." Distilling all this to a workable definition, a Graphic Designer should be someone who deals with the creation, planning, development, and execution of visual graphic treatments and applications on all "flat" surfaces. This is a seemingly reasonable definition, yet there are grey areas of Graphic Design where theoreticians and practitioners disagree, among themselves and with each other.

The Industrial Designer (who is basically concerned with the design and development of three-dimensional objects) prefers to think of Package Design as an area of expertise within the Industrial Design discipline. In reality, Package Design is a unique category with its own systems and procedures, very different from all others. Yet, even in its uniqueness, it is closer to Graphic Design in concept and development. Indeed, the best work in packaging is generally done by designers with a heavy background in visual "surface" design.

Interior Design deals with visual, wall (flat) graphics and color applications that are "graphic" by definition, yet fall well within either the Graphic Design or the Interior Design scope of expertise.

Many Graphic Designers work in video and film, yet both of these disciplines require specialized knowledge and the mastering of techniques outside the realm of Graphic Design. Both mediums are visual, but technology has spurred their evolution toward disciplines unique unto themselves.

Some think Illustration belongs within Graphic Design because it is traditionally associated with print design, requires many of the same skills, and is conceptually similar. Indeed, many designers are fine illustrators. In reality, however, Illustration is primarily concerned with drawing and mastering plastic mediums traditionally associated with painting and printmaking. Though most designers consider it essential for the student to master drawing and sketching, and though designers do paint and make prints, Illustration is not the area in which the Graphic Designer expends most of his working time.

We have pointed up some of the grey areas associated with Graphic Design, and given our opinion as to where they belong in relation to the designer. We have not as yet, however, defined *Graphic Design* itself. For this text *Graphic Design* will include the following disciplines:

1. Corporate Identity Design and Corporate Communications Design: the design of images and graphic materials for corporate use
2. Print Design for Advertising and Collateral Design: print ads and all types of support advertising (pos-

ters, billboards, mailers, brochures, sales promotion items, etc.)

3. General Publications Design: mass-audience books, magazines and newspapers, and other publications
4. All Types of Graphic Signage Design: commercial identifiers, environmental, information, and directional graphics
5. Package Design: the visual development of all types of packaging materials

# *The Education of the Graphic Designer*

Almost all professional designers working today are products of universities or art or design schools. Fifteen years ago, such schools could not offer the total intellectual and creative training needed to prepare designers for careers. Today, typical design graduates leave the carefully constructed academic environment more or less ready to enter the profession. The portfolio has been manicured to the best of their and their instructors' abilities, and they have benefited from at least two years of concentrated, professionally oriented training. Usually, if their talent is merely adequate and technical proficiency is evident, it is enough to insure some kind of position somewhere.

To the prospective student looking for the "right" design school, a professional approach is the measuring stick of a competent design program. Elaborate, professionally oriented programs are now becoming a part of our educational process. Schools where no design programs existed five years ago, have suddenly realized the need to compete for a growing number of professionally minded art students. The pressure for "relevant" design programs is on in earnest. Yet, who is to decide what is a relevant design program? This and other major concerns loom large on the horizon, and questions are being asked by design professionals and educators alike.

The balance between theory and practice in design education is a delicate one. An imbalanced education can be dramatically pinpointed in the professional end-product, but is not so readily apparent in the learning process itself. Unfortunately for the student, it is at the educational level that important decisions affecting your whole life must be made. It is relatively easy to change jobs or even areas of interest within a profession, but it is a herculean task to "redo" an entire education.

Too many "relevant" design programs are turning out designers who are nonverbal individuals. Especially true in the Graphic Design field, this is an ap-

palling circumstance for artists who deal in art for human use. Almost as bad, many designers are sadly lacking in the intellectual and philosophical traditions of art, something no real artist can afford to be without. Design requires individuals who have a broad background and range of interests. It also demands artistic balance. To be a successful designer, a person must have a very wide understanding of the world in which he or she lives. Most American designers have these characteristics, but the number who don't is far too high.

Perhaps Graphic Designers don't take their medium seriously enough as a social and environmental statement? Is this due to an inadequate education in art history? Is the Graphic Designer not enough like his or her counterparts in other fields? Painters, sculptors, architects—all, in roughly the same amount of educational time, begin to fabricate an intellectual approach to their work which applies in one form or another over the continuing span of their careers. Why not the Graphic Designer?

Looking at it honestly, the student who chooses a Graphic Design education is often learning theory separate from skill, with no real integration between the two: theory may be taught adequately; skills may be taught adequately; but the bridge that links them is weak. A sense of purpose and philosophy and a basic understanding of art and art history are important prerequisites for the successful artist in all fields, the Graphic Designer included. Likewise, learning to generate and channel conceptual thinking, organizing and mastering skills of communication through traditional artistic—as well as *verbal*—means, and understanding *design development procedures* as exercised in real practice, are vital to building the bridge between theory and developed skill. This "communication bridge" is sadly understressed by both professionals and educators in design.

The motto of one major design firm is: "We are in business to give the client, not what they want, but what they need!" This idea can be tough to practice when an organization depends upon profits, but it is a fine philosophy to aspire to. One of the critical flaws in design education is that, in too many instances, it is "in business" to give the design profession what it *wants* and not what it *needs*! For educational institutions, which are not mainly in business to make a critical end-of-year profit, this is a sadly flawed policy. The pressure to gain and retain a "highly respected profile" in design education sometimes generates patronage attitudes. Higher education in design is not meant to *service* the design profession's needs. It is meant to produce the potential for excellence in design.

As a young designer fresh out of college, you *will* be tolerated by the professional world for your lack of experience and unproven skills, at least temporarily. You will not be tolerated for your lack of creativity, incompetence in basic *artistic* skills, or your inability to conceptualize. Understanding and training in the "bridge" areas of design before you start your career will enhance your overall effectiveness on the job. To quote one professional designer, "Young designers catch on quickly to the routine of *how* to do things, but we don't have time to teach them *why* to do things!"

American design education is far better today than it has ever been in the past, and it is getting better every year. The most dramatic improvement in recent years has been at the state university level, where the majority of American students gain their education. No program, however, is so perfect that it could not benefit from adjustments in its curriculum on a constant and steady basis. The design student can and should contribute to the refining of curriculum, as should the concerned professional. In the final analysis, it is the talent of an individual that determines the ultimate degree of professional creativity that is attainable. Education is only the glue of creativity . . . not the spur.

# The Challenge for the Future of Graphic Design

Every designer should be constantly aware of one very important fact: the painter or sculptor, as an artist, owes the public nothing, but the designer, as an artist, owes the public a great deal. The painter's end-product, if badly conceived, will affect hardly anyone. The designer's end-product, if badly conceived, can visually or physically disrupt the lives of many people. The painter's work rarely reflects the needs of the public; the designer's must reflect those needs to a great degree. This responsibility to the public is one of the major differences between design and the nonfunctional fine arts.

Designers, at their best, bring together the grace and timelessness of beauty, the functional excitement of human use, and the power of mass production, making them the ultimate "public" artists. Art to use— living, working art; hold-in-your-hand art; buy–discard– buy-again art; art that can be absorbed into daily life—is the most powerful of all art, and the designer is responsible for it. This responsibility *must* weigh heavily upon the designer's personal integrity. Designers at their worst—without responsibility and integrity, with minimal training and talent, working to no personal standard—diminish an incredibly fine heritage, pollute the contemporary environment, and establish a poor base for the standards of the future.

The designer's basic challenge is to help make the world an integrated, visually unpolluted environment. This almost superhuman task will never be totally accomplished, but attempting even a fraction of it re-

quires the very best-trained minds and talents. Many things are beyond the designer's control, and the best of ideas can become mundane, but when the designer offers anything less than his best creative effort at problem solving, he or she is cheating the recipient: the public who must ultimately put up with second-rate solutions. Designers also cheat themselves and their profession by compromising their most basic standards. When the public accepts poor design, they are negating the role of the designer and compromising their environment.

Many interchanges on the present and future aspects of design are traded by designers, but the bulk of these interchanges are directed inward amongst themselves and those professions linked with design. Unlike associations of other professions, designers have no natural inclination toward "high profile" publicity, or the organizational propensity for promoting public awareness. Designers have few truly effective associations such as the theatre, medical or legal professions which promote design as a whole. The designer cannot successfully achieve the ideals he or she aspires to without learning to master the business of self-promotion. Success in educating business and the consumer to the importance of good design requires first educating the designer to the point where he or she is capable of effectively educating others.

There is no reason that the design of a package, magazine advertisement, or television commercial should not be as carefully considered and designed from the human viewpoint as that of a good bus, building, or highway. If it is easier and more enjoyable to drive on a well-designed superhighway, it is likewise easier and more enjoyable to view a creative television message, read a beautifully designed magazine or book, or pass by a beautifully designed graphic on the street. If it were possible to create such things by simply being "creative," there would be no need for designers. The designer's role is specific, and so is the designer's relationship to those who are in decision-making positions concerning his end-product.

Understanding business practice is also essential, if the designer is to effectively garner cooperation from the business community. Without a working knowledge of marketing theory and how and why people buy and use things, the designer cannot effectively solve communication problems. A designer without this knowledge is like a physician well versed in the science of medicine, but who is unable to relate it to the physical and mental needs of the people who come for consultation and cure. That physician is an incomplete healer, and, in allegorical comparison, that designer is an incomplete environmental healer. Communication is a two-way street. Designers must show they can maintain their half before fairly expecting anyone else to do the same.

## *"Wrist Work" Versus "Brain Work"*

All successful artists are masters of the mediums they work in. This is true of all the arts. It is certainly so in good design: designers must master such mediums. Knowing and being expert with one's tools is essential because it makes the process of translating ideas to a presentable form easier—and the easier and quicker the mechanical tasks, the more time there is for creative thinking.

As a designer, at least sixty percent of your working time will be spent involved with uncreative, time-consuming, and possibly tedious tasks. And the process of building one's ideas for presentation is usually the designer's own responsibility. The beginning designer is especially concerned with performing basic skills. In most cases, beginners adjust and refine their own layouts and designs, produce their own comprehensives, and specify, as well as order, their own type. Experienced designers oversee the development of key-line art and the constant series of last-minute revisions that inevitably occur. These responsibilities leave precious little time for creative "brainstorming," and—when you allow for the fact that being creative is not a clockwork activity that you can punch in and punch out as you please—the designing part of design is often steeped in frustration. It is unfortunate, with all our modern technology and machine intelligence, that we have not come up with a workable system that will allow the designer to spend more time "up front" at the conceptual stage of development. Until machines replace hand-power, the designer must pay his or her dues, and learning by doing is still the quickest way to design "freedom."

# FOREWORD

This is a book that is badly needed. I predict it will be welcomed not only by the students to whom it is primarily directed, but by many other designers who wish to broaden their understanding of the range and scope of the graphic design/communications field. Happily, the information presented and the attitudes and philosophical points expressed apply not only to that specific design discipline, but will be useful as a base for implementation of many other types of design projects as well. Young designers of all persuasions who are eager to expand their design horizons and practice potentials would do well to read this volume!

As an industrial designer who has been privileged to watch the slow growth of design—in all its aspects—as a cultural and commercial force over the past several decades, I have joined those who have lamented the unsatisfactory pace of this acceptance, and the lack of adequate documentation of what we do and how we do it. Thus it's good to see, in this book, a tool that might help accelerate our growth, and will certainly aid those designers who are eager for new perspectives by adding an additional dimension to designs' literary shelf.

The many points and implications of what Mr. Blanchard says must be continuously repeated to our consciousness and our consciences. Consider the vitality and variety that design provides for human use—both physical and emotional; the responsibilities of leadership which the designer must assume; the inevitability of change and the resistance it evokes; and the fact that although Graphic Design is recognized as *the* communications discipline *all* design deals with communication, whether it be architectural, product, package, or identity. The author urges us, and rightfully so, to be interested in what goes on around us, and involved.

Finally, the pragmatic information about the elements of design and how we utilize them to their optimum is invaluable, especially if we note the admonition that they, too, are subject to rapid technological and human factor changes. We are reminded that if we are victims of a closed mind we may win a few battles but we *will* lose the war.

I suggest that this is *not* inevitable, however, if we follow through in the ways this book suggests.

William M. Goldsmith   FIDSA, FSTA

# GRAPHIC
# DESIGN

# THE CONCEPT

## Chapter 1

Being creative is not a particularly novel enterprise; everyone is creative to some degree. Creativity in the arts is a finely tuned mechanism that functions with the development of a discipline.

## Information Gathering: Basis for the Design Process

To the artist, the *process* is often more meaningful than the ultimate product. This is also true for Graphic Design. In Graphic Design, however, the process is more specific, and subject to fixed sets of problems and rules. For the beginner, demanding requirements can make creating easier (by simplifying), but for the professional working in the creative mix of marketing, copy, and design, the process of designing can be more difficult and the ultimate objective harder to achieve when grappling with complexities essential to a problem. Rather than succumb to the limitations that always accompany a project of any complexity, the designer learns to utilize them to *clarify* and *define* the paths open for developing alternative solutions.

Understanding a problem's scope is essential to developing a design solution. One comes to an understanding of the problem by *communicating effectively* with (1) the people who have the problem and (2) the people (nondesigners) whose job it is to deal with nonvisual aspects of the problem. *All* design problems have nonvisual aspects that must be addressed before design solutions can be achieved. The designer cannot—nor is he or she expected to—deal with all of these aspects. Information gathering and analysis of that information is a team process, and the designer must be an effective member of that team. When the designer is not, the ultimate solution to the problem is very often less than successful.

How much time is spent in making initial stabs at a solution is critically affected by an understanding of the input. The tenor of a whole project is established by the early conceptual process. Excitement generated by the accuracy and viability of concept alternatives affects everyone involved in a project . . . even the client, who many times is included at very early stages in the creative development. Selling an idea is easy when that idea is logically developed. And an easy sell (a right solution) is desirable from everybody's standpoint.

1

Marketing is the information ingredient in design. Marketing professionals are essential team players in the design arena. The solutions themselves are "sold" from a marketing standpoint, as a marketing solution *achieved* through the practice and use of good design. *Good design for its own sake is rarely understood by clients with a marketing problem to solve, even when that problem is essentially caused by bad design practices.* All major graphic design problems are also marketing/human-factor problems.

In design practice, addressing the clients' problems and marshaling the facts begins the moment one leaves the client's office. Proposals must be written which outline objectives and costs, and working timetables agreeable to both sides must be arranged. People within the design group—marketing/business people as well as "creatives"—must be assigned to the task. Research and fact-finding must be correlated. "Meeting time"—introducing the client and the problem to the office—takes place. Strategy sessions are always necessary, sometimes with clients themselves participating. Exchanging initial ideas and impressions of the client and his problem, and analyzing the pros and cons of the present situation, are part of the orientation to the assignment. Designers involved in team efforts usually do this in an informal manner as a primer to the project launch. Only after these labors are completed does the "formal" creating begin.

## Roughing Out Ideas: Putting Information to Work

That the designer begins designing long before he or she puts a pencil to paper has been established. The "head" process (information) is, most definitely, designing. The next logical step is the "draw/think" or visual-conceptualizing stage. With all of our information solidly in place around us, what is often called the "most difficult" part of design is not so difficult after all. This is where our learned skills—our practical knowledge of tools and processes, our understanding of typography and design principles—enable us to develop ideas to the point where they are understandable (presentable) to others. Factors like psychology and preference, visibility, learning, intelligence, taste, level of sophistication—the intangibles—at once take precedence over other variables at this stage. Here the designer takes complete control of the situation and is rarely questioned while the concept takes form under his or her guiding hand. The "draw/think" step is a uniquely personal time, and every designer experiences it in a different way. To teach a single method of "draw/think,"

then, is difficult. There is no right or wrong way. Methods that produce results are "right." Learning someone else's way is only good up to the point that it complements your own sense of order, your own design intuition.

The "draw/think" step is a two-phase process: (1) roughing out ideas and (2) image making, or manipulating those rough ideas into cohesive entities through intuitive decision making.

Part of the roughing out process involves a certain amount of stimulation (conscious or unconscious) from existing graphics, usually current examples of someone's idea of the best work being done. The success of the graphics annuals and professional periodicals is due, in great part, to the designer's desire to see and develop a feel for what contemporaries are doing! This "seeing" (being attentive to others' work) is a healthy reaction that affects our own ideas and development. Creating in a vacuum is difficult and undesirable, and for the student designer, all but impossible. As a student, you should be encouraged to use hallmark examples of work in your field to stimulate your "draw/think" capabilities. Knowing that professional designers often utilize the same process to "get them going" should help you understand that no idea is so totally original it hasn't been influenced to some degree by another. Using such "starter" techniques to aid your conceptualizing (or "concepting," to use design jargon) does not signify a lack of creativity. Rather, it indicates an awareness that one's contemporaries are needed as touchstones for your own creativity.

Many design schools advocate a standard approach to "concepting": in the roughing out phase, get down on paper as many ideas as possible, in whatever time is allotted. There are several reasons for this: (1) it gives you a greater range of visual ideas for consideration and manipulation in the image-making phase of "draw/think," and (2) it keeps you from "locking in" on one idea too early and overdeveloping it, to the detriment of other possibilities. There are valid reasons for this "classic" approach used in design teaching. And ideally, it would be nice if everyone could be taught to approach concepting in this manner. Realistically, however, not everyone thinks or functions at the same level or at the same speed. Molding everyone to a standardized approach denies the very originality and variability that makes the creative process unique.

On the other hand, the essence of human nature also makes it difficult to put an idea down without tinkering with it. This weakness can trap even the most sophisticated designer, let alone the student just approaching the medium. (This can be unconscious, too. Often, what is perceived as a different idea by the designer is really nothing more than a variation of the previous idea.) Tinkering in the roughing out phase is only valid as long as it does not inhibit the development of another idea already forming in the artist's mind. This "not seeing the forest for the trees" syndrome is caused by failing to realize that an idea is *just* that, an idea! What may appear as sheer genius to the designer at the outset may be something less in the clear light of mutual evaluation and comparison. Nevertheless, one should not give up a certain amount of tinkering, nor should one be overly concerned at the inability to "shotgun" a lot of ideas in a short amount of time. Generating two or three *really valid, different* approaches good for image-making is *more* than adequate, and neither the designer nor the design student should be judged a creative failure by comparison with someone more facile at brainstorming.

The product of the roughing out phase is the "thumbnail." *Thumbnail* is Graphic Design jargon for the preliminary sketching done by the designer. Originally the word referred to the size of the sketching—traditionally quite small. Now, however, the word has become generic and is loosely used to mean all types of quick idea sketches, really a misnomer. Although strongly supported by design traditionalists, the value of the small thumbnail sketch in concepting—as a vehicle to quickly lay out an idea—is questionable. Admittedly, the organizational thumbnail is helpful in coming to grips with the complexities of folios (multiple layout spreads for publications) and for doodling something down so as not to forget a possible direction. The restrictive aspects of working so small, however, often make it impossible to express the essence of an idea. Even though the thumbnail is exclusively for the designer's benefit while working, it is always helpful if even it, in its roughest state, can communicate a thought process to someone else.

It is very important to keep in mind that not all graphic ideas begin through drawing, thumbnails or otherwise. Neither do all graphic ideas progress during the concepting stage by drawing alone. While we are probably saddled with the word *thumbnail* as a general way of identifying idea development (because of tradition), we should by no means restrict ourselves to working up all ideas from small, quick drawings. "Sketching," a term the dictionary defines in a much broader sense than just rough drawing, is really a more accurate way of describing the visual product of the "draw/think" step. The process of idea development must be done in whatever way is most comfortable and productive for the designer doing it. In many instances the product being designed dictates the size, nature, and complexity of any sketching that is done. If one achieves significant results by pushing large shapes of paper around on a wall-sized format—as a preliminary to developing a fixed graphic image—then that way is the "right" way to begin "sketching" for that project. Teaching that every

roughing out process must begin through the development of the traditional small "thumbnail," simply because that's the way it has always been done, is not valid. There is no reason why the sketching process cannot be as varied as the job at hand, and as individual as the talent of the designer.

# Image Making: Intuitive Decision Making and Creativity

With the roughing out process established, the designer steps back logically, and visually, to get an overview of the creative avenues he or she has opened. The merits of one direction or another are carefully weighed, and decisions to "work up" an idea are made. These decisions are often group efforts involving other designers (often at a higher level of responsibility) and nondesigners who are also involved in the project. Even so, the designer doing the initial creative exploration is still best able to determine the strength of a graphic idea because of personal involvement. The designer should clarify and direct others' opinions as to the possibilities inherent in the emerging idea—through his or her verbal skills and ability to sell the idea. All other considerations being equal, image making is allowed to develop before a final judgment is rendered by the creative team. At the image-making stage, the designer is completely dependent upon his or her own skills, background, and training to create a visual graphic from the workable ideas that is relevant and in good taste.

In developing the graphic image, the designer draws from a pool of talents dominated by three principle commodities: (1) intuition, (2) past experience, and (3) current values. These are *not* vague references, just as these aspects of real life are not vague. Each designer's pool of talents and commodities differs, and so do the graphic images an individual creates. Seeing things differently from others is the principle hallmark of the creative personality.

Intuition plays strongly in the designer's ability to let one factor inspire and influence another as the work proceeds. Previously unseen variables are created, experimented with, and incorporated or rejected all according to the designer's ongoing intuitive sense. Even though something may be aesthetically "correct," if the designer's intuition says that it is really not working in the present context, it should and will be wisely eliminated in favor of other options.

Intuitive sense is also a factor in evaluating an idea or a graphic's "appropriateness"—both to the product or problem and to the client. Working from basic information surrounding an assignment, the designer develops what is usually vaguely termed "a feel" for the design subject that cannot be totally accounted for in the facts and figures of the problem. Most designers are justifiably inarticulate about this sensitivity because it is not easily identified, and as long as it is in good working order, no one takes the time to question it! The designer who works directly with the client soon discovers this sense as he or she begins to "second guess" aspects of the relationship with the client. This sense of "second guessing" develops early and may be taken for granted without fully realizing what it is. Perhaps you, as a student, have found it easier to develop "the right" ideas and images for an instructor whom you are more familiar with, whose ideas and background you are aware of, someone whose personality you have some insight into. Don't view this as merely ingratiating behavior; it can be a very positive factor. Like it or not, a designer is a salesperson, and like any good salesperson, he or she will use this sensitivity to cement a positive designer-client relationship.

Past experience enables the designer to avoid major pitfalls in the image-building process. It is an accepted fact that maturity is always a productive force in a creative career. Truly creative artists get better as they get older, with very few exceptions. Unfortunately this especially crucial commodity is the one asset few young designers have early in their careers.

For the designer, past experience is more than just past experience with design problem solving. Repeatedly we have emphasized that effective designers must be well-rounded individuals with a range of interests beyond the scope of their personal talents. The designer brings many things to the drawing board . . . most of them in his or her head. General knowledge about many things aids in the concepting process. As your base of general knowledge expands, your ability to cope with problem solving expands. Specific knowledge about areas within the design field make it easier to exercise the creativity fostered by your general knowledge and background.

Specifically, the most creative concept in the world is a bust if it cannot be effectively adapted to the medium in which the designer must work. Past experience with a medium tells the designer where to begin, what limitations he or she must contend with, and just where to place the greater part of the effort that is put into an assignment. The young designer should concentrate heavily upon developing as much experience as possible, in as many areas as possible, as quickly as possible . . . to make a better, more capable designer, and in so doing hasten his or her career development.

The weathervane for the professional designer is that system of values and trends which currently affects general attitudes in society. These values are constantly changing and the designer, as a manipulator of visual mediums, should be at the forefront of this change. That is not to say that one's own personal values need change, only that an awareness of societal change is necessary. One of the real problems that plagues designers is the inability to grow after a certain point of success is reached in a career path. Fear of loss, lack of personal insight and of trust in one's own abilities, and lack of imagination can all contribute to this occurrence.

Of course, the reverse is true, too. Designers are the very manipulators of change itself . . . designers in all areas and in all disciplines. Because of this pivotal position, the designer is many times severely criticized for too eagerly anticipating a trend, thereby creating artificial needs and material values unnecessary to society. These criticisms are justifiable, and the cause-and-effect relationship has been argued seriously by many from both sides of the issues. But what these issues do, in fact, point up is just how crucial the designer's role is in the shaping of society. Unfortunately, most designers do not see the importance of their role. Compared to other artists, the designer often comes across as a very *modest,* almost timid conveyor of ideas and philosophy. This is a paradox that can be traced, at least in part, to the educational process that designers are put through. Many programs do not stress the impact of the designer's role to any *accurate* degree. Perhaps this is because design is a relatively new medium compared with architecture and painting, theatre and dance, or other historically influential arts.

Whatever the reasons, the very immediate nature and practical necessity of graphic design requires persons well trained and able to stand up to the demands of the medium as well as individuals who have something to say and have learned the courage to say it *realistically* and creatively.

Spontaneity in design is directly attributable to one's ability to understand the contemporary aspects of environment, attitude, and response. Staying "contemporary" is important for everyone who wishes to lead a well-adjusted and reasonably happy life. For the designer, keeping everybody "contemporary" is a way of life . . . not always well-adjusted, nor happy, yet always necessary!

# THE COMPREHENSIVE
## *Chapter 2*

*C*omprehensive, or "comp," is the term which identifies that piece of art used to present the idea to the client. It is most often a carefully done sketch (sometimes a tightly done rendering) that gives the client a good idea of what the graphic image will be as a printed piece. The comprehensive is an important part of the design process, because nonvisual people tend to have difficulty in recognizing the essence of an image when viewing rough sketches. It is also only natural that a client would want to see the solution to his or her problem as a reality rather than a suggestive outline. Asking "What's it going to look like?" is understandable human nature.

Comprehensives vary widely in their degree of finish from one discipline to another. The presentation of an idea for film or video, or for a print ad, will rarely be as tightly done as the comprehensive model for a package design or the dummy for an annual report. Fabricating comprehensives can be a major design expenditure, running up the cost of an assignment quickly, so great care is taken with the idea-selection process before the go-ahead is given to develop a comprehensive. The concept is decided on, and all "bugs" are ironed out, in a fine-tuning process that is a prelude to the comp itself.

## *Fixing on the Good Ideas*

In Chapter 1, we mentioned the role team judgment plays in picking the good ideas from the mediocre or bad ones. The designer's *verbal* influence weighs heavily in that process, in terms of rationale and explanation of the emerging sketching. In deciding the approaches to be finalized in comp form from the graphics of the image-making process, the designer's *visual* influence (skill-task development) can make or break an idea. How well he or she actually *designs* the idea, how good the "pool of talents" is, in other words, can have a definite effect upon those people whose job it is to make the decision to go to comp. A good idea badly done often becomes a "bad idea"!

In fixing on the good ideas, marketing input first used earlier as background information again becomes a measuring tool; this time in judgment of the relevence, effectiveness, and appropriateness of the graphic image itself. Questions often asked are: "How well does the image help convey the verbal message or the 'personality' of the client business?," "Is the visual message clear?," "Is the visual image powerful enough to stand up to the importance of the verbal idea?" And last, but not least, the question "Is it a good graphic design?" must be answered.

It is easy for the designer to become too personally involved with an image, sometimes to the point where staying objective becomes difficult. Remember always, it is best that all concerned be as objective about a job as possible. The problem of objectivity is no more a criticism of the designer than of any other individual who is intimately involved in the development of something. Team (or committee) judgment helps avoid many of the often subtle complications that can arise in judging creative efforts. The team approach insures that the concept and graphic are on track with the desires and original objectives of the design firm managing the client's problem. If belief in point *C* as a solution to the problem is established by the firm in the information-gathering phase of an assignment, it is necessary to get there logically through points *A* and *B*. Remember, *the logic of a solution will always appeal to a client when properly presented, whereas the beauty of the image may not!*

The team process of isolating the good idea(s) for presentation can be painful, even when the idea's creators are being as objective as they can. Even the best of committees—because of the nature of group decision making—tend toward compromise, and if there is one action a creative individual despises, it is compromise! The flower is always more meaningful to the gardener who grew it, and try as you will, it is often difficult to get others to see your flower exactly as you wish. Realistically too, committees do kill good ideas for no better reason than conservative consensus—or even lack of consensus altogether. Unfortunately, due to the cautious aspect of human nature, dazzling people with innovative creativity can sometimes have the opposite effect (especially in business), frightening them away from the proposed solution. This is one of the principle reasons why major changes in graphic imagery are often done in several transitional stages.

Each individual within the concept-evaluation team will bring different ways of looking at the problem. Ultimately, the concept and graphic that stand the closest scrutiny survive. In almost every circumstance other individuals than just you, the designer, will help determine what work will ultimately be shown to the client. This is not to be viewed as an injustice! Fixing on the good ideas should no more be the total responsibility of the designer than it should the total responsibility of any other specialist. No matter how much we broaden our intellectual base, designers *are* specialists, and like all other specialists, we have a naturally intensive, singular viewpoint to present on an issue. There

are too many ingredients within any given solution to a problem to be judged by one creative specialist—be that person a writer, artist, or marketing genius!

## *Fine Tuning the Concepts*

After the decisions on directions are made, the ideas to be comped are refined by the design team through a series of decisions relating to typography, color, and final compositional arrangements. Once again, the designer's judgmental skills come into play. Suggestions will be made and reasons will be given for different approaches by all involved, but usually the designer will be responsible for weighing the pros and cons of the alternatives and coming up with the "right" combination of ingredients. This process, usually ongoing throughout the preparations for the client presentation, consists of little, almost "fussy," adjustments to the art as it is being comped. A consummate sense of detail really shows up in this stage of design development. Subtleties not considered before become all-important to the success of the total image.

Often other hands and skills in addition to the designer's are employed in the comping process. When this is the case, the designer functions in a director's role, and patience and skill at interpersonal relationships are required to get the best results. In larger design firms the involved handwork required in comping is done by junior designers or specialists in production art. This frees up the designer's time to coordinate other aspects of the presentation or to begin thinking about another assignment. Because comping is labor intensive, the benefits of its being done by persons whose hourly rate is less than the designer's are obvious. In small design situations where the division of labor is not broken into hard-and-fast cost categories, the designer may very well do the actual comping, providing he or she has the necessary equipment in studio.

As mentioned at the beginning of the chapter, comprehensives vary greatly according to the needs of the design discipline in which they are being formulated. Examples in this range of variations might be generalized as follows:

1. *Comping for television and film.* "Storyboarding" a written script is the usual way television ideas are presented to clients. Storyboards consist of frames of action (usually drawn figures and situations) illustrating dialogue or descriptive copy as it proceeds throughout the allotted time of the sequence. "Highlighting" of the most important aspects of the script is done to keep the overall number of frames within presentable proportions. The type of drawing most successfully used for storyboard presentation is highly stylized

and simplified in composition, with flat bright areas of color very much like a newspaper comic strip might appear in its original hand-drawn state.

Television art directors spend considerable time perfecting their drawing styles, to present ideas clearly and attractively. Many times the images presented give a better impression of the idea than the words do. Most agencies hire art directors as much on the strength of their drawing skills as on their concepting abilities. Larger agencies may even hire illustrators who specialize in storyboarding and do nothing but presentation work. The size and format of the frames that make up a storyboard vary according to the working preference of the agency. Some agencies develop printed pads of outlined storyboard frames to save drawing time.

Storyboards are developed around ideas that relate to a theme concept and presented to clients in multiples along with scripts. Not all ideas that are scripted for a campaign are developed in storyboard form. Due to time restrictions, only the strongest or central ideas are fully drafted in presentations. Other supporting themes are presented in "key frame" drawings, larger, more complex sketches which attempt to illustrate an idea in one single image to the accompaniment of a script.

All in all, the completed presentation, ready for review, will have a studied casualness to it that is anything but casual. It has been carefully constructed to reflect the tone of the overall concept: nonspecific in detail, slightly vague in personality characterization, and open to variation and change without losing the basic identity of the original thought. The drawings and the scripts, to the word, will present an entirely positive psychological aspect. The spontaneity of the campaign concepts must be reflected in the physical elements of the presentation, and this is basically the responsibility of the illustrators and art directors who develop the imagery.

2. *Comping for packaging design.* Of all the graphic design disciplines, packaging requires the most meticulous and illusionistic style for a comprehensive. The reasons for this are simple. To be fairly judged, a developing package must be viewed in relation to its shelf competition, either singly or in multiples. This can only be done if the proposed package appears to be a finished entity. Also, because packages are rarely if ever presented singly or in isolated view in retail circumstances, multiple facings are critical to judging a potential design's shelf impact and general character. For this to be done properly, each unit of the design must be as near like every other as possible to simulate the nature of real printed packaging. This is best accomplished through mechanical processes.

The packaging designer develops ideas and images in exactly the same manner as a designer practicing in any other discipline, until the decision is made to go to finished comp. At that point the situation often develops differently. There are several ways to achieve the finished graphics necessary to packaging design.

When no more than a few packages are required or where existing packages are being minimally updated, mechanical elements such as press-down type, stats, color Xerox, and color-key processes may be used. Hand lettering, a dead art in other design disciplines, is often used to individualize a logo or product name. Done as black and white art, these stylized elements are then translated to color and applied to the package with color-key cells. Actual photography, tightly rendered drawings depicting the product, colored papers and films, and possibly even rub-down "Greek" type may complete the realistic look. All manner of materials and methods may be necessary to achieve the desired results, and sometimes much experimentation is required.

Some designers are skilled enough to do hand comping, and indeed it is sometimes preferable to actually hand paint a package from scratch. This requires a mastery of mediums, patience, and skills usually beyond the reach of young designers, and even among seasoned professionals it is a skill looked upon with great respect. This meticulous handwork is rarely done for more than one or two comps because of the time and cost restraints.

For major package redesign, new product packaging development, and other activities where there is a need for an exact final image—or for finished multiples, anywhere from ten to two hundred or more—limited silk-screen runs are printed. This requires the development of keyline art. From the approved concept direction the designer creates a tight sketch or three-dimensional "rough comp" of all surfaces incorporating all agreed upon changes. Photographic images and drawings are finalized, logo and typographic treatments are rendered, type is set, and the keyline takes shape according to the corrected sketch or rough comp. The actual proposed package is then printed, cut, formed, wrapped or whatever, and presented "en masse" to the client for evaluation.

When silk-screening a package is not practical, where it cannot be done, or when only one or two units in a finished form are necessary, a process similar to silk-screening is done in which layers of transfer material are hand printed and applied to paper or to the base material of the package. The effects achieved by this method are similar to actual screen printing but are much more perishable.

3. *Comping for collateral and corporate design materials.* In the design of booklets, catalogues, and other multiple-page materials dealing with products, services, etc., comping is usually done only for

cover ideas and for a few key "spreads" (inside page layouts). The one exception to this is the annual report, which is often detailed minutely, page by page, for executive consideration. The use of rub-down lettering, color-key materials, and photographic elements and stats is usual in comping collateral materials. Rarely will there be a need for the degree of finish seen in packaging design. Marker rendering the various ideas to be presented is adequate in most every instance, and "pencils" (pencil layout drawings outlining objects and copy for placement) are used for spreads that repeat the same basic design motif over and over again.

For booklets as complex as a product catalogue or a narrative instructional piece, the designer will not lay out every spread for presentation to the client. If the general design format or theme is not acceptable, then much time will have been lost in applying that theme throughout the piece. Usually several ideas are presented for consideration, uniformly comped (as mentioned above), with two or three spreads and a cover representing each idea. Once the decision has been made on a direction, the designer will then put in the considerable time necessary to lay out the entire book. The finished layout, either of a combination of color sketches and pencils, of all pencils, or of perhaps even all marker rendering, will then go back to the client for approval before keyline art is initiated.

The format for presenting catalogue or booklet designs may vary, but generally the graphics are arranged either in flat page spreads or built into three-dimensional "dummy" book form. In many instances the designer will request an actual made-up sample booklet from the paper supplier in the stock he or she is recommending for presentation, along with the design variations. This enables the client to get a feel for what the printed piece will be like.

4. *Comping for print advertising and promotion.* Print advertisements and promotions are usually comped in a loose marker technique similar to that used for TV storyboards. Type, always an important aspect of print advertising, is rendered by hand to approximate the feel of a particular face, and body copy is indicated with undulating or ruled lines blocked out to desired proportions. Once again, the concept is to capture the general feel of the idea without belaboring it with exactly rendered imagery. Some situations and clients require an exact projection of what the real ad or promotional piece will be. When these circumstances arise an image formulated in the usual marker style discussed above will be carried to tight comp stage in a manner similar to a package design. Type will be set, the actual image will be illustrated or photographed, and the ad will be constructed with colored films and papers, stats and color-keys, or transfer cells (color-keys that can be applied to a surface in a manner similar to transfer type).

As with designing for corporate and collateral materials, several design (and copy) solutions will be presented for· consideration. In the case of print ads where there is only one surface to design, variations in graphic imagery and format may be developed for each idea or copy variation, and themes may be explored in greater detail without expending large amounts of design time.

5. *Comping for display and point-of-purchase materials.* Like packaging design, comping for display and in-store (point-of-purchase) materials can often be an expensive and detailed process. Since the great majority of these materials are three-dimensional, graphics must be considered and designed from that standpoint. Flat sketching of the three-dimensional object with graphics is done for preliminary presentation within the design group and sometimes for presentation to the client. Where existing constructions are utilized, graphics are often applied to the actual surface during the graphics' development, and a full-blown comprehensive, perhaps as tightly done as a package, may result from these studies.

Marker sketching usually takes on quasi-architectural quality, showing the display from various angles, similar in nature to, but looser than, the rendering done for product design. A considerable number of sketch variations may be done before fixing on a three-dimensional application, and that application will evolve according to the realities of the display unit.

Where original display materials are being created, design development is a two-stage process with each stage affecting the evolution of the other. Graphics may dictate construction and vice versa depending upon the type of materials used and the amount and type of space available. An actual production run of displays is very small in comparison with a production run of packaging, which will average well up in the hundreds of thousands. Because of this and other factors, such as special dye-cuts, folds, and assembly parts, limited printing runs for presentation purposes are not common. The company contracted to make the display will fabricate an original construction from the designer's plans, to be sure it can be produced within the estimated budget, but it will not be printed with graphics. This construction or a recommended existing unit will be reviewed by the client separate from the graphics. If a three-dimensional comprehensive incorporating all elements of the project is required, more than likely it will be a carefully detailed hand comp utilizing some or all of the mechanical aids discussed previously. Needless to say, the detailing of such a large piece is a time-consuming and expensive process.

6. *Comping for corporate-image programs.* If comping for packaging design is the most meticulous and illusionistic method, comping for corporate imagery is certainly the most elaborate. Corporate identity design is a paradox in that it is the most elemental of design processes in the developmental stages and the most complex procedural design process in its implementation stages. Symbol design is perhaps the "purest" design development; that is, it is the least subject to the outward restrictions of format, method, or presentation. The designer may approach the development of a signage or corporate symbol in the same way a fine artist will approach the development of symbolic shapes within a composition. The end result of the designer's efforts may be just as abstract a reference to a set of ideas as the fine artist's finished work is to its real-world subject.

In many instances, symbols are developed and finalized in black and white before being translated to their color state. This is easily achievable because of the relative simplicity of symbolic imagery and does not require the elaborate mechanical processes necessary to comping in other disciplines. The real involvement in the detailing of a corporate identity image is in the application of the symbol to its various usages. At times this can be very complex—in size variation, surface application, and material reproduction.

Usually in corporate identity development, the image (finalized as it would appear in its applied state) is presented with several recommended applications before any elaborate systems implementation is undertaken. Often, the implementation of an image to all of its corporate usages is a stage of development contracted separately from the concept. When a systems application book is prepared along with the approved image, it is elaborately detailed and prepared by the design staff and printed in a limited run similar to that of the package multiples.

# Recrossing the "Bridge"

Designing and creative thinking does not stop when the pencil is laid down. A good three quarters of the job is still ahead after the comprehensives have been finished. This is no exaggeration.

What step comes next after designing the concept and building the comprehensive? The student designer most often will answer "setting the type and doing the keyline . . ." This is a simplistic answer that reflects ignorance about the real workings of a design assignment—but one not likely to be corrected in the classroom.

The evolutionary process of designing as taught in most university programs places almost all its emphasis on basic skill development and creative concepting, both usually permeated with a heavy dosage of design methodology. These are certainly the basic building blocks necessary to the design learning process, but not to the *exclusion* of other equally important aspects of designing . . . aspects that are obvious to any working professional. Let it be pointed out that the factor of time is often the culprit in the exclusion of material from academic programs and not the attitudes of faculty and staff. But the fact remains that many of the important "bridge" relationships of design are totally neglected.

Because of this, we will spend a few chapters in careful consideration of that "three quarters" of design involvement . . . selling, producing, finishing, proofing, and delivering the job. For the greater part of this information, we will take an actual job—a complicated, contemporary piece of design—and follow it, step by step, as it comes together as an actual printed piece put in the hands of the client. By doing this, by concentrating on the specifics of one assignment, we may better see all the components, relationships, and efforts that go into making up the total concept of design.

# SELLING THE IDEA

## Chapter 3

The importance of convincing others about the significance and viability of your creative product is as critical a part of the total creative process as any other. All of the creative concepting efforts, all of the fact-finding and marketing research that has gone into a project, can be counted a waste if the job is not presented vigorously and convincingly with good business acumen and with finesse and style.

## *The Presentation*

### SELLING YOURSELF

Presenting is more than "showing your wares." It is selling ... a very personal selling, because your product is usually your own or your associates' abilities. Every good salesperson sells him or herself first, before the product. Personal credibility always adds to the aura of the product or service, and in the design profession, where the product is so tangibly open to personal interpretation, credibility can be the key factor in a designer's ultimate success or failure.

Designers have, traditionally, not been the best of salespeople. Those designers who have been gifted salespersons have succeeded spectacularly in the profession. Unfortunately, they can probably be counted on the fingers of your hands ... with even a few fingers left over! Why is this? Why do gifted and intelligent creative artists go through life unheralded by anyone but their peers and financially unrewarded (by comparison to other professions) for their efforts? A criticism often leveled at designers is that they, like other artists, fail to think in terms of the "whole issue," that the "creative personality" speaks from a minority rather than a majority interest and lacks the perspective to generate effective persuasion. We must face the fact that this charge is, in great part, factual, or else why would it be heard again and again? Yet although the criticism is valid, its basis is not. The "creative personality" is no more or less *able* to be effective in these circumstances than any other type of individual. The simple, but apparently not so obvious, answer is that the creative personality receives little or no formal training in the business "arts" of managerial strategy and persuasion. Design curriculums are uniformly devoid of business classes of any type. The necessary specialist mentality of design is carried too far in this respect and the "bridge" relationship goes undeveloped. In order to function persuasively and deal effectively with "whole issues," the designer must *learn*! If training in design salesmanship is not *available* to the designer (for whatever reasons), changes in habits and thinking will never be effected. When the student learns how to sell design as well as he or she learns how to create it, and carries that learning into the professional marketplace, the designer's position relative to other professionals will change dramatically!

## SELLING THE CREATIVE PRODUCT

The initial presentation of work to a client is probably the most crucial point in the evolution of a design assignment. First exposure and the relative reactions to it set the pattern and tone for the entire client-agency relationship that will follow. It is often very difficult to change subtle attitudes and opinions that develop from first impressions; conversely, "getting off on the right foot" with your client will establish their confidence in your ability to make wise design decisions for them later on in the project. It doesn't take a genius to understand that doing well on a first assignment (well enough to please the client) is the *only* way to get the second assignment and develop any worthwhile account relationship.

The obvious question to address, then, is "What makes for a good client presentation?" There are a number of factors that can be tightly controlled by the team making the presentation. Note the use of the word "team" as opposed to "individual." Many design agencies believe it is better (whenever possible) for two people to handle the responsibilities for a major presentation. A lot is riding on the proposal, of course. And marketing questions often come up as well as design in relation to the visual product. With design and marketing personnel working together, in support of each other, they can be very effective in dealing with the entire scope of the project, as well as in handling specific questions that arise in either category during a presentation. The psychological aspects of having "two heads" to deal with the situation is also a plus factor.

From the client's viewpoint, designers who are knowledgeable about the product and the problem and conversant with its aspects at their level are most impressive in presentations. Remember that in hiring your design firm, they expect you to become familiar with their situation as a matter of course. Reassuring them that you have "done your homework" is exceedingly important to their feeling comfortable about design solutions you are presenting. Coming across in such a manner is the number one priority to be addressed when presenting.

Allow the client to become involved in the selection process, without condescension from the designer; this is also essential to successful presenting. This will help insure that the client does not let irrelevant subjective prejudices enter into the evaluation process. People are always more positive and cooperative when they feel they are contributing effectively in the creation of something. In reasonable situations, this always works to the advantage of the design team and the solution being recommended, providing the case for that solution is strong enough . . . which brings us to the next important point in presenting.

Always be sure you have built a strong case for your recommendation. Marshal as much hard-core data in support of your rationale as you can. Remember that you are dealing in a very subjective and interpretive medium. Your client will rarely have the aesthetic sophistication to understand, let alone appreciate, the subtle ins and outs of design relationships. What will be respected is factual material that supports your reasons for doing things your way. Even when you are dealing with corporate creative people—client's art, copy, or creative director, for example—who will probably respond to subtler creative issues, real evidence in support of your proposal will often swing the balance of the decision to your favor.

Be flexible and intuitive enough to back off of a design particular that is causing the client some problems. "Winning the battle but losing the war" is deadly in client-agency relationships. Don't be stubborn about using *only* your ideas. You could be wrong, and an alienated client will have you in an "I told you so" position later. Stubbornness does not inspire confidence in your abilities and will dig you your design grave quickly! There is never only one way to do something, and the design team should be prepared with "alternative avenues" to preserving the recommended solution, should the need arise. Being firm about a particular color, style of type, or sizing of an element is good up to a point, but if it increases the chances of a recommendation being rejected, the wise presentation team will show their willingness to search for satisfactory alternatives.

This relates back to the criticism leveled at designers that was mentioned in the beginning of the chapter. It is a tragic mistake for designers to allow their egos the luxury of being inflexible on the issue of "design integrity." *Design integrity is an optional issue seen from varying viewpoints.* God is the only designer who has never been successfully argued with in matters of aesthetics, and even in God's case, many have tried! One of the most satisfying accomplishments a design organization can credit itself with is arriving at a solution to a problem *in spite of* the difficulties placed in its way!

Leave the client with the feeling that you have

*paid attention* to all the variables that arise during a presentation. Taking notes in detail and even summarizing the body of the meeting in writing, both to the client and to design staff, is an excellent way to insure that your interpretation of the client's directives is accurate—as well as impressing the client with your effectiveness in group encounters. This reflects upon your ability to be "businesslike," an aura every successful designer and design organization must project.

Lastly, an effective presentation engenders a positive feeling of excitement about the product and the efforts put forth by the design firm, and about the recommended solution to the problem. This is necessary to carry the client momentum on a project at a crisp pace, to insure real enthusiasm toward upcoming aspects of the project (aspects that are often tedious), and to help instill in the client's mind the "rightness" of your solution. The best recommendation of all is a client who is truly happy with the results that you have achieved. After all, much of the design business is done by referral and recommendation from satisfied clients.

# PRODUCING THE JOB

*Chapter 4*

The majority of graphic design produced includes some type of photography and/or illustration as an integral part of the concept. This usually requires hiring and supervising a specialist in these areas to accomplish the aims of the designer.

## *Choosing Photographers and Illustrators*

Both the illustrator and the photographer function in a different environment from the designer. By comparison, designers are "generalists." Designers may illustrate or photograph (many do, quite successfully), but actually, the designer is as far removed from the function of each of the above as from the function of the writer or other creative talents.

Most photographers and illustrators are selling a very specific product, and especially in the case of the photographer, a product that requires involved technical know-how to successfully achieve. Generally, their work and their talents are represented by others who devote full time to that end. Unlike designers who must cope with and contribute to a "blitz" of information and ideas, the photographer and illustrator work totally within their own self-made environment doing very much "their own thing." This is the very reason their specific talents are so invaluable to the function of graphic design. One need only look through an illustration or photographic annual to see the tremendous diversity, not only of technique, but of "personal vision" that is available to choose from. The designer's job is to choose the best talent for the job at hand; not always an easy task!

The art director-designer has less of a task in dealing with the illustrator than with the photographer. The illustrator can always give you exactly what you want, given careful direction and sufficient input. The only technical limitations are in the characteristics of the medium the illustrator uses and in his or her abilities.

With photography, as marvelous a science as it is, there are always things that are technically impossible (or at least not feasible because of time, cost, etc.). Illustration can be changed as it develops: new ideas or changes in attitude can easily be incorporated into the emerging image. But as an art director of photography, you must have a very good idea of what you want and how to achieve it before you begin. There are very few ways of changing the character of the image once the process has begun because of the instantaneous nature of the medium. Because of this, the art director-designer must spend considerably more time in the development of a project that utilizes original photographic elements . . . often more time than it took to create the idea to begin with.

At this particular juncture in the swing of fashionable preference, photography is used much more often than illustration in the day-to-day developing of design. Because of this, we will spend some time here in looking at the relationship between photographers and designers and the workings of a photographic assignment from the viewpoint of the art director (as it relates to the design-job example at the end of Chapter 10).

Photographers tend to specialize in one or two areas rather than try to run the gamut of commercially applicable photography. When doing a layout that requires a photograph of food, it is customary to look for a food photographer; when designing a brochure or book that requires situations with people, to look for a location and model photographer; when doing a catalogue or annual report for heavy industrial products and services, to hire an industrial photographer; and everyone must realize that magazines such as *Vogue* and *Harper's Bazaar* do not usually go to studio portrait photographers to shoot action, high-fashion model spreads for the clothes they are pushing. It is only common sense for the art director to look for a photographer with experience in and a flair for the kind of photography he or she needs done.

If the art director has no specific photographer in mind for an assignment, it is easy enough to find one. Publications listing photographers and showing their work are quite common and easily obtainable. If there is indecision concerning who should get the assignment, the art director will usually call in three or four photographers or their representatives ("reps") for a closer look at their work and a discussion of costs and possible scheduling for the project. Many complex assignments require more than one type of photographic specialty, and the art director will either split up the assignment between photographers or search around until one is found whom the art director feels can adequately handle the entire project. Studios which specialize in photography are excellent sources in this respect because they often have the varied staff and experience necessary to handle complex situations. Sometimes the art director (or the client) will choose to go to a "name" photographer for various reasons. Perhaps using a celebrity who has built a reputation from doing a certain style of imagery might increase the chances of a suc-

cessful job, or the client may simply want to capitalize on the name value of the photographer.

In the case of our design assignment (a catalogue), it was necessary to "shop around" for a photographer conversant with product *and* model photography, someone who could work comfortably "on location," photographing people interacting with the products, and at the same time would have a studio and equipment complex enough to manage unique individual shots. Because of the complicated nature of the assignment (which will soon become apparent), a studio was chosen to handle the photography.

The assignment, from the Brunswick Corporation's Recreation Centers Division (BRC), was an all-inclusive one, not simply a design problem. The development of a marketing strategy was necessary (what should the catalogue do and how should it do it). Once a relevant theme for presenting the products was decided upon, the copy had to be written (what do the products do for the consumer, and why should they buy from us rather than from someone else). The design alternatives were developed along the marketing theme at the same time the copy was being written.

The catalogue itself—presenting the line of balls, bags, and shoes sold through each center's pro shop—is a high-profile glamour presentation of products and their uses. It is looseleaf, a ring-bound collection of pages presented on a counter display unit for convenient use by recreation center patrons. Aside from the development of the project as stated above, a number of corollary pieces to support the catalogue had also to be developed. These included a graphic design for the display backboard, with a "pocket" brochure distilling the product line information in a take-away format interested patrons could use for future reference. In addition, an introductory poster and a sales kit acquainting the center managers with the new catalogue were also proposed. Needless to say, this required considerable project coordination on the part of the art director and his staff, both in design and in keyline supervision, as well as production detailing and art direction. With all of these aspects to deal with, the art director wisely chose a familiar photographic source with considerable experience in catalogue work of this kind.

## DEVELOPING WORKING LAYOUTS

Producing "working" layouts off of the accepted design direction is absolutely necessary for the development of keyline art as well as for reference in photographic production. Aside from the fact that the designer must work out every detail of each layout to his or her satisfaction, the client will often want to approve such detailing as well, especially if the products have a critical "face" (display angle). Many times, layouts will vary considerably from spread to spread, and pencil tissues showing these variations and how they affect the design and the products are necessary to everyone. In the case of our catalogue, the design direction called for photographic material on every page. For the photographer to understand the job at hand, a complete series of spreads was given to orient him to the designer's (and client's) demands in terms of size, location, and importance of specific products and product-use situations throughout the catalogue. The page-by-page layouts were also used as a production record to check off what had been done and to estimate what needed to (and could) be done in realistic working segments. This became crucial in the location sessions, where there was a fixed amount of time daily to work. From these working roughs, the art director and the photographer also determined the number of shots, their size and complexity, and whether they would be studio or location photographs. This was necessary for the photographer to make an accurate estimate of the cost of the project and to see that it dovetailed with the art director's budget for photography.

The designer's pencil layouts will be used for other reasons as well. Consideration must be given to where the copy will fall, how much there is, and if it needs to be edited or increased to effect the best mix of copy and design. The client will also approve finalized copy before type is set and keyline art is initiated. Our catalogue consisted of 34 pages (68 printed front-and-back surfaces), no two of which were exactly alike. The basic keyline art was constructed around the designer's layout for each (in this case, looseleaf) page. Small adjustments and revisions were made at the keyline stage in the catalogue's evolution. This is common practice in projects of any complexity. In dealing with complicated formats of any length, complete, detailed layouts are necessary if for no other reason than to keep the designer's (art director's) "head straight" (i.e., as an ongoing reference throughout the project).

## MODEL SELECTION AND PRODUCT COLLECTION

Working with the art director, the photographer and his production assistants first determined the number of models that were necessary for the location shoot and then set up interviews with each model (with the client present) to verify that they were right for the job. More often than not, this is a crucial part of the shoot itself.

Clients are always very concerned that the models associated with their products have the "visual attitude" that most accurately reflects the characteristics of their audience or consumers. The model selection process can often be a tedious, time-consuming venture.

In our example, the Brunswick people responsible for the project have a very distinct profile of the people who frequent their recreation centers. This makes it relatively easy to select the correct model types to be used.

Four groups of people were chosen corresponding to the marketing data profile: (1) a man and woman in the over-55 category, (2) a man and woman 35 to 45 years old, (3) a man and woman under 25, and (4) a boy and girl 8 to 12 years old (to be photographed alone, as well as interacting as the children of the couple in the 35-to-45-year age group. A 3 year old was also used in the same capacity. The children were important to the ambience of the catalogue as the emphasis at Brunswick Recreation Centers was on family involvement. Once the selection had been made, the photography studio booked the models for specific shoot dates previously agreed upon by the client, the art director, and the photographer.

Representative samples of the products to be included in the catalogue were gathered together by the client (two or three of each) and shipped to the photography studio for "prepping" (preparation for the photo sessions). This is a common practice when shooting products in a studio setting. Because of the intensity of photofloods and strobe lights, even the minutest flaws in a product are magnified. Therefore, each item for the catalogue is carefully checked over by the photography crew and nicks and bumps are smoothed over and the most nearly perfect product is selected to shoot. In the case of the bowling balls, the surface sheen was heightened by applying a coat of liquid soap! The bags were checked to see that all seams were properly sewn and that there were no scuffs or scars in the material surface. All shoes were brushed, laces aligned and straightened where needed, and the soles were checked for flaws.

Even though this is "routine inspection" by all photographers before shooting, every product presents a different set of problems that must be solved in order to benefit from the optimum effects of a photograph, and it is the art director who is ultimately responsible for seeing that the product is properly ready to be photographed. In the case of complicated settings, difficult prepping, or unusual shooting situations, it is the art director's responsibility to have a representative from the client on set who knows corporate policy concerning display of the products. The photographer is working for the art director unless otherwise specified, and "the buck stops" with the art director for all practical purposes!

Photographers will be the first to agree: it is hard enough satisfying the demands of an art director; it can be chaos taking directions from other sources, perhaps conflicting ones, less knowledgeable in the technical aspects of the graphic arts. The art director must take charge of the photo session and see to it that things run smoothly and efficiently, that responsibility for details is delegated to the proper people, that the photographer understands what is wanted from each shot, and, above all, that the client (if present) is satisfied with the way the shoot is proceeding. In addition to this, a sensitive art director will allow the photographer as much latitude in interpreting the product as is possible and will defer to the photographer's technical understanding of the photographic medium. This will help insure the best possible results from the effort. All of this is a difficult assignment for an art director, sometimes a superhuman task.

## SETTING UP THE SHOOT

The art director and the photographer together decide (1) the actual number of working hours it will take to complete the required number of shots and (2) in which order they will be shot. The photographer's production assistants will arrange the details of transporting products to the location and blocking out the time periods at the location site necessary to complete the shots, of getting models and equipment to the site on time, and of all the other aspects of the assignment relating to the actual shooting of the products. In the case of our catalogue, one of the Brunswick centers was used as a location setting and arrangements with the center manager were made for blocking out the necessary number of lanes, on-site equipment, and time needed.

Because a model's time starts at $100 an hour and up, it is crucial that the time a model spends on a set be used to the fullest! Many sessions require the work of professional makeup artists and propping assistants (individuals who deal with special costumes or items used in the shoot), and this time must also be figured into the working schedule. In our case, neither of these two aspects of photography were necessary. The models were responsible for their own makeup and were directed as to which articles of wardrobe to bring with them. Since we were using an actual bowling center as our location backdrop, artificial propping was unnecessary.

If it is not already obvious to the reader, it will be stated here again, that the designer on a project is usually always the art director on that project. It is a very rare instance when this is not the case, for who has a better feel for the design or is more capable of making decisions that will affect it than the project designer? In the last analysis the totality of the project is always visual. The words and the pictures, the paper, are all visual elements. These elements either work together to the benefit of all or fail to effectively communicate the message. Thus the responsibility for one or the other rests on the designer's shoulders more than on anyone else's.

**1**

**1, 2, 3** Shots of photographer and camera crew on location.

## TAKING THE PICTURES

Once again the photographer and the art director must make a critical decision affecting both the budget of the project and the quality of the imagery that will come out of the assignment: that is, to decide which format to use to take the photographs.

Most commercial photography for projects like ours is done using transparent positive film (transparencies) exactly like the slide film you might use in your own 35mm camera. When the need arises for prints (for extensive retouching that cannot be accomplished successfully in the transparency medium), dye transfers or other similar processes are used. For our project we did opt for the dye transfer process in one instance, which will be discussed later.

There are four formats widely used in the graphic arts to accomplish the aims of photographers and designers. They are (1) the 35mm format, (2) the 2¼ × 3¼ format, (3) the 4 × 5 studio camera format, and (4) the 8 × 10 studio camera format. The smaller formats have distinctly different applications than the studio formats. They are for location or studio photography, where there is movement or stop-action work. They are the formats most commonly used when working with models. The 4 × 5 and 8 × 10 studio cameras are quite large and are used for product and set photography where the atmosphere and elements can be strictly controlled by the photographer. Our assignment was fairly typical in that we found it necessary to use more than one format to accomplish our aims. As a matter of fact, we used three.

Because the cost of making good film positives for printing (necessary to make negative printing plates) is so high, printers prefer to "gang" photographic images together and enlarge them to the actual printing size in groups. This obviously is a labor-saving method much less costly than enlarging each image to "pos. film" separately. For the printer to accomplish this gang imagery, the photographer must shoot products and images that will ultimately be printed same size, "in pro," or all the same size to begin with. For instance, in our catalogue, all of the bowling balls are shown same size relative to each other. The photographer shot all the balls under controlled circumstances, in the studio, with a studio camera, on 4 × 5 film—"in pro." This enabled the printer to "take them up" together (to make his film positives) on a single sheet of film to the actual reproduction size. The action (model) photography showing product usage throughout the catalogue (see color plates 2 & 3) was shot on "2¼" transparent film (with a Hasselblad camera) "in pro." The printer then "ganged" them to three specified sizes: (1) same size as the original image, (2) up 150 percent, and (3) up 600 percent. Not every shot in our catalogue (nor in most jobs) could be ganged together. Some images shot "2¼" out of necessity were used in odd sizes that required bringing up "to size" individually. Such images were kept to a minimum, however, and the catalogue was *designed* specifically to keep the plate-making costs within a reasonable figure.

The bag and shoe product images were "in pro" on 8 × 10 film, shot with the same or similar lighting. The cover image, a complex issue requiring consid-

**2**

**3**

**4, 5, 6** 2¼ out takes—
Pabst Blue Ribbon

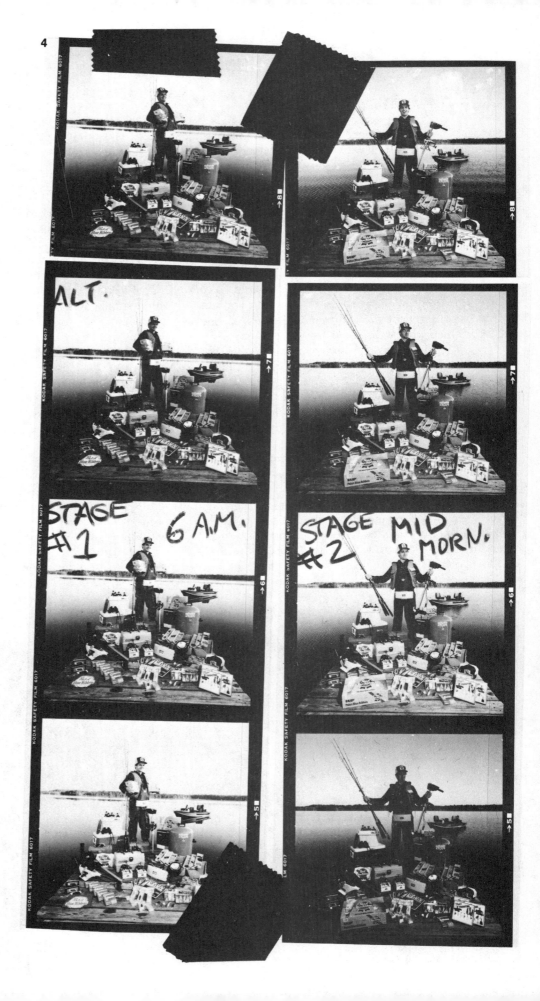

6

erable detailing and correction by a retoucher, was also shot on 8×10 film. All the 8×10 images were used "same size."

Such is the "in pro" process for creating photographic imagery.

On set, under the lights, the photographer is constantly checking with the art director concerning the compositional details of the photograph being taken.

On location the art director will request certain combinations of clothing for models to wear, will pair off models and group them to his or her satisfaction, and discuss what is wanted out of each shot with both the model(s) and the photographer. After a last check through the lens, the art director will then step back and let the photographer do the job and get the most from both model and action. When the photographer feels that the shot has been adequately "covered" with enough good poses representing the action, a halt will be called and the photographer and art director will regroup everyone for the next shot. This process will be repeated systematically until all the required shots are accomplished. It is a process that rarely goes as smoothly as everyone would hope. As is true with any complex project involving complex factors (human and otherwise), the range of variables is unpredictable. Tedious problems can arise totally beyond the control of the best-ordered plans. Weather can postpone or interrupt an outdoor shoot. Models can get sick or not show up. Products can be defective, or perfectly maintained strobe lights can refuse to flash. Great shots, "in the can," can in reality turn out to be unusable because the model blinked or looked the wrong way. A thousand possibilities exist, good and bad. A shoot can be both totally exhilarating and totally exhausting, an experience-builder like none other in the design profession.

## REVIEWING THE TRANSPARENCIES

When the day's shoot is done, the film is sent out for processing, and, within half a day to overnight, the transparencies are ready for review by the photographer and art director. If the shot has been "bracketed" (one or two exposures below and above the correct exposure—the case with most studio product shots), the art director and photographer will choose the best bracket of each shot (that bracket that best represents the true aspects of the product). If—as is the case with action and/or model shots—there are a number of different poses for a circumstance, the art director and photographer will evaluate the grouping (sometimes as many as ten to twenty frames) and choose the one that most attractively accomplishes the aims of the situation. Sending film out

is done on a daily basis throughout the shoot, unless it is not possible—at a location site for instance—to get the film to the lab. In this way, the photographer and art director can see if a subject or a product needs to be reshot. If this is the case, it is always done before the shoot "winds down"—before the location is left, the lighting or weather changes, or before the models are booked for another job. When this task is fully accomplished (usually at the end of the shoot), the art director and the photographer will review all of the chosen transparencies together to see that the project has been adequately covered. At this point, the art director will take the recommended transparencies to the client for review and together they will decide (usually on the art director's recommendations) what retouching if any needs to be done.

## RETOUCHING THE ART

In the case of our catalogue, little or no retouching was necessary for the 8×10 bag and shoe product shots, so carefully were they prepped and shot. The 4×5 ball shots required extensive retouching because of the reflective surface of the balls. The "blowback" from the strobe lights created "hotspots" (circles and odd-shaped white glare spots) on the surfaces, which needed to be removed. Since our product shots were all "dropout" halftones ("floating" images separated from any background props), they were shot on plain paper "sweeps" (long rolls of backdrop papers that come in a wide variety of colors). Even with this method, a certain amount of residual "halo effect," ghosting around the peripheral edges, took place. This was caused by the sweep paper being reflected off the surface of the balls. This ghosting needed to be toned down, yet not completely removed, or else the balls would have flattened out visually and lost the illusion of dimensional roundness necessary to be photographically convincing. With the product support shots, for those which showed models holding up or otherwise involved directly with product, selected retouching was done to color balance all products. This was necessary because ideal studio settings and lighting gave a truer sense of color than did the strobe-reflecting product of the location action shots. All retouching of this type was done on the actual transparencies or on enlarged duplicate transparencies.

There are two methods of retouching: (1) transparency retouching, and (2) reflective art retouching. Transparency retouching, as stated above, is done right on the actual image by chemically stripping away layers of emulsion and building back up the layers with different shadows, colors, and so on. Amazing effects can be created by a skilled transparency retoucher, and

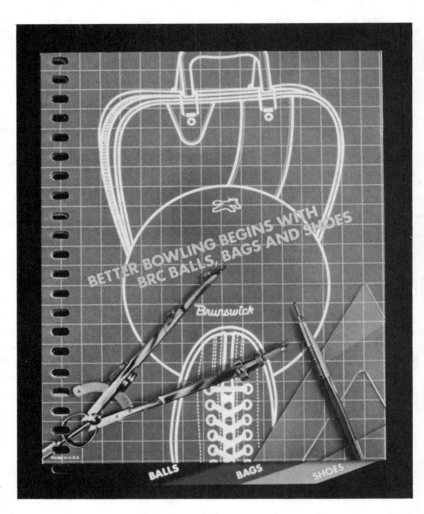

**7**  Cover of Brunswick catalog
Brunswick Recreation Center Catalog,
permission of Brunswick Corporation.

in recent years, more and more art directors are requesting this type of retouching over the more traditional dye transfer method. The newer method saves money (the average dye transfer runs over $300), and more importantly, it allows the use of the actual image, and not a reproduction print that is one step away from the original.

The one place in our catalogue where a dye transfer print was necessary was the cover. Because of the complex elements and the meticulous reality the pieced-together subject required, the dye transfer technique offered a more flexible format . . . and this is still its strong point.

Dye transfer color prints made from color transparencies are faithful reproductions—color emulsion layer by separate color emulsion layer—of the original. The technical aspects of doing such printing warrants a whole chapter in itself, but this information is readily available in many books on the techniques of color photography and does not relate directly to our subject here. Let it suffice that given a selection of dye transfer prints, the art director has at hand the most flexible (if not the most accurate or the cheapest) method of doing intricate and extensive retouching. In recent years other, cheaper printing methods, some with color fidelity almost as good, have come on the market; it is possible to use them when reproduction quality is not as critical as in a situation such as our catalogue. But dye-transfer reflective-art retouching remains traditional for improving the imagery of photographic material. Many art directors still swear by it as the *only* way to insure excellent, controllable reproduction, and printers (a traditionally conservative lot) feel more comfortable with the time-proven process.

Our cover concept, as originally developed by the designer, was a still-life reality difficult if not impos-

**8–13** Following is a sampling of printed pages from the Brunswick Recreation Center catalog.

Brunswick Recreation Center Catalog, permission of Brunswick Corporation.

**8**

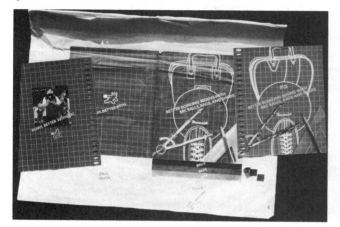

**11**

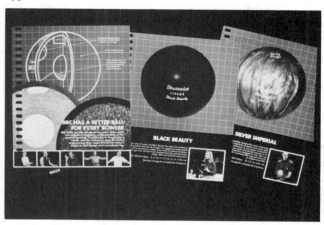

**9**

**12**

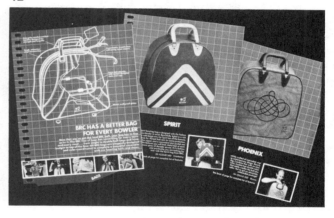

**10**

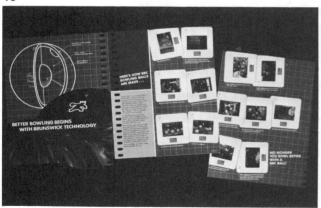

**13**

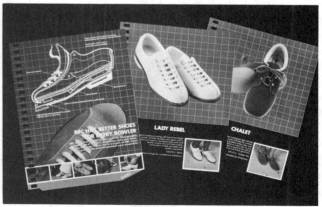

sible to duplicate as one piece through the medium of photography. Because of complex problems with parallax and other limitations of lenses, the answer was apparent: do it in pieces and "strip" them photomechanically together in the form of a dye transfer, to be retouched to the point where the total image was one of photographic reality. It is true that a "photographic realist" illustrator could have done the job equally well, but probably at a much higher cost, and certainly in much more time. Expediency, familiarity, and manageability dictated the former approach, and that was how it was done.

The still-life elements of the cover (the angle, the compass, and the mechanical pencil) were positioned on a blue sweep paper exactly as they would appear in the finalized art. The grouping was shot actual size on $8 \times 10$ film. The transparency was then given to a photographic color service who developed a same-size dye transfer image in the center of a larger ($20 \times 24$) piece of photographic paper. The peripheral excess of paper was used by our retoucher in expanding the background color area to the required size. At that stage, then, we had an actual-size paper image of the still-life elements, a mimetic reproduction of the transparency on paper.

As is true of most dye transfer orders, a selection of prints (three to four), varying in color balance, were given to the art director, who would select the one he felt best represented the coloration of the objects. Wisely, he consulted the retoucher chosen to finish the work on the print for his opinion as well. In our case, the retouching to be done required meticulous detailing as well as color balancing of background tone and adjustment of reflected light. It was important that the retoucher be comfortable with the image he had to transform, and his experienced opinion weighed heavily in the selection.

It is important here to point out the essential element that separates the great art director from the run-of-the-mill one: that is, *understanding when to defer to the specialist's judgment during the creative process.* This sounds simple in print, but is surprisingly difficult to put into practice in everyday on-the-job circumstances. Because of the pressures of decision making that accompany a project the size and scope of ours, it becomes easy, after a number of successes, to believe that your judgment is infallible, that because no one is as heavily involved in the project as yourself, no one else has quite the "overview," no one is more "capable" of making correct judgments concerning the elements of "your" assignment. This is not an uncommon delusion in many intense professions requiring personal commitment where a project or problem may turn on one series of decisions. The best, most effective

art directors (like the best leaders in any area of endeavor) use as much expert opinion and consider as much technical advice as possible before making a judgment on a project under their management. One of the real problems in our profession is still the artistic ego; that ingredient that convinces you that the God-given way to the final solution is always *your* way, by right of talent! Artistic ego is a necessary and wonderful aspect of every gifted individual in our profession, but it is also a never-ending source of frustration and trouble for those who cannot learn to control and use it as a positive force.

The catalogue cover posed several special problems for our art director and retoucher. When photographing metallic objects, it is often difficult to make them appear physically "real" because of reflective patterns of dark and light that can flatten out or change the appearance of the object in the photo image. This was true of our compass (see color plate 24) where the highlights had to be modified to make the object appear more "real" than it was. Small areas of color were added to block out disruptive shadows, grey and white highlights were modified by bleaching to heighten certain characteristics and prevent the loss of shapes over the entire image. The gold of the pencil bezel was made brighter and more "metallic," and all the cast shadows of the objects were deepened to snap them out of the background color. Finally and most critically, the retoucher "blew in" (with an airbrush) a uniform opaque blue over the existing photographic blue to flatten and intensify the background area. He then added the architectural grid pattern and our "camera-ready" image was ready for the printer. The stylized mechanical drawings of the bag, ball, and shoe were done separately in black line art and stripped in photomechanically during the separation-making process to complete the image.

The art director/designer was responsible for every step in the process, from ordering the dye transfer selection to supervising the retouching of the image. His judgment was final in determining options, in deciding how far to carry the retouching of the image, and in finalizing the art. Bad judgment on his part, poor supervision, or failure to communicate accurately his wishes to either the dye transfer printers or the retoucher could have crippled the job through wasted effort and the cost of redoing what should be done right the first time.

## INITIATING THE KEYLINE ART

Keyline art for the project was begun long before the retouching of the cover was complete—indeed, before the photography itself was finished. Working from the designer's page-by-page tight pencils and the finalized approved copy, the keyline artists constructed the basic keyline boards and set the type according to the designer's specifications. With the base elements together, work was begun on the line drawings for the cover and each section page (see color plate 14) and, as the transparencies came in for each section, sizing and stating of images for position placement on the boards began.

The stage of "minute adjustment" had arrived. The art director, once again, was responsible for coordinating keyline efforts with his staff, the production director, and keyliners working on the assignment. As each board was completed, it was checked over by the production director and then brought back by him to the art director for approval or discussion and adjustment. More often than not, it was for discussion and adjustment. This was not a reflection on the abilities of the keyline personnel to interpret the designer's sketches, but rather a genuine problem that always exists when translating layouts to actual art. The visualization of items and images yet to be developed rarely if ever has the exact feel of those same items and images when they are laid down in place on a keyline board. Adjustments in continuity from page to page, resizing of headline types from original specifications to better complement the "real" photography, resetting detail type because of a "widow" here or an extra line length there, careful rematching of grid patterns, minutely increasing character spacing in headline type to carry better in reverse areas, plus the inevitable "typos" and client changes to copy—all were time-consuming, nitpicking aspects of our catalogue requiring the most careful husbanding and visual sensitivity. The single overriding issue was clear to everyone involved: if changes were necessary, now was the time to make them, while there still *was* time, and while the costs were negligible. As anyone involved in the graphic arts will tell you, having to make changes in 4-color process artwork in the film or proofing stages is a costly business, both in money and in personal stress!

When everything is right, when everyone agrees (or some are overruled), the boards are reviewed in their entirety and a careful set of record stats (same-sized photostats) are made. The art director and the production director then go through the keylines and "mark them up" for color break in those flat-screen color areas common to the whole book or that serve as background for type or photography. In the case of our catalogue, this meant calling out screen tints (percentages of each of the 4-color process colors—black, yellow, magenta, cyan) from a printer's color chart to insure that the colors we wanted were attained through the proper mix of process inks. This was especially critical with our uniform blue "grid" ground. Under nor-

mal production runs it would have been advisable to specify a fifth "private" color (a laydown of solid ink from an extra station on the press) that would insure excellent consistency of application with no variation from page to page. This problem of color variation is always present in production runs where large areas of ink are to be laid down repeatedly throughout a printed piece. In our case, this problem was not as great a factor because our production run was so small that the entire job was run on a proofing press, a small, high-quality press used by printers for proofing a job, for client approval, before the actual large run on a bigger press. The proofing press allowed us to achieve a background blue that was a mixture of process color rather than a separate (more expensive) private color. Each board, when "speced" (referring to "specifications") for color, will carry callouts identifying photo areas as "4c," flat color areas marked for percentages such as "10% K (black) overall," "60% B," "30% Y," "SR" (solid red)—one of our designates for a purple background tone out of which type was reversed.

To achieve a solid, deep, lustrous black ground for the reverse copy on the back of each product page, a 60 percent screen of Process Blue was laid down before the black plate (always the last plate to be printed) was applied. This also was carefully specified by the art and production directors.

## ESTIMATING PRINTING

In most cases, designers responsible for following through with the print production of their work do not simply choose a printer out of a hat. Even when the designer and the printer are on familiar working terms, every job must be estimated well in advance of the printing date and a cost figure affixed to it, so that the art director may offer the client a complete estimate of the expenses involved in producing the assignment. To do this accurately, the art and solidus or production director must review the job with the printer. The complete pencil roughs are used for this, and the printer will make an estimate, based on discussions with the design team, concerning the amount of printed pieces needed, the type of paper to be used, whether it is process, and if there are any special considerations to be noted such as a private color. Whether or not the photography is in "pro" is important at this stage. A printer is usually chosen on the strength of past performance, but if an estimate is deemed too high in relation to the other costs of producing the job, another printer may very well be given the assignment! Getting more than one estimate for a printing is a common practice. Competition is very keen among printers, the costs involved are substantial, and often there is wide margin for adjustment on individual aspects of the assignment. Exactly because of this, it is essential to nail down the printing estimate in a very finite manner.

Once again it is the art director's responsibility to do this, or to see that it is done. Forgetting to include an aspect of the job in the printing estimate and then finding out later down the line that it is crucial to the success of the piece is an agonizing learning experience well worth avoiding by knowing your job or by listening to someone who does—such as your printer.

## A FINAL WORD ON
## RECORD STATS

Taking record stats of keyline art is always advisable, for many reasons, not the least being to avoid loss or destruction of the actual keylines. To rebuild keylines from record stats is much easier than starting all over again, working from memory and the designer's pencil tissues! The loss of keylines is not a far-fetched notion; for one reason or another, it happens many times.

## SUPERVISING PRINT
## PRODUCTION

One would assume that once the artwork has been put into the printer's hands, the job of the design team is done. This is only partly true. While the majority of the people involved with the assignment can ease up and go on to other assignments, the art director (and many times the production director) must still be available to look at color proofs, and often be ready to go "on press" during the proofing and production runs if problems arise that will require formal approval. Generally printers will always seek a written approval to proceed with the printing of the job. This is done to protect themselves and is only natural. It is the art director who assumes the responsibility by signing off on the proofs and initiating the production run ... and the art director had better be right!

It is the rare designer who has not had the experience of being on press. Printing presses often run round the clock, production changes and adjustments are tedious, and an "afternoon" of on-press approval can sometimes run into the small hours of the morning.

The art director's basic responsibility is to see that the job gets printed to his or her satisfaction (and the client's). The worst possible nightmare of any design assignment is breaking your back turning out a creditable job only to have it negated by bad printing. That is not to imply that printers, if not sat upon, will ruin your job. On the contrary, the wise art director *will* choose and *listen* to a good printer who knows the capabilities and limitations of print machinery. Here is some sage advice: get friendly with the best printers as fast as you can! Good printers will knock themselves out to give you a reproduction as true to your concept as the artwork allows. They stand to gain from a good sample, too. Good printers will tell you when you are overreaching the technical capabilities of their medium.

The good printer will also want you around so he can explain what he is doing and seek your approval or decision when there is more than one alternative at hand. So you see ... even within the medium of another professional the art director must take responsibility for his or her creation.

## DELIVERING THE JOB

Strange as it may sound, a design firm often is called upon to make sure the products it creates are delivered "to the field," whatever and wherever that may be. Since the client relies upon the design firm to coordinate delivery of materials to its sales force or manufacturing facilities, the firm's involvement in an assignment clearly extends right up to the "in-the-hand" stage. Although the art director is most apt to delegate the responsibility of following through with these aspects of the assignment to others, he or she will be aware of the process and responsible for seeing that it runs smoothly.

Our catalogue required some special consideration concerning delivery. Since it was a kit of several pieces, an adequate mailer had to be identified that was large enough to facilitate all articles and sturdy enough to insure a safe arrival. Two hundred fifty kits had to be mailed to many locations around the country, all to arrive on a specified date. If some center managers received their kits significantly before or after others, coordination of the project would have been interrupted and complaints from the field would be forthcoming, reflecting on the corporate executive responsible for the project. Be assured that such displeasure would be passed along to the design firm!

In reflecting over the progress of our catalogue from concept through delivery, you will see that well over half of the designer/art director's involvement required *verbal* directives and decisions about visual matters. This should underscore the absolute necessity of having good capacity for communicating thoughts and ideas without the use of a pencil. Although being able to doodle out a talking thumbnail to reinforce a directive is always helpful, under deadline pressures or on-the-spot decisions that is not always possible.

Recall our initial statement, that three quarters

of a designer's job still lies ahead after the comprehensive development. Understanding this process—even anticipating it in advance—is as important to the education of the graphic designer as knowing the rudiments of typography, printing, and other technical aspects of the visual arts. Understanding a second point is important, too: you, as a student, most probably receive one assignment at a time and have a certain number of hours or days to complete it before you begin another. In real life this is a fairly rare occurrence. The average working designer is juggling two or three jobs at a time, all overlapping in production and completion schedules.

Not everyone majoring in Graphic Design will *want* to be a part of this demanding role. There are many designers who want only to be left peacefully alone at the drawing board, who happily leave such involvement to others. Their choice means they sacrifice their ability to control their creations, once out of their hands. This is fine—if they choose knowledgeably. What is important is having the knowledge beforehand, so that you have some basis on which to judge what is, and what is not, your cup of tea.

# LINE AND SHAPE
## Chapter 5

That the basic elements of art are the foundation for all aesthetic judgment and practice may seem childishly obvious, yet many designers, in their eagerness to be inventive and original, often forget these essentials in their practical work. This aesthetic "amnesia" is not strictly a professional disease; it seems to manifest itself the moment students enter their subject of major interest. Unless it is diagnosed and corrected at an early stage, it is often fatal to the growth of the creative professional later on. Overdeveloped style can be symptomatic of visual "amnesia." Indeed, style can easily become the god of design, and pressures to set, or adhere to, trends do warp the judgment of artists and contribute to questionable design problem solving. Good design is never out of style. Good design needs no elaborate rationale or justification. Good design certainly can vary according to the tastes and trends of the times; but underneath the flair and show of momentary fashion, the basic elements are always in evidence.

It is impossible to get too much education in basic design. The fledgling designer, eager to try his wings in the shifting winds of applied design, must be careful not to abandon the seemingly "elementary" essentials of the artist's craft. Applying basic design judgment may become second nature as one becomes sophisticated in a medium, but it is wise to foster a conscious awareness of the "cradle arts" and use them as a check and balance system in your work. Knowing the basic rules often leads to new variations on them, and helps establish new realms of aesthetic practice. Revolutions in thinking are rarely made out of ignorance or neglect of basic principles.

Because of the specific nature of this text, we cannot thoroughly review all information pertaining to basic art studies. We must assume that the student entering the Graphic Design curriculum has, at the very least, a basic understanding of the elements and principles of design. Of course, there are many excellent books available on art fundamentals for the reader who wishes to know more.

It would do well, in light of our emphasis on essentials, to spend at least one chapter discussing the two design elements upon which the entire fabric of Graphic Design is constructed—that is, line and shape. Without line and shape there would *be* no Graphic Design, nor, for that matter, any other two-dimensional art form. Let us discuss them, however, *from the working designer's viewpoint,* not from the lecturer/instructor's viewpoint, and relate them to practical work experience. Line and shape will be addressed in this chapter.

If line and shape are the basic structure of Graphic Design, typography is the running thread that holds that fabric together. As a practical extension of the theories of line and shape, the rules that govern their usage are very much applicable to the written word. Chapter 6 will discuss typography—once again, from the viewpoint of the professional designer.

Color is a prime psychological mover in communication mediums. While it is not as essential to graphic design as typography, it is rarely disassociated from the designer's efforts. Certain attributes of color, such as value and saturation, are critical even to the application of black-and-white graphics, typography, and printing. Technical aspects of color specification and color reproduction are usually only vaguely understood by the design student. Since these are the most critical aspects of color for the professional designer, the sooner the student becomes familiar with terminology and procedure (even if practice in application is limited), the better able he or she will be to cope with professional problems. Chapter 7 is devoted to the use of color in Graphic Design.

Finally, there is a short chapter (Chapter 8) on layout, that ritual series of methods by which the designer sorts out and assembles the elements. There has been so much excellent material already written on the history, philosophy, and methodology of composition and layout that, as is the case with basic design study, we need not repeat such information here. What we can do is relate layout to the designer's daily work, as we do in other chapters, and to cover another important aspect that seems heretofore neglected—that is, *the perspective on layout of people who work with graphic designers: the marketing professional, the copywriter, the printer, and ultimately the client/purchaser*. Most classroom situations allow the designer to develop layout, size and place elements and typography, and create emphasis more or less without the related marketing and conceptual copy input. While this may be thought irrelevant at the beginning levels of design learning, it is most certainly *not* irrelevant at the more advanced levels.

One concept that will be repeated in one form or another throughout this text is that the design of *anything* is a useless exercise unless that design fulfills its basic requirement of communicating its use or message clearly. Because copywriters, printers, and clients *do* see layout *differently* than the visual artist, this issue is a vital topic.

Before speaking of line or shape, let us ask ourselves, what does the lowly dot or point mean to the working designer? It means a great deal, not only as a point of origin from which the designer begins designing, but as the crucial component in the printed imagery that is the designer's end-product.

# *The Dot or Point*

We are taught that the dot is the simplest unit of visual communication, a focal reference for the eye and a psychological as well as physical beginning for more complex visual ideas. We know that the dot is an extremely strong visual device, with the power to attract and hold the eye wherever it is found. A single dot or point is static and has no direction. In combinations or groupings, the dot can lead the eye and establish a measure of motion and of space. It can imply and define shape, and when in great numbers and complex juxtapositions, dots or points allude to reality, as in continuous-tone reproduction for printing.

**14** When dots merge, visually or actually, they become a line, a totally nonstatic element.

Measure: If we think of a line as a continuing progression of dots or points starting at one place and ending at another, we are dealing with one aspect of a line's measure: length. As a two-dimensional graphic device, a line's measure also includes width, and in the physical world, a linear form may have the third dimension of breadth. While a line can be any length or width, it must be perceptibly longer in dimension than it is wide, or else, by definition, it may fall into the category of the dot, or even that of shape.

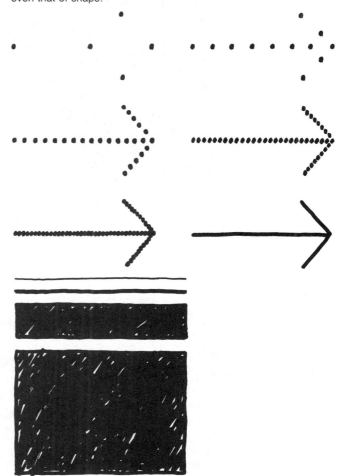

As the Graphic Designer's work and reputation is entirely judged on the printed image, the dot which controls that image and how it is used by the printer needs to be completely understood by the designer. We will discuss this at greater length later on in the text. For now, it is important to keep in mind the complexities involved in the concept of the dot or point. Those elementary rules of design, those artistic references to the function of the point are very much in evidence every time the designer sits down at a drawing board to compose elements. Viewed as a position of departure for a concept, for the graphic line that begins that concept, as a basic element in the translation of the graphic concept to the finalized printed image, and as a vehicle to control the consistency, value, brightness, and clarity of that image, the dot, in all of its simplicity, is perhaps the most complex paradox the practicing professional designer will ever deal with.

For the printer, the dot is everything. All imagery is broken down into patterning composed of dots in the plate-making process. The concept of full color—the reproduction of reality on the two-dimensional surface—would not exist without the dots, which overlap and juxtapose to create the effects our visual process interprets as "natural" color. The only means the printer has of controlling and varying the reproduction process is by manipulating the size and character of the dot and by regulating the amount of ink the dot represents from plate to paper.

As a design student, your experience and even your concern with dots is minimal. Yet, the stronger you build your "bridge" between theory and the technical aspects of your art, the more you will come to understand and share the printer's viewpoint concerning the importance of the dot, and also see just how critical it is to the realization of your own work.

# *Line*

Line is a man-made graphic device used primarily as a communication tool. It exists in nature as edge, separating one mass from another. Line is the essential element in visualization for the graphic artist. Tremendously varied as a concept, the line in basic art study is defined in terms of its specific attributes. Its properties—*measure, type, direction, location,* and *character*—help establish its usages in the mind of the artist. Perception is a key factor in the definition of what is and is not a line, and relationships to human sizing affect our understanding of line. In the intimate, human scale of the artist—at the drawing board or easel, dealing in structured compositional area—line divides or unifies the pictorial format and defines shape.

   The designer works most often with linear tools. The pencil, pen, marker, the brush, all are essentially linear. Controlling the tool to create sensitively requires not only understanding of the tool, but also complete understanding of the attributes of line. Master drafting of any kind cannot be achieved without this combination of knowledge.

   The designer uses all aspects of line in his or her daily work. The ability to produce basic concepts in

**16** By their very nature, lines fall into types: rectilinear and curvilinear. Rectilinear lines are essentially straight from beginning to end and, when joined together, form angles. Rectilinear lines are most often associated with geometric constructs, and two of the three basic shapes, the square and the triangle, are defined by rectilinear lines. The angularity of rectilinear lines creates visual abruptness and excitement in compositional arrangement.

Curvilinear lines are generally associated with organic properties found in the natural world. Their aspects are, for the most part, random and uncalculated, and a greater degree of freedom and lack of stability characterizes their configuration. Curvilinear lines are inherently more graceful in application to the compositional format, and establish a sense of rhythm more easily than do rectilinear lines.

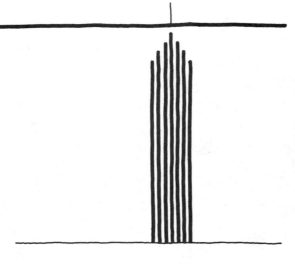

**17** Direction: The direction of a line is what moves our eye around a composition. There are four basic directions for human orientation: vertical, horizontal, diagonal, and circular. These directions imply certain psychological characteristics the artist can utilize.

A horizontal line's direction can imply harmony and stability. In concert with the verticality of the human body, we orient our universe in terms of horizontal ground-plane relationships.

Vertical lines imply a sense of aspiration and dignity, a transcendental effect. Man has always been preoccupied with the upward mobility of his spirit. The architecture of the Gothic cathedral used visual linear verticality to impart a feeling of spiritual "uplifting," a bridge to heavenly attainment. Graphically, vertically directed lines "heighten" the compositional effect and create a graceful, dignified character.

**18** Diagonal direction is the most unstable force effect and, consequently, the most dynamic in application. Diagonal direction effects a soaring or plunging attitude depending on the orientation. Composing with the use of strong diagonals implies stress, and is threatening to the stability we seek to surround ourselves with.

Circular or curved directional forces and linear movements have an all-encompassing effect and evoke a natural harmony and warmth.

Graphic line directions, used singly or in concert with each other, enable artists to express the emotional content of the material they are working with.

**19**  Location: the location of linear elements in a compositional area can serve to unify and balance or divide and compartmentalize that area. The relative significance of the same linear element as a unifying or divisional device changes depending upon its positioning within the format.

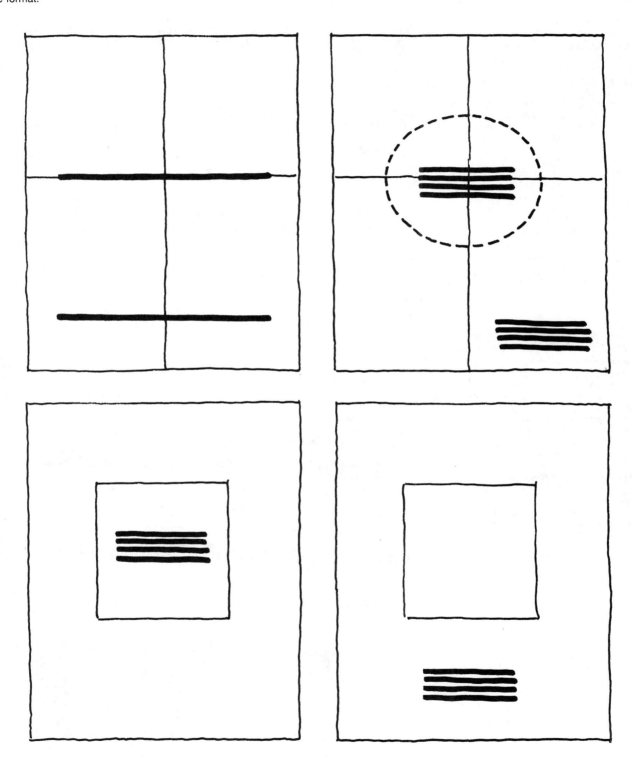

**20**   Character: A line's character is generally perceived, by degree, in two ways: (1) hard/fast lines, and (2) soft/slow lines.

The medium or tool used to draw a line helps determine where a line fits in relationship to these categories. Although a hard line does not always constitute a fast line, nor a soft line a slow line, more often than not they will be closely related in this manner. The degree to which a line characterizes either of these categories will be determined by the artist who is exploiting the tools and creative possibilities of the situation. An architect or draftsman rendering a building will utilize certain linear characteristics to give a crisp, hard/fast technical feel to the work, while an illustrator, sketching the structure from a more interpretive and expressive viewpoint, might very well use a slower, softer line to capture the essence of the building.

A graphic designer might choose a typeface because its linear construction makes it read "fast" or "slow."

A harder, faster linear typographic feel which is the combination of type style and drawing instrument.

A softer, slower linear typographic feel which is the combination of type style and drawing instrument.

**21**   Samples of the linear variation produced from differing designers' tools.

A penline constitutes a hard/fast line. It is direct, its edge is well defined, and the eye perceives it as a line very quickly. A drybrush line, on the other hand, because of its subtle and constantly changing edge and fluctuating density, is a soft/slow line by comparison. Its distinction from its background is not so obvious or quickly comprehended, and the eye is more apt to linger over its surface. In simple context this categorizing has little meaning, but when viewing a total work, the nature of that work is established, in great part, by the linear character of the constructs that make it up.

a visually convincing and appealing manner is directly related to how well the designer uses line as a sketching, storytelling device. The designer builds composition and layouts for ideas based on linear constructs, graphic and implied, and produces continuity in work through the use of linear direction, again both graphic and implied. The aesthetic sensitivity achievable by mastering the usage of line is most apparent when using line as a building device for mass area, tone, texture, and color.

All good designers have a sensitivity to the linear aspects of typography, as well as to its effects as a mass element in composition. Indeed, the designer is constantly employing the linear effects of typography in the image-making process. One need only observe a grouping of typefaces together to understand the tremendous variety they offer. A designer insensitive to these characteristics, both in single letter and mass configuration, will never successfully use type on a consistent basis. Perhaps to the untutored eye the differences in the paragraph effects of a Caslon versus a Baskerville roman are a puzzle. Through education the designer knows the effects of the two faces are so markedly different *because of* the subtlety of their linear construction. Understanding this means also realizing the potential a typeface has.

In forming perspective, line is used to define planes, which in turn define the limitations of volumetric forms and create the illusion of three-dimensional space on the two-dimensional surface. Without a foundation in the linear aspects of perspective space, the designer is a conceptual cripple with limited artistic function. The Graphic Designer cannot afford the stupidity of limiting him or herself to thinking and conceptualizing simply in two dimensions.

The techniques used in the development of problem-solving visualization are dominated by the element of line; other elements are secondary to it. In many instances, an idea will be accepted or rejected on the strength of the linear idea, before it even gets to the comprehensive stage, where other elements such as color, texture, tone, or scale may enhance its value as a solution. Each stage of a creative project has a "look," a character which establishes the level of development and sets the degree of evaluation necessary. The logic of progressive development requires such a system. At early stages of any creative assignment, latitude must be established and accepted . . . latitude for creation as well as for interpretation. To fix on a precise image or goal at too early a stage is counterproductive to the growth of a creative product. Line becomes a critical factor in dealing with the styling and presentation of ideals in this sense. Learning to master and use the *vagaries* of line is an important process for the designer.

Designers who have not mastered the basics of line cannot draft or draw well. And designers who do not draw well are at a decided disadvantage in Graphic Design. Drawing is one of the more *teachable* creative disciplines. If you justify yourself by saying "I just can't draw," you imply you have no aptitude for it—and you are fooling yourself. Drawing requires a good eye and a thorough understanding of line. If you don't have the "good eye," you also have no business being a designer . . . and that's the hard fact of it!

**22**  Totally linear effects in an ad layout . . .

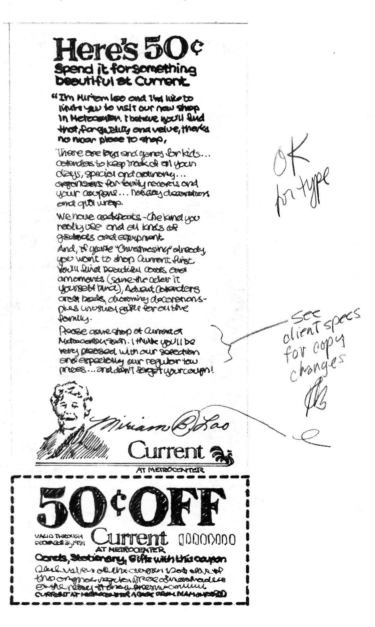

**23**    . . . and in perspective sketching.

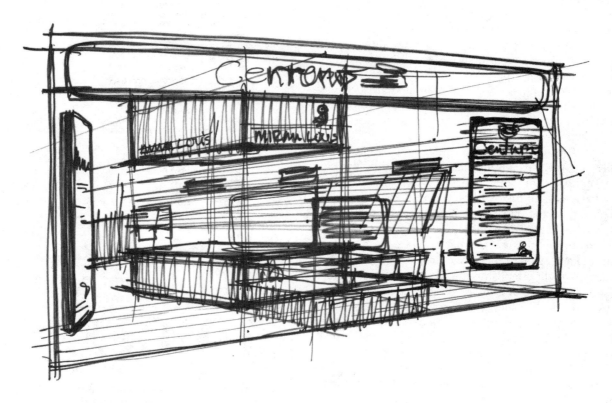

**24**

This is an indication of how type character

appear as line.　When blown out of context,

it becomes more apparent that they are

judged first by the eye as horizontal linea

constructs.

scale is relevant to judging individual letters as linear constructs

scale is relevant to judging individual letters as linear constructs

e is relevant to judging individual letters

udging individual lett

ndividual l

ridual

# *Shape*

It is often said that shape alone is the basis for Graphic Design and that other elements are secondary. Yet, since shape is an *extension* of the linear concept, the two appear to be of equal importance to the work of the two-dimensional designer. One first conceives a shape by drawing or visualizing its boundary. Boundary—or edge—is a linear concept. As an extension of the linear concept, shape is characterized by linear closure. Linear closure creates area, and as all basic art students learn, area is the distinguishing attribute of shape. All shape must have area, and all area is dilineated by edge—graphic or visual or implied.

As we have stated earlier, "Without line and shape there would be no Graphic Design." What is more, line and shape also represent all that is *necessary* to the creation of Graphic Design. Color is certainly not necessary. Neither is form. All texture and value can be achieved through the creative use of line. In terms of a basis for function, line and shape are symbiotic and cannot be viewed as two separate entities.

## THE PERSONALITY OF SHAPE

Designers work with shape as a compositional tool, much as they work with line as a graphic indicator. Like line, different shapes have different characters and convey differing attitudes. The personality of a shape can increase the effectiveness of composition and message by contradiction, by contrast, or by reinforcing through similarity. Rectilinear geometric shapes incorporating sharp angles create activity and tension and are strong attention-getting devices. More regular rectilinear shapes such as squares, rectangles, and shapes with curvilinear definition convey a much greater sense of equilibrium and order and act as stabilizing elements in compositional usage. Even in their extreme complexity, organic shapes project distinctly differing personality profiles. The rectilinear variation in the fissure cracks in a dried mud flat convey different characteristics from the intricate, fluid curvilinear balance of a chambered nautilus.

If we properly view the whole concept of compositional format itself as shape—that is, graphic area limited by linear boundaries (edge)—we see that the format has personality that can affect, to a greater or lesser degree, the entirety of the graphic message. Most often, the designer works with formats based upon the square or rectangle, but there are many notable exceptions. Package design, product graphics, and signage many times present difficult formats for the designer. Ultimately it is the size and shape of the format and its inherent personality that dictates basic guidelines in problem solving. Where the format is detrimental to the presentation of the message, the designer will restructure the compositional area within the larger format, perhaps echoing the personality of the format or possibly contrasting or complementing it with another, depending upon what works best with the content of the message. For instance, the orderliness of a square's personality for establishing a graphic message might be the very thing for an unlikely or odd-shaped format. As an example, one of the more restrictive shapes that the designer must deal with in the presentation of graphic imagery is the surface contour of a commercial jetliner. The available area for graphics, and the shape of that area, is a real challenge from the design standpoint.

There are many similar situations where graphic messages are subject to the restrictions of formats that, of themselves, project strong shape personalities. Experiment for yourself. Try composing one or two simple shapes with a few paragraphs of copy accompanying them, first in a circle, then in an oval or other paraboloid shape. In seeking to establish a relationship between the elements you are working with, your first instinct will be to restructure the compositional area to accommodate them. The difficulties in designing within (and relating to) such shape formats as compared with a square or a rectangle will quickly become apparent. Whether the personality of shape is the limiting format itself, or whether it is the active communicating ingredient within the composition, it is a realm for continual interpretation on the part of the designer.

## SHAPE: ITS DESIGN POTENTIAL

It is essential to remember one thing. The character of shape within a layout is a vehicle to convey the message; it is not the message itself. When designing, it is all too easy to be seduced by the beauty of shape and its personality, and to lose perspective on the potential communication value shape may offer. Shape can be appreciated in its own right within the larger context of the message when its personality is used effectively. However, if the shapes within the layout obscure or overpower the message, the basic reason for the graphic as a piece of communication is lost. Looking for a more creative way to design the shape of a block of copy, for instance, other than as a square or rectangle, is justified as long as the information is easily readable and the shape reflective of the larger graphic idea of the message.

The potential, for instance, of sharp-angled shapes in expressing a message about stress is great . . . much greater than the potential of a circle. That potential can be utilized in varying degrees of subtlety in combination with other elements. The potential may exist for conveying the idea without the need of a verbal

# DIFFICULT GRAPHIC FORMATS

LIMITED AREA OF
READABILITY FOR GRAPHICS

DESIGNER MUST
CONSIDER ALIGNMENT
PROBLEMS FOR FORMAT
IN ON-SHELF CIRCUMSTANCES

BIGGEST PROBLEM IN
CAN DESIGN IS CREATING
EXCITEMENT IN VERY
RIGID FORMAT WHILE
MAINTAINING PRODUCT
READABILITY

GROCERY STORE IS <u>MOST</u> DIFFICULT
OF ARENAS FOR GRAPHIC SURVIVAL!

25

---

26    # DIFFICULT GRAPHIC FORMATS

UNUSUALLY NARROW FORMAT
APPLICATIONS TEND TO LIMIT GRAPHIC
POSSIBILITIES WITHOUT RE-STRUCTURING
OR MODIFICATION

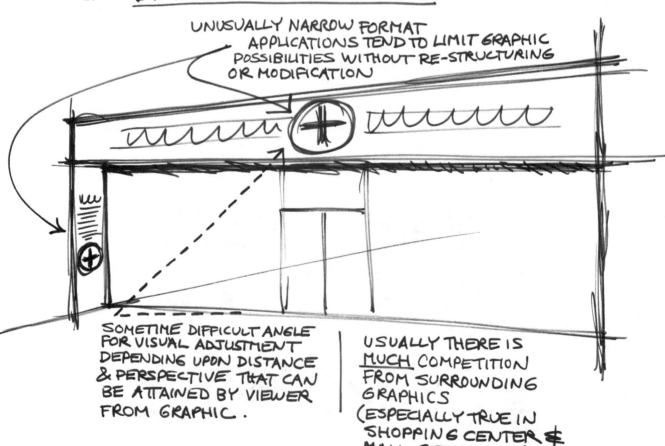

SOMETIME DIFFICULT ANGLE
FOR VISUAL ADJUSTMENT
DEPENDING UPON DISTANCE
& PERSPECTIVE THAT CAN
BE ATTAINED BY VIEWER
FROM GRAPHIC.

USUALLY THERE IS
<u>MUCH</u> COMPETITION
FROM SURROUNDING
GRAPHICS
(ESPECIALLY TRUE IN
SHOPPING CENTER &
MALL SITUATIONS)

**27**

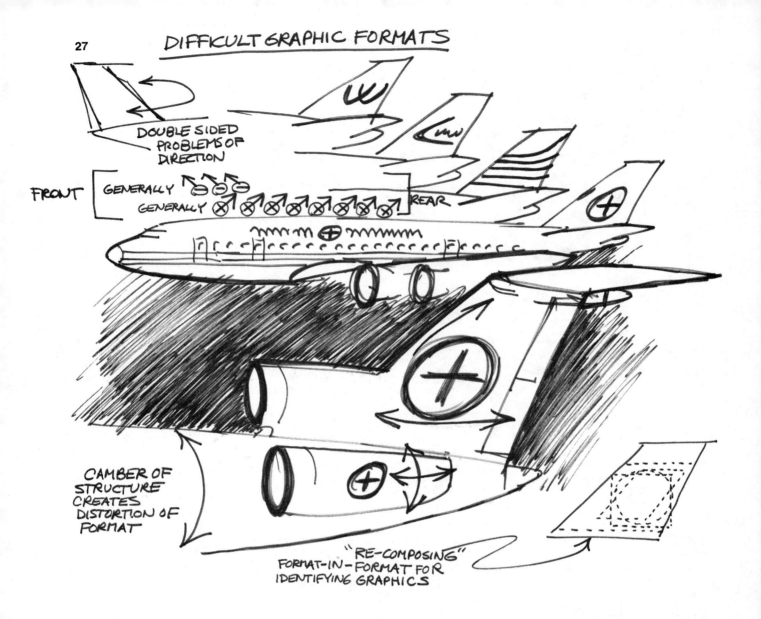

DOUBLE SIDED
PROBLEMS OF
DIRECTION

FRONT

GENERALLY

GENERALLY

REAR

CAMBER OF
STRUCTURE
CREATES
DISTORTION OF
FORMAT

"RE-COMPOSING"
FORMAT-IN-FORMAT FOR
IDENTIFYING GRAPHICS

**28**

STRESS

STRESS

STRESS

message at all. Indeed, this is the very essence of symbolism. But a message like "stress" is simple. If the message being conveyed is more complicated, as most messages are, the shape's design potential is useful up to the point, once again, where it does not conflict with the essential message. Sensitivity to the potential of shape is a key factor in the creation of good graphic communication.

## SHAPE IN GRAPHIC ART

1. *The Literal Shape.* Shape in graphic composition often represents the configuration of known, recognizable objects. Literal shape is employed by the designer to directly confront the viewer with preconceived imagery. Because "a picture is worth a thousand words," one would think that a literal shape needs no design interpretation to make it effective communication. This is sometimes true, but the fact of the matter is that the object itself is never as important as the viewpoint from which the object is presented *or* perceived. If this were not true, if the literal shape always presented itself most effectively as the message alone, without viewpoint or comment, there would be little need for the talents of creative communicators in any art discipline.

A unique presentation of literal shape and imagery in the graphic format is often *required* to heighten the effectiveness of the message. Because of this, the designer's creative task can sometimes be more difficult when working literally than when working with shape in an abstract, interpretive, or symbolic manner. Literal shapes in a dynamic composition undergo varying degrees of transformation and become individualized as part of the visual language of the designer. In this visual language, that realm of personal creative variation common to every artist, the literal shape can be applied in as highly interpretive a manner as the abstract or symbolic shape. Taking the ordinariness of the literal and making it extraordinary by designing it *while* retaining its shape recognition is a creative way of dealing with literal shape.

Taking the literal shape out of context is another effective way of designing shape. When an object is separated from its real surroundings and isolated or mixed together with other, unrelated shapes (literal or symbolic), or with a format that is unrelated to the literal shape, the unique attention-getting possibilities of the image can be exploited. The literal shape is used extensively in modern graphic design. Visual identification, either as photograph or illustration, has undergone extensive metamorphosis in the last fifteen years, so much so that it has caused a minor revolution in the photographer's approach to the medium and a renewed stylistic renaissance in illustration rivaling that of the 1930s.

2. *Interpretive or Abstract Shape.* Abstract shape in graphic composition can effectively be used to establish balance. Once again, the copy block is a good example of this. The designer views copy as shape and uses it as a balance against other elements. As such, it is a heavily influential factor, especially in book, magazine, and brochure design. As an abstract component of the total design of a piece, it is a dynamically flexible element in all types of graphic composition. The typographic style of copy is often used as a decorative ingredient in design and may balance by contrast. Whether a one-word headline or a mass of body copy, its shape configuration has great meaning in relation to the pictorial material of the composition. When typographic shape is played against itself, as when typography is the only element of a composition, the shape variation factor becomes very apparent. This can be seen in much of the poster work of the Bauhaus.

Abstract shape as color or value mass has always been a powerful factor in graphic communication. Used in support of illustrative or typographic material, it can help to structure the compositional area, its character (as discussed earlier) being a significant factor in the visual rationale of the total image. When it is used to interpret aspects of the literal, in a stylized sense, abstract shape can combine to formulate imagery that conveys the idea even more quickly than the literal shape.

Abstract shape can be used to control the direction and duration of the observer's attention. The designer can use shape in much the same manner as the painter: to lead the eye around the compositional format or toward the central message. This visual control aids the transition between divergent elements. The rhythmic movement established by this visual transition serves as a unifying device for the composition.

Until very recently, all the major movements in painting were concerned entirely with the central tenets of modernism: (1) nonillusionism, and (2) maintaining the integrity of the picture plane (flatness). To a great extent, the graphic designers of the late 1940s, the 1950s, and early 1960s followed this trend, but the practical aspects of the designer's work has always necessitated dealing with the concept of space on the two-dimensional surface to some degree no matter what the current stylistic dogmas.

Shape is the major means by which the designer deals with this allusion to form and space—shape in conjunction with line through the systems of linear perspective and the concepts of volume and the spatial plane. The abstraction of shape to form spatial effects, the styling of shapes in combination for symbolic spatial reference, are both common usages in graphic communication of all periods when the literal image does not adequately fill the requirements of the concept.

Historically, the graphic designer may be less

**29**

involved with the technical aspects of the illusion of space on the two-dimensional surface (the mechanics of linear perspective) than the architect or the industrial or interior designer; but the conceptual idea of spatial shape has always been important in graphics. Besides its utilitarian function, it gives the designer infinite devices for expression with or without the rational conclusions that are absolutely necessary to these other disciplines.

## SHAPE AS SYMBOL

For the graphic designer, the development of visual symbols is an exercise in the design of shape. There are many variables in the evolution of symbolic communication, but the common visual denominator for symbols is shape. Indeed, the ultimate summation of visual symbols is shape. Because of this, a discussion of symbolic communicating seems essential at this point.

The basis for symbolic communication lies in people's response to stimuli that relates to similar stimuli acquired from their past experience. Symbols create imagery that triggers perceptual experiences associated with what the stimulus represents. (For example, see Figure 29.)

One does not have to stop and think to be affected by strong symbolic stimuli like these. We have internalized such symbolic references to the point where they are accepted on almost a subconscious level.

Visual symbols function in five basic ways: (1) to identify events, (2) to describe the nature of objects, (3) to establish forms of behavior, (4) as positive-negative evaluators, and (5) as a general frame of reference for comparison. Shape becomes symbolic when it performs one or more of these functions.

Visual symbols, along with all other types of symbolic communication, fit into three general categories: (1) conventional symbols, (2) personal symbols, and (3) universal symbols. *Conventional* symbols are written words, representational sketches, and color that is strongly associated with ideas and events. Many visual symbols fit into this category. *Personal* symbols express an individual's past experience with life. They are formed around attitudes and beliefs and become representative of them. Such symbols are difficult to change. *Universal* symbols are those things that are basic to all humanity. Life and nature are manifest through universal symbolism. Art and science communicate with many universal symbols.

## *Using Symbolic Shape*

1. *Conventional Symbols.* Most conventional visual symbols are interpretations of literal shapes. More than simply pictures of things, they represent larger ideas. An idealized drawing of a matronly woman on a bottle of cough syrup or a cold remedy from the turn of the century was more than a literal shape, a picture of a person. It was a powerful symbol as well, and it conveyed a "mother knows best" attitude that still has a psychological holdover in today's marketplace. The basis of many contemporary trademarks is in the adaption of the literal-shape configuration. One need only walk through a supermarket to observe smiling faces, scratching chicks, dancing fish, colonial mansions, top hats, crowing roosters, and hundreds of other conventional symbols representing as many different ideas. Some of the world's largest corporations express their identities through the use of conventional symbols based either strictly or loosely on literal shapes such as Prudential's rock, Shell Oil's shell, and so on.

2. *Interpretive or Abstract Symbols.* Classic hobo signs are good examples of interpretive symbolic shape. They are codified markings giving pragmatic information about what will be found in a particular place by future visitors.

Abstractions of letterforms are a very common symbolic usage. By themselves—or in combination with other letterforms or imagery—letterforms run the gamut from conventional application to high abstractions of shape and pattern. Most applications of letterforms as symbolic identifiers are seen out of their conventional context, to make them more distinctive and memorable.

Following is a further sampling of letterforms in a wide spectrum of corporate usage. The range of possible applications is as infinite as the imagination of the designer. Notice the range of applications from literal word symbol shape to highly interpretive abstraction of shape.

### INTERPRETING A CORPORATE SYMBOL

Let's take a look at a well known (and well designed) corporate symbol and interpret the design logic behind its component parts. Interpreting should be easy in the case of our example because the design *communicates* the involvement of the company so simply and directly.

The symbol is the corporate mark for the International Paper Company. It is applied in various ways as an identifier of the company's business involvement: on letterhead stationery and business cards, on the sides of trucks, on rolls and cartons of paper, and on buildings within corporate properties. It is a visually strong identifier, memorable, and easily applied to many sur-

faces and translated to many sizes.

Pictograms, abstracted shapes that are distillations of events in our environment, are so common to our culture that we take them for granted. They are illustrative examples, storytelling segments of interpretive symbolic shapes.

**41**

**41** International Paper Company

**42** The circle: earlier in the chapter we discussed the personality of shape and its implications when used to personify an idea. The circle is representative of continuity and timelessness; it is the most self-contained of shapes. Universally, it is used to suggest a complete sense of balance and order. More literally, paper comes in large rolls.

**43** The tree form: here it is used in an interpretive, abstract way to indicate the company's primary business involvement, the manufacture of paper products.

**44** The components of the tree form: the tree form itself is made up of the initial letters of the company name. The careful design of the letters to form the tree shape is calculated to reinforce the psychological totality of the image.

**45** The reasoning behind the elements of the mark is soundly based. Although the image is beautifully crafted from an aesthetic standpoint, nothing was done for the sake of design alone. There are no wasted artistic gestures here. Visual elements and symbolic ideas meld together in a perfect symbiotic message. Unfortunately, not all symbols can or do convey such a sense of function.

THE CIRCLE

THE COMPONENTS OF THE TREE FORM (I.P.)

**42**          **44**

THE INTEGRATED COMPONENTS

THE TREE FORM

**43**          **45**

**46** Futura Black as a possible inspiration for the Ansul Company mark.

**47** Stymie as a possible inspiration for the IBM mark.

**48** Eurostyle as a possible inspiration for the Abbott Laboratories mark.

**Futura Black**
46

STYMIE
47

Eurostyle
48

**49** A. B. Dick Company

**50** Container Corporation Of America

**51** Foulds Inc.

**52** Standard Photo Supply

49

50

51

52

**53** Snack bar; picnic area; Smokey the Bear (Forest fire prevention)

53

## THE EVOLUTION OF A SYMBOL

If we were designing a symbol shape, consciously or not, we would progress through some or all of these stages in the evolution of our conceptual thinking.

It might seem that we have wandered far afield from our initial premise, which was a review of line and shape from the working designer's viewpoint, but in actual fact we have not. At the outset we stated that shape was an extension of the linear concept and that line and shape are interdependent, symbiotic elements in the work of the graphic designer. In the same context, symbols are interdependent with shape, and every exercise in symbol development, in great part, is simply a sophisticated application of the essential attributes of shape. There are, of course, many other complicated aspects to the development of a symbol, but at the artistic level it is impossible to separate the concepts of shape and symbol.

54

55

56

57

58

59

**54**   The nonvisual conventional conceptual word symbol.

**55**   The literal picture/shape.

**56**   The literal picture/shape "symbolized" (as in a "cameo" logo application on a package design such as discussed earlier).

**57**   Segmentation of the literal picture/shape in symbolic usage (same application).

**58**   Interpretive distillation of the literal picture/shape (elementary descriptive "cartoon" image).

**59**   The interpretive distillation "symbolized."

**60**   Universal symbolic abstraction of the concept of bird.

**61**   Figurative stylization in symbolic form (stylized patterning).

**62**   Complete abstraction of shape symbolizing the concept of bird.

**63**   Complete abstraction reinforced with the conventional conceptual word symbol and presented as a specific communication device.

**60**

**61**

**62**

**63**

# TYPOGRAPHY*

## *Chapter 6*

ANTIQUE OLIVE

**H**arry Fat, Shotgun, Skin and Bones, Fat Face, Snell Roundhand, and Rondo Bold are not the names of shady characters from a "B" gangster movie or a Dick Tracy comic. They are characters of another kind. They are but a few of the thousands of typeface "characters" at the disposal of the designer. Harry Fat and friends are examples of the trendy variations in type that come and go as quickly as the styles in women's fashions. Trying to keep track of every new hybrid variation would be next to impossible, and the great majority of these typefaces have very limited use for the designer. In looking for a novelty face, the designer need only open any number of type books and leaf through them until something that suits his or her needs is found. While delightful and effective usage can be made of "oddball" type styles, they are outside the mainstream of typography and design considerations.

Although the designer does use type books to select the right face or faces to solve any given problem, it is essential that he or she be familiar with the large group that comprises the all-around "usable" spectrum of typefaces. Without a working knowledge of these "classic" families of type, it would be difficult indeed to design anything that incorporates the written word. To be able to think "Century Medium," "Univers 45," "Optima," or "Goudy Oldstyle," and have a clear idea in mind of the general feel, weight, and character personality of each, is a practical sense all good designers have learned.

For the design student, learning mainstream type families and their variations and the characteristics that make them unique, early on, can make life a lot easier in the classroom. Following is a list of the most used and generally the most versatile typefaces available to designers.

---

*All sample paragraphs in this chapter are set in 10 point type with 2 point leading.

| | | |
|---|---|---|
| **Alternate Gothic** | Craw | News Gothic |
| Avant Garde | Egyptian | **Olive Antique** |
| Baskerville | Eurostyle | Optima |
| Bernhard | Folio | Palatino |
| **Beton** | **Fortune** | Perpetua |
| **Bodoni** | **Franklin Gothic** | Plantin |
| **Bookman** | Futura | **Souvenir** |
| Caledonia | Garamond | **Spartan** |
| Caslon | Gill Sans-Serif | Standard |
| Century | Goudy | **Stymie** |
| Cheltenham | Grotesque | Times Roman |
| **Clarendon** | Helvetica | Trade Gothic |
| Clearface | Kabel | Univers |
| Cloister | Korinna | **Venus** |
| **Compacta** | Lydian | Weiss |
| **Cooper** | Melior | Windsor |
| COPPERPLATE | Memphis | |
| **Corvinus** | Microgramma | |

BODONI

Many of these faces vary only in subtle ways; some are used much more regularly than others and have been popular for years. Generally speaking, there are very few design problems that cannot be solved satisfactorily with one or more of these "classic" type families.

By calling them "classic" typefaces, we do not mean there are no other beautiful or versatile faces available to the designer. There are many. Indeed, new variations on letter designs seem to be coming out on a regular basis, and contemporary type designers are as busily creative as their historical counterparts ever were. There are many excellent periodicals available that deal with contemporary typography development. The one most easily obtained by the designer is *U&LC* (Upper & Lower Case), a FREE newsprint format publication that speaks, in an off-hand and humorous way, to other issues and subjects as well. For subscription information write to: U&LC
216 East 45th St.
New York, NY     10017

**65**  Our alphabet of 26 letters is one of approximately two hundred identified by scholars. Fifty of these alphabets are in use today. Ours, the "Roman" alphabet, is the world's most widely used.

When Roman craftsmen carved letters in stone, they found that the grooved stroke made by the chisel seemed to bow out or bulge visibly toward the middle. To compensate for this illusion, stone cutters swelled the ends of the strokes slightly. This turning out with the chisel created a graceful, highly legible letterform that reflected more of the character of the hand calligraphy on which the stone-cut letters were based.

The letters on the column of Trajan in Rome are considered to show the ideal proportions of Roman form. They are still used as a guide by type designers. This detailing of letter-strokes by stonemasons is a probable origin of the serif letter.

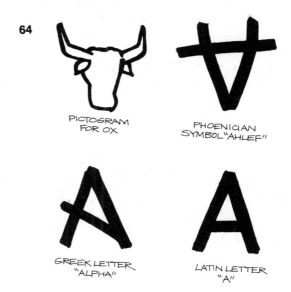

**64**

PICTOGRAM FOR OX

PHOENICIAN SYMBOL "AHLEF"

GREEK LETTER "ALPHA"

LATIN LETTER "A"

**64**  The journey from pictograms and drawings to symbols and finally letter-forms was an entirely logical one. Letters were first drawn with instruments that made uneven, variable lines as opposed to uniform strokes. Reed pens, brushes, and the stylus, all contributed to the development of the letter as we know it. Habits formed over centuries dictated stylistic parameters that helped form alphabets.

The first formal alphabet known preceded our own and was used by the Phoenicians and other Semitic cultures of the Near East. The Phoenician word for "ox," for instance, was "Ahlef." The symbol for this sound looked a great deal like the head of and ox. Later Greeks took the symbol from the Phoenicians, turned it upside down, and pronounced it "Alpha." Alpha was then translated into "Ah" in Latin, and the present day shape for "A" came into being. Other alphabets, derived from symbols of other cultures, developed along stylistic lines reflecting the attitudes and values of those civilizations in which they were based. One need only look at the hieroglyphic writing of Egypt or the delicate calligraphy of China or Japan to understand the tremendous cultural differences reflected in handwriting.

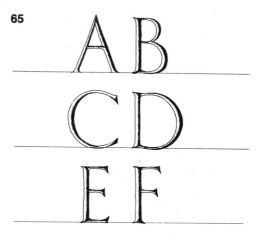

**65**

FREE-HAND SKETCHING OF LETTER FORMS FROM THE COLUMN OF TRAJAN

# Garamond

The invention of a "true type," a typeface that would appear uniformly "printed" in character, is generally credited to a Frenchman. His name was Claude Garamont (later spelled Garamond). With Garamont, a profession was born. He was the first full-time typefounder or maker of type. Garamont's face and derivatives of it were used as the principal type for 200 years. It is still the prototype of the "oldstyle" romans. He placed great emphasis on the design of lower case letters, blending their shapes and creating a pleasing uniformity while retaining a sense of grace and character.

# Caslon

The movement away from Garamont's type began in the latter half of the 17th century, and in 1722, William Caslon I, an Englishman, cut a revolutionary new face which he called "Oldstyle." The Caslon face, while devoid of distinctiveness in individual character design, tended to "read" as a whole very well and give the overall appearance of solid simplicity and strength. It became popular immediately and became the mainstay of a whole family of Caslon types that would follow. Caslon enjoyed widespread usage in the American colonies and became a "standard" in U.S. printing.

# Baskerville

The first type "designer" (as opposed to type-founder or maker) was an Englishman named John Baskerville. Baskerville was a wealthy manufacturer and amateur printer who designed on paper a typeface that was, in its own right, as revolutionary as Caslon's had been. His face, a redesign of Caslon, was straighter and more mechanical. He flattened his serifs and heightened the thick and thin aspects of the characters. Baskerville also contributed to the development of printing technology. Among other things, he created a finer grained ink and printed his type-face (more delicate than Caslon's) on smoother, slicker paper stock. Unlike Caslon, Baskerville did not enjoy immediate success with his type-face. It took 40 years to gain acceptance, but when it did, its popularity circumvented even the universally favored Caslon Oldface. Benjamin Franklin was one of Baskerville's main proponents in this country. Baskerville's type represents the first major "transitional" roman.

# Bodoni

Firmin Didot, a member of a famous Parisian printing family, introduced a crisp, sharply cut letterform that he printed on an improved press developed by his family's firm, F. A. Didot. Improved papermaking techniques of the time made available a woven paper that added to the precise impression achieved by Didot's face. Didot is better remembered for giving Europe a fully developed type measurement system (named after him) than for being an originator of modern roman letters, however.

Giambatista Bodoni, printer for the Duke of Parma and a prolific type designer, receives credit for the "modern" roman face. Although his letters were not as "pure" or radical in concept as Didot's, his influence appears to have been greater, and history has given him the "lion's share," perhaps unduly. Didot's typeface, very popular in Europe, is not available in the U.S. Instead, we have utilized the large family of Bodoni types.

# Firmin Didot Bold

# Bodoni Bold

# Bodoni Ultra Bold

**67** This type has been set in Atlantic/Plantin 36 point and 9 point, 1 point lead. By putting a pica rule on each line and comparing the regular set against the Italic, you can see that the Italic "sets up" to a tighter measure.

# *Italic Type:*

*"Italic" or slanted type originated in the 16th century in Venice. Aldus Manutius, a local printer, sensed a growing trend for cheaper books. He developed a new type based on existing roman designs married with characteristics of the informal hand-writing of the time. Manutius called this type "Chancery", or in Italian, "Chancelleresca". His Italian contemporaries called it "Aldine" in defer-ence to him, and in the rest of Europe it was known as "Italic", referring to the type's Italian heritage. The combined effect of the slanted letters was graceful and because slanted letters could be designed narrower than their upright counterparts without affecting their readability, more words could be printed on a page thus cutting down on the number of pages and the amount of paper used in a book.*

"Italic" or slanted type originated in the 16th century in Venice. Aldus Manutius, a local printer, sensed a growing trend for cheaper books. He developed a new type based on existing roman designs married with characteristics of the informal hand-writing of the time. Manutius called this type "Chancery", or in Italian, "Chancelleresca". His Italian contemporaries called it "Aldine" in defer-ence to him, and in the rest of Europe it was known as "Italic", referring to the type's Italian heritage. The combined effect of the slanted letters was graceful and because slanted letters could be designed narrower than their upright counterparts without affecting their readability, more words could be printed on a page thus cutting down on the number of pages and the amount of paper used in a book.

**68**

Sans-Serif and Revolution:
The Industrial Revolution and the age of mechanization made new demands on the development of typography. Alphabets designed specifically for the process of printing and to serve the needs of commerce and advertising came into being. A new plethora of display faces, heavier, cruder, more easily cut, attention grabbing faces, were put into mass use. The first heavy faced letters were introduced by Robert Thorne at the Fann Street Foundry in London in 1803. Other types followed. Heavy serified "Egyptians" were introduced by Vincent Figgins in 1815.

**TYPE TYPE TYPE TYPE TYPE TYPE TYPE TYPE**

# EGYPTIAN BOLD EXTENDED

William Caslon IV, one of the better known type designers of the period, first cut a type of uniform thickness without serifs. He called his letters "Egyptian" also, but the terms "gothic" and "grotesque", which earlier had been used to describe Northern Renaissance black text, were now popularly applied to all these new "mechanized" types. Hundreds of variations of these faces soon blossomed in peacock fashion, and literally all sizes, weights and styles were available. Sans Serif faces flourished briefly in the 1800's, but did not gain permanent acceptance until the early twentieth century.

# Gill-Sans letters

Sans-Serif Refinement in England and the
Bauhaus Revolt: **The English played a major role in
the refinement of Sans-Serif type. Edward Johnston
and Eric Gill were important contributors.**
*Johnston designed a well-balanced, beautiful sans for
the London Underground, and Gill Sans is still a major
offering in most commercial type books.* **This is the
Gill face in its differing aspects.**

# Futura Book letters

Out of the chaos of the turn of the century, a new
group emerged intent dealing with the realities of the
age of technology and its need for designers. The
Bauhaus originated at Weimar under the leadership
of the architect Walter Gropius and was intended
primarily to be a combined art and technological
school. The movements of Cubism, Constructivism,
DeStijl, and Dadaism heavily influenced the
typographic work of the Bauhaus designers.

Its teachers such as L. Moholy-Nagy, Herbert Bayer,
and Joost Schmidt, sought to break down the barrier
of gothic tradition that still permiated German
typography and book design, and build an aesthetic
based on geometric fundamentals. Herbert Bayer
designed an ''ideal'' type face in reaction to the black
text Fraktur of everyday usage that he felt would
communicate directly and clearly, and along with other
designers, established a blueprint for a new typography
governed by mechanical logic. Bayer went so far as
to suggest that capital letters were simply redundant
and unnecessary, and ''designed'' them out
of his alphabet.

One of the lasting faces to come out of the
Bauhaus movement is Futura. It is still widely used
today and represents the now ''classic'' principles
of the new typography.

# The Revolution in Typography

ROCKWELL

In the "old days," type was either handset or set by
operators on clattering, Rube Goldberg-style machines. Although Monotype and Linotype machines
are still pounding out molten lead characters and lines
today, conceptually they are dinosaurs of the past.
Aside from the handset headline, which is still demanded by some designers and art directors, it is safe
to say that almost all type orders are processed by the
"cold type" method. Cold type is all type set by computer, by photocomposition, and by all systems in general that are not cast from molten metal ("hot type") or
are handset ("foundry type").

BOOKMAN

**In 1949, photographic composition of
type was introduced on a wide scale. As the
name implies, type is produced in lines on film
or photographic paper by a photographic line-
composing machine. By rotating the lens, the
letters can be shaped and distorted in various
ways to produce all the standard typographic
variations within a given family (condensed, expanded, italic) as well as customized effects
such as curving a line to any desired shape,
pitching and angling to perspective planes, and
even turning of words and sentences in 360°
circumferences. All of these procedures are expensive compared with the normal use of film
lettering—that is, for headlines and copy set in
regular lines.**

CALEDONIA

Typographers generally agree that photoset
type is more precise than characters reproduced from
hot metal moldings. Because the image is reproduced
on photographic paper, it can be blown up much larger
without losing its sharpness. Both letters and words can
be "kerned" back (brought closer together) to make the
total effect of the copy-block tighter. The designer can
choose the exact amount of kerning desired, all the way
to and including overlapping of letters if needed. Kerning cannot be done with hot metal methods.

CENTURY

The modern slayer of the hot type "dino-
saur" is the computer. Virtually all modern typesetting systems are computerized. Advanced Photo-
optic and Photo-scanning typesetters, as well as
digital scan setters and even laser-generated imagery, are common today where even ten years ago
they would have been considered science fiction. Indeed, the world of typesetting technology is changing so fast that equipment that was new six

**70**    An example from the Shore Typography Display book showing options in headline "colorspacing" (kerning).

## SHORE | Display

To assist you in ordering phototype headlines colorspaced to your visual needs, we have set five different styles of colorspacing in Sans Serif and Serif type styles. All Shore phototype will be colorspaced Visually Normal unless you specify Tight, Very Tight, Touch or Overlap.

**Advertising Typography**

Advertising Typography

NORMAL

**Advertising Typography**

Advertising Typography

TIGHT

**Advertising Typography**

Advertising Typography

VERY TIGHT

**Advertising Typography**

Advertising Typography

TOUCH

**Advertising Typography**

Advertising Typography

OVERLAP

months ago may already be outdated! The phenomenon of direct-entry (direct input) phototypesetting, machines that have input and output capabilities all contained within one unit, and their interfacing capabilities with word processors, have made in-house typesetting a growing reality in many business enterprises.

CASLON

The advent of computer typesetting has created a "cottage industry" where once huge typesetting firms dominated, for they were the only ones that could afford the space and machinery necessary to serve many clients. Now, with the lease or purchase of many different computer typesetters and the myriad software fonts and type families that accompany them, smaller "boutique" typesetting shops suddenly find themselves able to compete profitably with their larger brethren, and in some cases, to even undercut the larger firms' pricing structures by a substantial margin. The "mom & pop" typesetter phenomenon is well underway and will prosper with the continuing advances in computer technology.

CHELTENHAM

What does all of this mean for the designer? Over the long term, it means an improvement in the communication effectiveness of the graphic medium. As systems technology improves, subtle variations and graphic touches previously too costly or impossible to achieve will become commonplace. As advanced systems move "into the office," they become more controllable. As art directors, designers, and even business managers inevitably learn to master the new typography, whole new ranges of possibilities will emerge to influence and change the entire graphics industry.

CLARENDON

**On a more immediate level, the computer typesetting revolution means it is easier to have a one-to-one relationship with your typographer, to get—generally—better service than before. Dealing with a service representative who is closer to you and your problems makes for better communication, and if he can already know your working habits and anticipate your needs, so much the better for you. When you enter the professional world and find yourself dealing with a typed manuscript from a copywriter ready for type specification, you will appreciate the special attention you may get from your more "local" typographer. Not that the traditional type houses are insensitive to personal service—the phone order is still the predominant procedure when ordering type. But designers are suddenly finding the big type houses more attentive to their business needs than in the past . . . their reps are more often seen on the designer's personal horizon!**

CLEARFACE

The image of the typesetter is also changing with the advent of the smaller cold-type shops. Once, the typographer, like the printer, was steeped in the elbow grease and lore of mechanized nineteenth and early twentieth century typesetting. Today, people with professional training in art, business, and technology are entering the typesetting field. Greater sensitivity to the demands of creativity is one result, and award-winning typographic detailing, not always the exclusive talent of the designer, is being seen. More than ever before, the business of typography is becoming a creative medium in and of itself.

CLOISTER

The one tremendous advantage the large typesetter still offers the designer is the variety of faces and mediums they offer. Being able to work with one set of books, to order everything from one source, simplifies the designer's task as well as creates greater continuity. Many smaller typehouses will not have a complete range in all of their representative typefaces. For instance, a small firm may have invested in Helvetica regular and medium, but may have chosen not to get the condensed or extended fonts in either weight. Also, because the big type designers patent and sell exclusive rights to the reproduction of their designs, unless your typographer has a system that includes a particular face, you will not have it available to you in your typographer's specimen book. What you might see instead is a lookalike, "spin-off" face.

PLANTIN

For example, the International Type Corporation (ITC), one of the major contributors to modern typographic design and development, sells the rights to represent and reproduce its faces. If one of its faces becomes extremely popular (as many often have), competing organizations may market a similar construction under a different patent name. These lookalike faces are so similar it is virtually impossible for the untrained eye to observe the differences. If you, as a typographer, have purchased a system that incorporates one of these lookalike faces, you of course, will offer it rather than the original. There is nothing wrong with these lookalike faces. They are used extensively—depending upon which typographer you use, what system that typographer has purchased, and the typefaces available under that system.

COOPER BLACK

**Nonetheless, these typefaces do vary, if only microscopically, from the original. For the designer with his heart set on Stymie, who has an experienced and discerning eye for the typeface, it certainly is an irritation to settle for a lookalike that is a shade different in lettercasting and proportion! These may be minor irritations to many designers, who are more practical with budgets or feel the total typographic effect is secondary**

**71** An example from the Shore Typography Display book illustrating some of the possibilities for letter distortion.

# Type Distortion

The Altergraph is a radical new distortion and reproportioning device which does an amazing range of distortion work without the use of mirrors, prisms, or lenses. The Altergraph will change one dimension of a headline, logo, or piece of line art up to four times increase or decrease. It will italicize or backslant in one-half degree increments to more than 30 degrees, as well as curve lines in many interesting ways.

The process works just as well on paragraphs of machine type to create unique type faces which are unavailable by any other method. For your next piece of unusual artwork, call Shore first. You will be amazed at the wild effects which you can achieve with this new service.

## Shore

Italicizes and Backslants to any degree

*Shore* **Shore**

Does "Plumb" Curves; both standard and customized

**ShoreShore**

Reproportions over an amazing range

**Shore** **Shore**

Does Circles and Arcs

**ShoreShore**

**72**  Some of the topography specimen books made available to Shore customers.

**to the visual picture development. But to the "stickler", to the lover of a well-turned and familiar "foot" or the particular rounding of a "knee," the rise or fall of an ascender or descender, to the designer captivated by the "feel" of an original face, there is no substitute!**

ALTERNATE GOTHIC

BENGUIAT

The major typesetters in large cities will carry *all* of the originals . . . all of the faces on our list at the beginning of the chapter, and more. Like as not, they will carry them in film, in hot metal, and to some degree in foundry. They will carry them in every conceivable weight and configuration. They will "bend" them to your specifications, and some of them will even have the sophisticated capability of distorting them beyond your wildest dreams! As well as this, they will carry hundreds of "boutique," "Harry Fat" style faces in film, and periodically come out with new "appendage" booklets full of them for your reference. To offer all this requires a great deal of space, equipment, and staff and, obviously, this drives up the cost of an order.

CRAW MODERN

So! Certainly it is to the designer's advantage to use *both* avenues of typesetting for his or her clients. Where there is a budget problem, or where you can get the *same* face more cheaply and quicker by using the small shop, where your relationship with their working establishment may be more intimate, it is wise to do so. Where you have a large job with a number of variations in size, font, and face, or where you need specialty faces or strange letter configurations and angles, it

is necessary to go to the long-standing experts with the sophisticated equipment to back them (and you) up. In either case, it is the designer's job to foresee and plan for these budget requirements wherever possible in advance of the situation. The way to do this, naturally, is to *know your typographers* and their capabilities.

## The Kinds of Typefaces

Type can be classified in different ways. Unless you are a student of the art form, steeped in the lore and history of calligraphy and type design, where categories according to time, place, and style are meaningful, broad classification of type is easiest to remember. As a practicing designer, you will find yourself arranging type in your head that generally corresponds with categories used by commercial typographers and found in type books that they supply to designers and design establishments. After learning basic information concerning the history and development of typography, the best classroom references for typography are *commercial type specimen books*. Typography texts are only good for teaching you *about* typography. A typography text so ambitious as to include even three quarters of the families, sizes, kerning specifications, character counts, and current boutique film fonts available from any of a number of big city typesetters has yet to be published! For your own benefit, get hold of a set of specimen books from a large typography house . . . even if they are out of date. Many used bookstores specializing in art and graphic arts will, from time to time, have specimen books. Your class could also request a set of books from a large typesetter in or near your city. You may have to pay for them, but the cost is well worth it.

EGYPTIAN

In terms of specific information about types, the designer and the typographer he or she uses must speak the same language. Since the designer deals with type houses almost on a daily basis, it is imperative to learn about and work with type in the contemporary sense and to be familiar with terminology and classification as it is currently being used in the marketplace. Since most type is ordered over the phone, given as typewritten pages marked with appropriate "specs" (specifications), or "talked" out with a type rep and set to fit an agreed-upon format, it is essential to keep the margin for error to a minimum.

ERAS

Broad categories of type—as generally arranged by typography houses in their type specimen books—are as follows:

1. *Serif Faces:* Most of the "classic" faces and derivatives thereof, with pronounced thick-and-thin strokes and formed serifs, make up the serif group. This

classification runs the gamut from the old styles to the transitionals to the modern families.

2. *Sans-Serif Faces:* All faces that exhibit strokes of even or near-even thickness or faces with attenuated strokes without serif ends (such as Optima) fall into this category. Tooled faces that appear closer to penned strokes (such as Lydian) are also included here.

3. *Square Serif Faces:* These are faces with the sans-serif characteristics of uniform or near uniform thickness, but with pronounced thick serifs such as Clarendon, Stymie, Beton, and Fortune.

4. *Script Faces:* Scripts are specialty faces designed to reflect the running characteristics of handwriting, with letters that connect either visually or physically. Most scripts are italicized and form two groups: (1) the formal group such as Commercial Script, Park Avenue and Snell Roundhand, and (2) the informal or casual group with a more irregular or brushed-letter look such as Kaufmann or Brush Script. No distinction between formal or informal is made in the script section of most type specification books.

5. *Decorative Faces:* This classification usually includes the black text gothics and their derivatives. It also includes a large number of serif and sans-serif "stylized" faces and other heavily ornate alphabets.

6. *Open, Shaded, and Three-Dimensional Faces:* Many of the standard faces have added effects that do not alter the basic design of the letters, such as the customized decorative faces do. These effects include outline letters, drop shadow letters, and other similar variations.

7. *Miscellaneous, Casual Faces:* Miscellaneous and casual types are similar to the decorative faces and, indeed, many are interchangeable with faces in that category. Most faces in this group are spinoffs of existing established faces, individualized to create informal and spontaneous effects. The typeface Ad Lib or Safari, for example, enjoyed a brief but intense popularity in some circles in the mid-1960s as a headline type (probably under many different names); it is an obvious informal stylization of one or more of the classic sans-serif grotesques. The majority of types in this category (as well as the previous two categories) have limited usefulness as they are only offered on film, 24 point or larger, and many of them have only been designed in capital letters.

## FAMILIES OF TYPE

Within each category there are many families of type. The families are divided into series, and the series are divided into fonts. Garamond is a family of type in the roman serif category. Within that family are different series of Garamond types such

as Garamond Light, Garamond Medium, Garamond Bold, and Garamond Extra-Bold. In addition to these, there are italic and condensed variations (in many faces there are extended variations also). All of these variations are separate series within the Garamond family. A particular size of type in any of the series is called a font (i.e., 24 point Garamond Bold Condensed is a font in the Bold Condensed series).

## THE POINT SYSTEM

Typographers measure the size of type by points. If you wish to speak intelligently about type to a typographer you must speak in terms of points, picas, and leading. Linear measures based on standard ruler designates have little meaning in the world of letterforms. This complex medium requires a specific language to communicate accurately, and it is the designer's responsibility to learn how to do this.

There are 72 points to the typographer's inch, 36 points to the half inch. The man responsible for working out the type measurement system was a Frenchman, Fermin Didot. Didot was from a famous Parisian printing family who, in addition to creating a uniform system for measuring type, developed a sharply cut type more appropriate to newer developments in papermaking that still bears his name. The Didot typeface is extremely popular into the present day, although its usage in this country is very limited. Americans have preferred and popularized another similar modern roman face developed about the same time: Bodoni.

**73** A complete "family" of type.

Garamond Light
Garamond Book
**Garamond Bold**
**Garamond Ultra**
*Garamond Light Italic*
*Garamond Book Italic*
***Garamond Bold Italic***
***Garamond Ultra Italic***
Garamond Light Condensed
Garamond Book Condensed
**Garamond Bold Condensed**
**Garamond Ultra Condensed**
*Garamond Light Condensed Italic*
*Garamond Book Condensed Italic*
***Garamond Bold Condensed Italic***
***Garamond Ultra Condensed Italic***

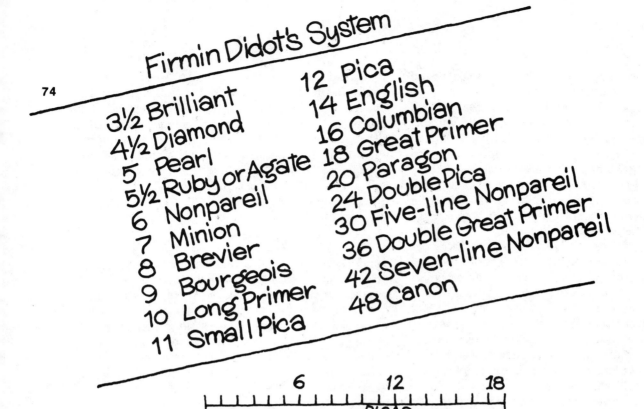

Firmin Didot's System

3½ Brilliant
4½ Diamond
5 Pearl
5½ Ruby or Agate
6 Nonpareil
7 Minion
8 Brevier
9 Bourgeois
10 Long Primer
11 Small Pica

12 Pica
14 English
16 Columbian
18 Great Primer
20 Paragon
24 Double Pica
30 Five-line Nonpareil
36 Double Great Primer
42 Seven-line Nonpareil
48 Canon

6   12   18
PICAS
INCHES
1   2   3

1 POINT = .0138 inch
12 POINTS = 1 PICA
72 POINTS = .9962 inch

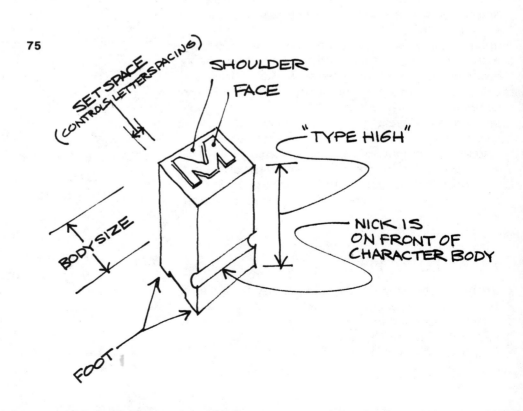

75

SET SPACE
(CONTROLS LETTERSPACING)

SHOULDER
FACE

"TYPE HIGH"

BODY SIZE

NICK IS
ON FRONT OF
CHARACTER BODY

FOOT

FOLIO LITE

Didot affixed a name to each type size or point that he identified (from 3½ to 48), and each point size became known by its name. While the measuring system established by Didot is universal today, the only two names to remain in common twentieth-century usage are Agate and Pica. Even the Agate measure, a system used for years by newspapers to calculate the depth of a column for article and ad space, is going by the way in favor of newer calculations and nomenclature.

CHELTENHAM ITALIC

*Pica, however, is a term that will likely remain with the typography medium for some time to come, because pica exists as the standard unit of linear measure for all type. Each pica is the equivalent of 12 points, and divides an inch equally into 6 handy units. Both typographers and designers use rules that designate points and picas as well as inches, and line and column widths are figured in picas. Leading (the amount of space between lines) is figured in points.*

FRANKLIN GOTHIC

**Measurement of type is taken through the height of a character, not the width. While the height of a particular font remains constant, the width will vary depending upon the letter (*i* being narrower than *w*). In theory then, a 36 point capital letter should be a half-inch in height. In fact, the actual letter or character is somewhat smaller than its point measure. This is because the point measurement is taken from the perimeters of the slug or base on which the character was (in foundry and hot-type technology) cast or carved. Didot really established his points based on the edge-to-edge measure of the body of each character. The space left between the edge of the slug and the character that sat upon it served as a control of minimum space between letters and as a ground for ascending and descending strokes. Following is a diagram of a typical foundry-type character.**

FUTURA BOOK

When technology made the jump to film and computer, the Didot system (upon which all types were designed or recut) was maintained for uniformity and for consistency with the historic visual logic of typography . . . with one radical departure: now that letterforms were no longer captive parts of wood or metal slugs, limitations on letter spacing were suddenly nonexistent. While classic spacing based on classic design is still respected (it was always possible to space out letters), the typographer and designer could now kern back characters and words to individual tastes. Line spacing was also affected by the sudden technological freedom. Foundry and hot-type line spacing was done with point rules (metal dividers of varying thickness). A 10 point type which sat on a 10 point body was separated, line by line, in this manner. Now (almost literally by the push of a button) the computer will track out spacing as you like it—that is, 10 point on 11 point body ("10 on 11"), 10 point on 12 point body ("10 on 12"), etc.—for any typeface.

ITC FENICE

The range of available type sizes usually goes from 4½ or 5 points up to 96 point. While there are typefaces in 1 point (and even smaller), their application is, obviously, very limited. The smallest standard size offered by most type houses is 4½. We can categorize point sizes from 4½ through 96 into two groups:

1. *Body Types:* Sizes 4½ through 6 point are generally used for legal or technical copy accompanying text material, or for annotations, etc. Eight through 12 point are standard text sizes, with 8 and 10 point being the most commonly used.
2. *Display Types:* Sizes 14 through 96 point are for display or headline type, with 24, 36, and 48 point the most commonly used. Fourteen point, often used as a text type as well, is really a borderline size between the two categories.

## HEADLINE AND BODYTYPE USAGE

GILL SANS-SERIF

To make hard and fast rules about what you can and cannot do with type is ridiculous. Just as with any other tool or medium, the aesthetic is subject to change. In the 1950s designers fashionably leaded out lines of type to exaggerated proportions on a page. In the early 1970s, overly enamoured with the possibilities of kerning, designers packed letters and words so close together that readability became a critical factor. Designers' attitudes change with the trend of the times, which is as it should be. However, to accept a current trend as gospel, or the ideas of a designer or spokesperson enjoying a brief popularity as basic truth is simply parroting another's opinion. There are designers who have never recovered from the romance of Helvetica during the late 1960s and early 1970s and are still specing it as if there is no other face! Attitudes about Optima being "old hat" or suddenly "not smart," or that Friz Quadrata or Baker Signet are a "new" answer, or carefully mimicking the typographic effects of the Bauhaus and thinking it a "fresh new trend," are incredibly stupid patterns of behavior and point up the immature aesthetic sensitivity many designers seem never quite to grow out of.

GOUDY

The design student, especially, is in a position to assimilate a great many ideas and attitudes. Why be controlled by one or two? Using common sense as a de-

GROTESQUE

signer is important. Learn to see *and admit* that if something honestly does not work it should be discarded, trendy or not. To be bound by an idiom is never wise unless it makes sense for the task at hand.

While hard-and-fast rules are suspect, we can make some general rules-of-thumb for type based on practical, commonsense experience. For instance, it is visually fatiguing to read a copy block that is set too tight or too wide. The size of a type affects the overall readable length of the line. A long paragraph of 8 point type "set solid" (no leading) to a 48 pica measure will most assuredly start to irritate the reader, while the same paragraph set to perhaps a 24 pica measure, with one point of leading, will convey the information much more effectively. *Never forget that conveying information is the basic reason for the existence of the medium of typography!* If the design of the page is such that it hampers this basic function, it defeats the purpose of supplying the information and, therefore, is badly designed. According to some sources, a copy block should be about as wide as an alphabet-and-a-half (39 characters) of lowercase letters. This is only one opinion, however.

HELVETICA

Extra space between lines aids readability . . . another commonsense attitude, especially for faces with larger, rounder body styles. Just as it is easier to read a typewritten page that has been double-spaced, so it is easier to read some faces if they are leaded. Legibility is the speed at which an individual type character can be identified. Even though a particular face may be paragraphed to the proper pica line width and adequately kerned (or not kerned as the case may be), its legibility can still be affected by leading. Many typefaces are simply not as legible as others, to begin with. No matter what the trendy winds of change say, serif faces *do* read better, en masse, than sans-serif faces do. Some sans-serif faces, such as Optima, were specifically designed to correct this inherent flaw of the sans-serif letter, and they do. But they are the exceptions to the rule.

KABEL

Letter spacing is extremely critical to headline type usage, especially with "all caps." Letter spacing can also be critical (although perhaps more subtle) in paragraph text. Badly spaced headline types are obvious offenders. But, in text usage, what works in one circumstance may not work in another. Some designers like to shape copy into tightly controlled blocks, while others prefer more open paragraphs, punctuated by subhead letter changes and paragraph indentions. Here again, the danger lies in trying to apply one philosophy to every circumstance. Although it is generally agreed that optically balanced words create better design harmony, there are times when uniform balance might not be as effective in creating the situation the designer wants.

## COPY BLOCK TERMINOLOGY

KORINNA

As a practicing designer, you will use certain key terms when discussing and designing copy blocks; words that will tell others associated with your project your thinking about arrangements and placement of type . . . terms that will become commonplace in your everyday vocabulary. They are as follows:

1. FULLY JUSTIFIED, OR JUSTIFIED R & L. When the left and right edges of a copy block or column of type are parallel and uniform (such as the column of this paragraph), we say they are "justified right and left." The majority of bulk information that you read in books, magazines, and other publications is presented in this manner.

2. FLUSH LEFT.   The flush-left copy block is the next most commonly used format for type presentation. The left side of a paragraph is parallel and the right side is allowed to end at random intervals producing a ragged effect (such as this paragraph). The human eye is fairly well conditioned to this arrangement because of typewriters, our own handwriting (which we are taught to margin to the left), and other, mostly cultural, influences that establish border limits on the left. "Tight rag" is the term used to indi-

**76**   Computer set lines where spacing has been adjusted. Further "fine tuning" can be made on the keyline board if the art director feels it is necessary.

# An example of badly spaced type.

# An example of well spaced type.

cate to the typographer that you want a variation of no more than 2 or 3 picas, maximum. This is a popular way to present copy blocks. Because the right side measure is arbitrary, there is little if any need to space out letters or words to meet a double margin requirement. In terms of specification, this makes both the designer's and the typographer's job easier. The effect is usually very handsome and can work equally well in the presentation of bulk information as full justification. Flush-left justification is often preferable for short copy. "Rag right" is also used as a term of reference to this kind of justification.

3. FLUSH RIGHT.   Flush right is the opposite of flush left. The right side becomes parallel and the left side is ragged. This is a more unusual method of presenting copy and the effect can be quite beautiful when done tastefully. It works best when the overall orientation of the design or layout is to the right. A greater challenge, flush right is more disruptive to the reader who is generally used to a left margin (compare this paragraph with the flush-left paragraph above). The designer's job is to integrate flush-right margins to the point where it appears natural.

4. RAG LEFT AND RAG RIGHT.   This combination offers the designer a highly unusual format in which to present written material. Copy blocks unbounded by parallel perimeters can take on any shape characteristics the designer chooses. Although the greater freedom rag R and L offers can make for exciting design, it also can create special problems that might make the overall solution more difficult. Shaping whole copy blocks is *really* designing with type, and rag R and L, in the hands of a good designer, can be stunning.

## TYPE PERSONALITIES

Just as differing shapes have differing personalities—and since letterforms *are* shapes—different types have different personalities. These personalities should be considered from the standpoint both of presentation and of how they relate to the subject. The way copy is arranged can either accent or stifle the type's personality. Some subjects are better presented in more traditional typefaces with tightly defined columns, while others benefit from freer paragraphing complemented by a more casual or flamboyant face. This is one of the judgments a designer must make about the material he or she is working with. The good designer will consider the appropriateness of each situation as it arises and design accordingly using common sense as a guideline, as we have so often emphasized.

With headline or display types, there is very little to restrict the designer. The many faces available allow for the creation of almost any desired effect. As we pointed out earlier, we are well into the age of the computer, where literally anything can be done to type. Once again, the only dictums that should inhibit the designer's creativity are appropriateness, taste, and whether the mood created by the display typeface is consistent with the character of the entire design format. In many instances the designer will choose to use a letter or series of words in a display face to abstract a new variation from, or will rework to form a distinctiveness unavailable in commercial types. This is common practice in packaging design where product names or designations are "logotized." In this respect, hand lettering, so widely used during the first half of the century, and now thought to be a dead art, lives on. Actually, the "reworking" of existing types through stating and drawing, restating and redrawing, and so on to the finalized image, is a more efficient means of achieving the same results and making quicker, minute adjustments without tedious man-hours lost, a better (if not more satisfying) solution to the old technology.

The ability to perceive and utilize a typeface for its appropriateness, personality, and design characteristics is a very important attribute of the really good designer. It is important, early as possible, to try to avoid developing a bias toward certain typefaces. Personal preferences can and should be exercised up to a point, but discretion is necessary also. Total commitment to personal preference is fine for the artist who is making a personal statement. Choosing the best solution for the *problem at hand* requires objectivity. If the type problem is approached with a view toward selecting that face or group of faces that relate visually and psychologically to the total content, then the design process is being well served.

## *OTHER FACTORS IN TYPE SELECTION*

*There are many instances where the printing process or the materials to be used restrict what kinds of type can be used. For instance, it would be unwise to use a face with delicate, hairline serifs or intricate detail for certain types of printing where methods of application are not precise because of extremely high speeds or material limitations. Flexographic printing is a good example of this problem and will be discussed later on in the text.*

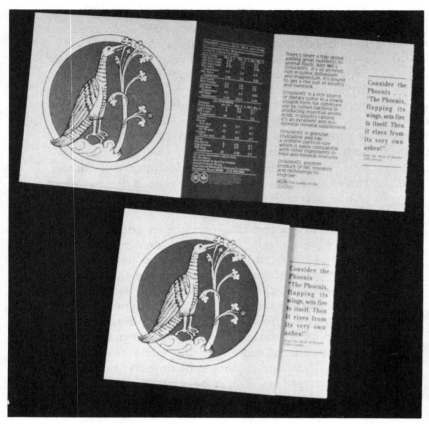

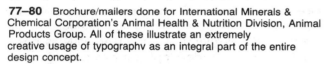

77

**77–80**   Brochure/mailers done for International Minerals &
Chemical Corporation's Animal Health & Nutrition Division, Animal
Products Group. All of these illustrate an extremely
creative usage of typographv as an integral part of the entire
design concept.

Permission of International Minerals & Chemical Corporation Animal Products Group.

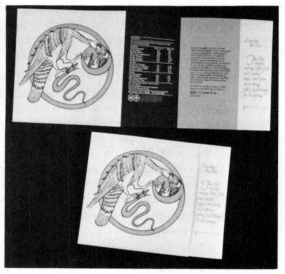

78

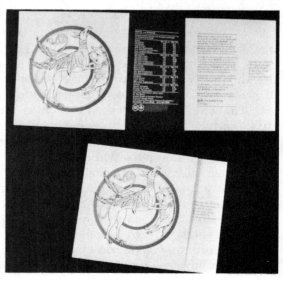

79

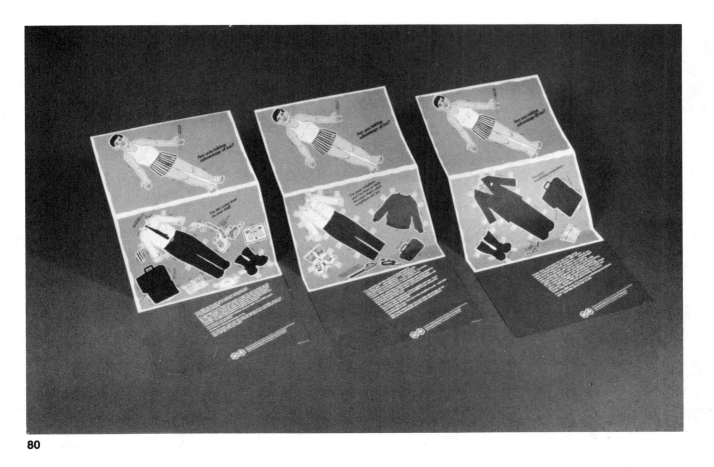

**80**

TRADE GOTHIC LIGHT

When working with copy that will be reversed out of a dark or colored ground, it is best to stay clear of light or extra light fonts, type that is very small, or type that, again, is too delicate in structure. Reversed typography has a tendency to fill in to a greater or lesser degree depending upon the porousness of the paper stock and the type of printing method being used; parts or even whole characters can, for all practical purposes, disappear.

OPTIMA

Paper, of course, can drastically affect the look of a typeface, depending upon the texture, absorbency, coloration, and surface characteristics. The same typeface, printed on newspaper, can have a completely different appearance when printed on an expensive cast-coat stock. More discussion of this appears in the chapter on paper.

## THE TABOOS OF MIXING, MATCHING, AND TURNING

PALATINO

Ask a copywriter what drives them up the wall about art directors and designers and they will answer almost unanimously that the designer does not respect that essential of language—punctuation! This is, of course, an exaggeration, but designers *do* tend to undervalue that capital letter at the beginning of the sentence or the consistent use of proper punctuation throughout a series of thoughts. Copywriters also are fond of underlining things for emphasis. This can sometimes be effective, but just as often it can be disastrous to the visual continuity of a type paragraph.

PERPETUA

SETTING TYPE ALL IN CAPITAL LETTERS ALSO SLOWS DOWN READING SPEED AS WELL AS USING UP ABOUT 50 PERCENT MORE SPACE. This is not to say that "all caps" should never be used. There will be circumstances when it might be preferable, and in short sentences, headlines, titles, and names of products, and so on, "all caps" is quite common. In every instance, the designer should be sensitive to the effects of capital letters before he or she specifies them. Likewise, specifying all lowercase letters can be terribly avant-garde or it can be just terrible! Careful thought should be given to the *readability* of *all* typographic material that is being designed—that can never be emphasized too often. And by the way, don't forget the period, exclamation ("bang"), comma, hyphen, leader dots, colon, semicolon, etc.! Certainly exception can be taken . . . if there is *justifiable* reason, aesthetic or otherwise.

SOUVENIR MEDIUM ITALIC

*Scripts and italics can be more difficult to read than upright letters, and careful thought should be given as to how and where they are appropriate. They can be extremely effective as an attention-getting device or to convey a sense of elegance and softness.*

HELVETICA CONDENSED

The problem of mixing typefaces and styles is always a difficult one, for both inexperienced designers and seasoned professionals. Many designers prefer to work entirely within one type family when solving a particular problem. A convincing argument can be made for this method, and there is certainly enough variety available *within* most type families to support this philosophy! Yet on the other hand, variety in type selection creates visual excitement and sustains interest. O brave designer that mixes and matches lavishly . . . and succeeds! A subtle tour de force will certainly have emerged. A good rule of thumb seems to be not to mix more than two or, possibly three, distinctively different typefaces together in any one design; yet, as always, even this rule has its rather glorious exceptions!

SPARTAN

A highly touted taboo is that you should never stack type vertically. Yet, if you were to take a close look at some classic design formats from the past, you would find even this taboo handled beautifully. It is *quite* reasonable to contemplate designing some typefaces in a vertically stacked format, not only that might read well, but that might hold together from a design standpoint, too. The key to designing with type in *any* situation is to *understand that thought must be given to the complementary characteristics of the configurations and their relationship to the content of the material being designed.*

STYMIE

No matter how a face is designed into a format, size relationships and weight distributions are critical factors when determining how one face plays off against another. Ask yourself questions like "Can one typeface work for headlines or accents, and another complement it as a body copy companion?" If you do *not* ask yourself these kinds of questions during your concepting process, you have missed opportunities for creating something that might just be extraordinary. A book on the Bauhaus designed set in Futura and its variations seems appropriate; setting it in Garamond, however, is questionable. But Garamond used as an accent type with the sans-serif Futura might very well complement it and be a more exciting design solution than type set all within the Futura family. It is safest to take the obvious course, but the obvious course is rarely the best learning device. Once you've learned the basics well enough to be comfortable with them, take a "flyer" and experiment. You've only a grade at stake. Later on in your career, if you haven't done your

**81** "Rough-comp" variations of three (out of a hundred probable) ways to design type forms in a vertically reading column. Find other ways. It is a good exercise in learning sensitivity for the proportion of letterforms as well as testing the range of your concepting ability!

experimenting and are not comfortable with your creativity, it might cost you something more valuable . . . your job! Apply that thought to every concept in this book

## REORDERS

TIMES ROMAN

The designer gets copy in two states: (1) rough copy, which is a conceptual work-up of the copywriter's ideas that aids in determining their viability, and is a rough guide for you, the designer, to follow in *laying* out your graphic ideas; and (2) finished, typed manuscripts ready for specification. No matter how accurate your estimate of space, no matter how good a job you do specing the type,

*Cheltenham Light Italic*

**Cheltenham Ultra Condensed**

*Century Book Italic*

**Century Ultra Condensed**

*Garamond Light Italic*

**Garamond Ultra Condensed**

*Clearface Regular Italic*

**Clearface Black**

***Bookman Medium Italic***

**Bookman Bold**

*Souvenir Light Italic*

**Souvenir Bold**

*Korinna Kursiv Regular*

**Korinna Extra Bold**

Kabel Book

**Kabel Bold**

*Franklin Gothic Book Italic*

**Franklin Gothic Heavy**

*Avant Garde Gothic Extra Light Oblique*

**Avant Garde Gothic Demi**

Lubalin Graph Book

**Lubalin Graph Bold**

Eras Medium

**Eras Bold**

**82** "Comprehensive" hand indication of various commonly used type faces.

ITC Cheltenham Condensed

*Snell Roundhand*

Helvetica Extended

**83** Quickly done "rough" marker indication of type. A designer who is comfortable with the tools and familiar with the character of typography can stroke out such indication literally in seconds and achieve the *"feel"* of a face more accurately than is possible with rub-down lettering and "Greek" type.

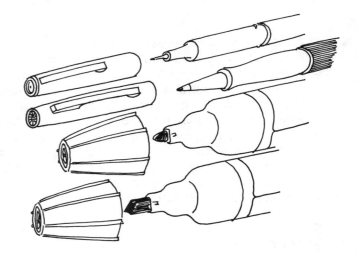

**84** Various marker pen nibs excellent for type indication at all sizes

there are usually always changes: "typos" (mistakes), copy changes requested by the client, changes in the original copy idea, bad line breaks, one-word widows, and a hundred other uncontrollable changes that make that final copy anything but final. Minute (and not so minute) adjustments in typography at the keyline stage are inevitable. The larger and more complex the job, the more changes there usually are. Obviously, everyone would like to keep the cost of changes down, but they seem always to be there, even in the most carefully planned job. The professional designer learns to contend with changes, typos, and the necessity of reordering type. Once again, having a typographer who is close to the job helps insure that any changes made are consistent with the original escapement and impression of the first proofs.

## WIDOWS

*TRADE GOTHIC*

Very few paragraphs of copy end in a perfect square shape. Last lines usually run a little short—too short . . . sometimes to one word hang-ons. Extra short lines are referred to as "widows" because they hang visually all alone in a sea of white (or colored) space. Many designers *despise* widows because they feel the spotty effect widows create in page layout is bad design. They try to avoid widows whenever possible by spacing out within the copy block, editing, or designing a rag right or left situation that will eliminate the possibility. Another, perhaps more radical, view is that the widow can often open up copy for a lighter design feel, in keeping with the "leading out" principle. Everyone, however—widow user or hater—tries to avoid the one-word widow like "it," "me," and so on.

## TRANSFER TYPE

*UNIVERS*

All designers and students are familiar with rub-down lettering. Produced under a number of patented names, several have become generic to the category, as the brand name *Kleenex* has to facial tissue. Rub-down, or transfer, lettering first gained wide acceptance in the 1960s, and it has been used mainly as a quick and relatively inexpensive way to produce a printed, typographic look. Hundreds of faces, sizes, and weights are available along with myriad borders, curlicues, and miscellaneous, standardized bric-a-brac.

*WEISS*

Transfer lettering is used mainly as a substitute for tight comprehensive hand lettering, and in that respect it is a "two-edged sword" in the tool cabinet of the designer. Too many designers use it as a crutch to escape practicing the skills of letter sketching and rough letter-comping, a very necessary ability for anyone involved in

layout. Letter sketching ability is directly related to a designer's understanding and appreciation of type design. Designers who depend heavily upon transfer lettering instead of drawing find themselves limited to those faces that are available in transfer lettering! Think how that limits one's ability to design with type. If Goudy or Cheltenham happens to be a good personality for a subject but is not available in transfer lettering or is not at hand in the designer's box of transfer sheets—tough luck. Odds are that the job will be done with whatever *is* at hand . . . and justifications made for it later. Cutting corners to cover an inadequacy in design skills is characteristic of a poor designer, yet many so-called "designers" would find it impossible to function without transfer lettering at their fingertips. Advocates of transfer lettering rationalize it as quicker to use. This is erroneous. It actually takes *longer* to accurately align, space out, and rub down each transfer letter than for a designer experienced in handstroking typeforms to comp type. In addition, transfer lettering is extremely *fragile* (it flakes up, does not bend or fold well, and cracks with age) and it is "colorless" as well (it comes most often in black and white only).

*BAUHAUS DEMI*

**The ability of the designer to get ideas down intelligently in sketch concept without mechanical aids is a must and using transfer type to get around the sketching process severely limits this ability. As a sign shop aid, transfer type has its uses, but in rough concept sketching or in a beautifully hand-rendered comprehensive it looks out of place. Transfer type *has* a place in the realm of design tools, but it is unfortunate that what was developed as an aid for designers has become a detriment to their talent development.**

## A WORD ABOUT THE PAST

*WINDSOR LIGHT CONDENSED*

The designer owes much to the past, especially in the typographical sense. The inevitable (and proper) motivation of the young designer is forward, toward new and exciting innovation in design technology and idea development. It is therefore often difficult for young designers to recognize the *timelessness* of the past's great design achievements, to accept their value as anything *other* than historical models of past trends. The fact that Caslon was designed well over two centuries ago does not make it any less *contemporary in design usage* than Helvetica, which was designed less than fifty years ago. Both faces are timeless as communication vehicles and in their exquisite sense of aesthetic proportion. For a designer to view the older as dated and the newer as timely (or vice versa) is ludicrous. Classic typefaces speak as do any classic art forms, totally above the limitation of periodic fashion. If you, as a designer, feel strongly about a particular typeface's ability to solve the problems set for you, *use it!* If your judgment is mature and creatively sound, to hell with anybody else's opinion about trends!

85

# PROOF READER'S MARKS

DELETE

LEFT OUT, INSERT

INSERT SPACE

TURN INVERTED LETTER

BROKEN LETTER

EQUAL SPACE

CLOSE UP

TRANSPOSE

WRONG FONT

LOWER CASE

CAPITAL LETTER

MOVE LEFT

MOVE RIGHT

ALIGN TYPE

STRAIGHTEN LINE

INSERT PERIOD

INSERT COMMA

INSERT SEMI-COLON

INSERT APOSTROPHE

INSERT QUOTATION MARKS

INSERT HYPHEN

INSERT INFERIOR FIGURE

SET IN SMALL CAPS

ITALIC TYPE

ROMAN TYPE

BOLDFACE

STET NO CHANGE

OUT, SEE COPY

SPELLING, SPELL OUT

PARAGRAPH

NO PARAGRAPH

RAISE

LOWER

INSERT SUPERIOR FIGURE

INSERT EXCLAMATION

INSERT QUESTION MARK

QUERY FOR AUTHOR

INSERT BRACKETS

INSERT PARENTHESES

INSERT EN DASH

INSERT EM DASH

INDENT ONE EM

INDENT TWO EMS

**86-109**  Following is a selection of faces from the Shore Typographer's Display book. They are arranged in the following order: Serif, Sans-Serif, Square Serif, Script, Open, Shaded and Three-Dimensional, Decorative, Miscellaneous and Casual.  The first line of each type sample is 24 pt.; the second and third lines are 12 pt.

All type specimens and specimen books used for illustration have been supplied by Shore Typographers, Inc., Chicago, Illinois.

# Baskerville Roman · abcdefghijklmnopqr ABCDEFGHIJKLMN

ABCDEFGHIJKLMNOPQRSTUVWXYZ
abcdefghijklmnopqrstuvwxyz  ff fi fl ffi ffl  1234567890 1234567890 .,:;'""()-&!?*$$¢'%%/£

# Bookman · abcdefghijklmnopqrstuvw ABCDEFGHIJKLMNO

ABCDEFGHIJKLMNOPQRSTUVWXYZ
abcdefghijklmnopqrstuvwxyz   ff ffi fi ffi fl fl  1234567890.,:;!?""-()&$£

# Bookman Bold · abcdefghijklmnopqrst  ABCDEFGHIJKLMN

ABCDEFGHIJKLMNOPQRSTUVWXYZ
abcdefghijklmnopqrstuvwxyz  fi  1234567890 1234567890 .,:;!?""-()&*$$¢°%/

# *Bookman Black Italic · abcdefghijklmno ABCDEFGHIJ*

*ABCDEFGHIJKLMNOPQRSTUVWXYZ*
*abcdefghijklmnopqrstuvwxyz  1234567890..;:!?""''--( )& $¢$¢ «»+°%/●○·■□·*

# Bauer Bodoni Extra Bold · abcdefghijklmn  ABCDEFGHIJKL

ABCDEFGHIJKLMNOPQRSTUVWXYZ
abcdefghijklmnopqrstuvwxyz  1234567890 1234567890 .,:;"''"?!O...-'&$$¢°%/'/

# Bodoni Ultra Bold · abcdefghijklm  ABCDEFGHIJ

ABCDEFGHIJKLMNOPQRSTUVWXYZ
abcdefghijklmnopqrstuvwxyz  1234567890 1234567890 .,:;'""''!?-()&'$$¢£%/

# Bembo · abcdefghijklmnopqrstuvwxyz ABCDEFGHIJKLMN

ABCDEFGHIJKLMNOPQRSTUVWXYZ ÆŒ
abcdefghijklmnopqrstuvwxyz æff ffi ffl fi flœ  1234567890 1234567890 .,:;'""!?()[]&*-$$¢£/96%//

# Bembo Bold · abcdefghijklmnopqrs ABCDEFGHIJKLMN

ABCDEFGHIJKLMNOPQRSTUVWXYZ
abcdefghijklmnopqrstuvwxyz  ff fl fi ffi ffl  1234567890.,:;'"!?()-$&£/

# Century Schoolbook Bold · abcdefghijklmno ABCDEFGHIJ

ABCDEFGHIJKLMNOPQRSTUVWXYZ
abcdefghijklmnopqrstuvwxyz 1234567890 1234567890 .,:;!?""-()&'$$¢£%/

Century Schoolbook · abcdefghijklmnopqr ABCDEFGHIJKLM
ABCDEFGHIJKLMNOPQRSTUVWXYZ
abcdefghijklmnopqrstuvwxyz 1234567890¹²³⁴⁵⁶⁷⁸⁹⁰.,:!?""''-()&*$$¢£%/

*Century Old Style Bold Italic Agency · abcdefg  ABCDEFG*
*ABCDEFGHIJKLMNOPQRSTUVWXYZ  ÆÇØ Œ*
*abcdefghijklmnopqrstuvwxyz  æçøœ  1234567890.,:;"!?-`````()&$$¢*

New Caslon · abcdefghijklmnopqrstuv ABCDEFGHIJKLMNO
ABCDEFGHIJKLMNOPQRSTUVWXYZ
abcdefghijklmnopqrstuvwxyz 1234567890 ¹²³⁴⁵⁶⁷⁸⁹⁰.,:;!?""''()-·$¢$¢%/⁰⁰

*Caslon 47¹ Italic · abcdefghijklmnopqrstuvwxyz ABCDEFGHIJKLMNOPQ*
*ABCDEFGHIJKLMNOPQRSTUVWXYZ  JQY*
*abcdefghijklmnopqrstuvwxyz  bᵈᵗ ff ffi ffl fi fl 1234567890 ¹²³⁴⁵⁶⁷⁸⁹⁰.,:;-""( )!?&$¢$⁰⁰%/%/*

Caslon 540 · abcdefghijklmnopqrstuvwxyz ABCDEFGHIJKLMNOP
ABCDEFGHIJKLMNOPQRSTUVWXYZ
abcdefghijklmnopqrstuvwxyz 1234567890¹²³⁴⁵⁶⁷⁸⁹⁰.,:;!?""-()..'&$¢%/$

**Caslon Black · abcdefghijklmnopqrs  ABCDEFGHIJKLMN**
**ABCDEFGHIJKLMNOPQRSTUVWXYZ**
**abcdefghijklmnopqrstuvwxyz äàèéößüú 1234567890¹²³⁴⁵⁶⁷⁸⁹⁰.,:;'-()&£$¢eˢᵉᵉ~——·ˆ··ˋ'(()**

**Caslon Ad Bold · abcdefghijklmnopqrstu  ABCDEFGHIJKLMNO**
**ABCDEFGHIJKLMNOPQRSTUVWXYZ**
**abcdefghijklmnopqrstuvwxyz 1234567890 ¹²³⁴⁵⁶⁷⁸⁹⁰.,:;!?'""-() $¢&ˉˢᶜ%£/£%**

Cheltenham Medium · abcdefghijklmnopqrstu ABCDEFGHIJKLMNO
ABCDEFGHIJKLMNOPQRSTUVWXYZ
abcdefghijklmnopqrstuvwxyz stᶜᵗr 1234567890 .,:;!?""”-()*&$

**Cheltenham Bold · abcdefghijklmnopqrstuv  ABCDEFGHIJKLMN**
**ABCDEFGHIJKLMNOPQRSTUVWXYZ**
**abcdefghijklmnopqrstuvwxyz 1234567890¹²³⁴⁵⁶⁷⁸⁹⁰.,:;'""()-?!ˈ&$$¢ᶜ%%/.**

Cheltenham Bold Extra Condensed · abcdefghijklmnopqrstuvwxyz ABCDEFGHIJKLMNOPQRSTUVW

ABCDEFGHIJKLMNOPQRSTUVWXYZ
abcdefghijklmnopqrstuvwxyz fffifffffi 1234567890<sup>1234567890</sup>.,:;!?'"-()`&$£¢%/<sup>¢%$£</sup>/

## Cheltenham Black · abcdefghijklmn ABCDEFGHIJKL

**ABCDEFGHIJKLMNOPQRSTUVWXYZ**
**abcdefghijklmnopqrstuvwxyz æ 1234567890.,:;!?''()-‾‵ˆ‶‶˙&B+/%£¢$**

Clearface Bold · abcdefghijklmnopqrstuvw ABCDEFGHIJKLMNOPQ

ABCDEFGHIJKLMNOPQRSTUVWXYZ
abcdefghijklmnopqrstuvwxyz fffiffiflffl 1234567890<sup>1234567890</sup>.,:;"""!?-()`&$¢%/£&&

## Clearface Heavy · abcdefghijklmno ABCDEFGHIJKLMNO

**ABCDEFGHIJKLMNOPQRSTUVWXYZ**
**abcdefghijklmnopqrstuvwxyz fffifffffiffl 1234567890<sup>1234567890</sup>.,:;!?"" "-–·()[]*$$¢°&£%/ ‵ˆ‶˜**

## *Clearface Heavy Italic · abcdefghijklmno ABCDEFGHIJK*

*ABCDEFGHIJKLMNOPQRSTUVWXYZ*
*abcdefghijklmnopqrstuvwxyz fffiflffiffl 1234567890<sup>1234567890</sup>.,:;!?"" "-–·()[]*$$¢&£¢%/ ‵ˆ‶˜*

Cloister Bold · abcdefghijklmnopqrstuvwxyz ABCDEFGHIJKLMNO

ABCDEFGHIJKLMNOPQRSTUVWXYZ Qu
abcdefghijklmnopqrstuvwxyz ctfffifffffiffl 1234567890<sup>1234567890</sup>.,:;-""'"!?()`&$¢%/$¢%£

Cloister Bold Condensed · abcdefghijklmnopqrstuvw ABCDEFGHIJKLMNO

ABCDEFGHIJKLMNOPQRSTUVWXYZ ÄÅÆÇÖØŒQ
abcdefghijklmnopqrstuvwxyz àåæçèéñöøøœü 1234567890.,:;'""!?()`&$¢ß-‾‾‾%%/

## Cloister Extra Bold Condensed · abcdefghijklmnopq ABCDEFGHIJKLMNOP

ABCDEFGHIJKLMNOPQRSTUVWXYZ Q
abcdefghijklmnopqrstuvwxyz ff ffi fi ffl 1234567890<sup>1234567890</sup>.,:;'"!?()-&$¢¢/

Cooper Light · abcdefghijklmnopqrstuvwx ABCDEFGHIJKLMNOP

ABCDEFGHIJKLMNOPQRSTUVWXYZ
abcdefghijklmnopqrstuvwxyz 1234567890<sup>1234567890</sup>.,:;!?'""-—[]*&$$¢¢%/£

**Cooper Black · abcdefghijklmnop ABCDEFGHIJKL**
**ABCDEFGHIJKLMNOPQRSTUVWXYZ**
**abcdefghijklmnopqrstuvwxyz 1234567890¹²³⁴⁵⁶⁷⁸⁹⁰.,:;!?""''-[]&\*$s£¢¢%/**

*Cooper Black Italic · abcdefghijklmn ABCDEFGHIJK*
*ABCDEFGHIJKLMNOPQRSTUVWXYZ ABDEFGMNPRTY*
*abcdefghijklmnopqrstuvwxyz 1234567890¹²³⁴⁵⁶⁷⁸⁹⁰.,:;!?""''-()—&\*$s¢¢%/*

**Craw Modern Bold · abcdefghij ABCDEFG**
**ABCDEFGHIJKLMNOPQRSTUVWXYZ**
**abcdefghijklmnopqrstuvwxyz 1234567890¹²³⁴⁵⁶⁷⁸⁹⁰.,:;!?""''-()&$s¢¢%/£**

*Craw Modern Italic · abcdefghijklm ABCDEFGHIJ*
*ABCDEFGHIJKLMNOPQRSTUVWXYZ*
*abcdefghijklmnopqrstuvwxyz 1234567890¹²³⁴⁵⁶⁷⁸⁹⁰.,:;!?""''-()&−−-[]'$s¢¢£%/*

ITC Garamond Book · abcdefghijklmnopqr ABCDEFGHIJK
ABCDEFGHIJKLMNOPQRSTUVWXYZ ÄÅÆÇÖØŒ
abcdefghijklmnopqrstuvwxyz äåæç fi fl ff ffi ffl ö ø œ 1234567890 4.,:;'""!i?¿()[]'--»°˙¨˜^˜&$s¢ß#%/

*ITC Garamond Book Italic · abcdefghijklmn ABCDEFGHI*
*ABCDEFGHIJKLMNOPQRSTUVWXYZ ÄÅÆÇÖØŒ*    °˙˜^˜
*abcdefghijklmnopqrstuvwxyz äåæç fi fl ff ffi ffl h m n ö ø œ z 1234567890 4.,:;'""!i?¿()[]'--»«&&$s¢ß£#%//*

Garamond Bold · abcdefghijklmnopqrstu ABCDEFGHIJKLMNO
ABCDEFGHIJKLMNOPQRSTUVWXYZ
abcdefghijklmnopqrstuvwxyz 1234567890¹²³⁴⁵⁶⁷⁸⁹⁰.,:;!?""''-..()'&$s¢%/£

*Garamond Bold Italic · abcdefghijklmnopqrstu ABCDEFGHIJKLM*
*ABCDEFGHIJKLMNOPQRSTUVWXYZ ABCDEGLMNPRTY RTY The*    -()&$s¢%/
*abcdefghijklmnopqrstuvwxyz a as ct e fi ff ffi fl ffl fr gy is k ll m n sp st tt u us v w 1234567890 1234567890 ¹²³⁴⁵⁶⁷⁸⁹⁰.,:;''!?*

***ITC Garamond Ultra Bold Italic · abcdef ABCD***
***ABCDEFGHIJKLMNOPQRSTUVWXYZ***
***abcdefghijklmnopqrstuvwxyz h m n z 1234567890.,:;""''!?()'-—&&$s¢£%/***

Goudy Old Style · abcdefghijklmnopqrstuv ABCDEFGHIJKLMNOPQ

ABCDEFGHIJKLMNOPQRSTUVWXYZ
abcdefghijklmnopqrstuvwxyz fffiflffiffl 1234567890¹²³⁴⁵⁶⁷⁸⁹⁰.,;:!?"'"-()&'$$¢£%/¶℔ct

*Goudy Old Style Italic · abcdefghijklmnopqrstuvwxyz ABCDEFGHIJKLMNO*

*ABCDEFGHIJKLMNOPQRSTUVWXYZ*
*abcdefghijklmnopqrstuvwxyz 1234567890¹²³⁴⁵⁶⁷⁸⁹⁰.,;"!?()˙-~~&℗℉//%$¢$ˢ⁴⁾*

**Goudy Bold · abcdefghijklmnopqrst ABCDEFGHIJKLMNO**

**ABCDEFGHIJKLMNOPQRSTUVWXYZ**
**abcdefghijklmnopqrstuvwxyz fffifIffiffl 1234567890¹²³⁴⁵⁶⁷⁸⁹⁰.,.:;!?"'"-()&'$$¢%/%/**

***Goudy Bold Italic · abcdefghijklmnopqrst ABCDEFGHIJKLMNO***

***ABCDEFGHIJKLMNOPQRSTUVWXYZ***
***abcdefghijklmnopqrstuvwxyz 1234567890¹²³⁴⁵⁶⁷⁸⁹⁰.,;:""'"!?()˙-~-&$$£¢%/***

**Goudy Thickest · abcdefghijklmnop ABCDEFGHIJKLMN**

**ABCDEFGHIJKLMNOPQRSTUVWXYZ ÆÇØŒ**
**abcdefghijklmnopqrstuvwxyz æçfiøœ 1234567890¹²³⁴⁵⁶⁷⁸⁹⁰.,;:''!?¡¿()-·*‹›°'''`^~&$$¢‹£ß%/**

**Goudy Heavy Face Condensed · abcdefghijklmn ABCDEFGHIJKL**

**ABCDEFGHIJKLMNOPQRSTUVWXYZ Ç.**
**abcdefghijklmnopqrstuvwxyz 1234567890¹²³⁴⁵⁶⁷⁸⁹⁰.,;:!?"'"'·—()[]&$$¢‹◦**

Melior · abcdefghijklmnopqrstuvwx ABCDEFGHIJKLMNOPQ

ABCDEFGHIJKLMNOPQRSTUVWXYZ
abcdefghijklmnopqrstuvwxyz 1234567890¹²³⁴⁵⁶⁷⁸⁹⁰.,;:!?""-()&*$$£¢%/

*Melior Italic · abcdefghijklmnopqrstuvwx ABCDEFGHIJKLMNO*

*ABCDEFGHIJKLMNOPQRSTUVWXYZ*
*abcdefghijklmnopqrstuvwxyz 1234567890¹²³⁴⁵⁶⁷⁸⁹⁰.,:;!?'""-()*$$¢%/£&*

**Melior Semibold · abcdefghijklmnop ABCDEFGHIJKLMN**

**ABCDEFGHIJKLMNOPQRSTUVWXYZ**
**abcdefghijklmnopqrstuvwxyz 1234567890¹²³⁴⁵⁶⁷⁸⁹⁰.,;:!?""-()*$$¢%/& £**

# Melior Bold Condensed · abcdefghijklmnopABCDEFGHIJKLM

ABCDEFGHIJKLMNOPQRSTUVWXYZ
abcdefghijklmnopqrstuvwxyz 12345678901234567890.,:;!?""-()&*$$£¢ᶜ%/

# Palatino Regular · abcdefghijklmnopqrst ABCDEFGHIJKLMN

ABCDEFGHIJKLMNOPQRSTUVWXYZ
abcdefghijklmnopqrstuvwxyz 1234567890¹²³⁴⁵⁶⁷⁸⁹⁰.,:;!?""-=()&'$$ᶜ£ᵗ%'/

# Palatino Semibold · abcdefghijklmnopqr ABCDEFGHIJKLM

ABCDEFGHIJKLMNOPQRSTUVWXYZ
abcdefghijklmnopqrstuvwxyz ff fifl. 1234567890.,:;!?''-()&'$¢

# Perpetua · abcdefghijklmnopqrstuvw ABCDEFGHIJKLMNOPQ

ABCDEFGHIJKLMNOPQRSTUVWXYZ
abcdefghijklmnopqrstuvwxyz 1234567890.,:;''-!?$&

# Perpetua Bold · abcdefghijklmnopq ABCDEFGHIJKLM

ABCDEFGHIJKLMNOPQRSTUVWXYZ
abcdefghijklmnopqrstuvwxyz ff fl fi ffi ffl ffi 1234567890¹²³⁴⁵⁶⁷⁸⁹⁰.,:;!?""-()&'$s£ᶜᶜ%%//

# Perpetua Black · abcdefghijklmnopqr ABCDEFGHIJKLMNO

ABCDEFGHIJKLMNOPQRSTUVWXYZ
abcdefghijklmnopqrstuvwxyz 1234567890.,:;''-!?O&/$¢

# Souvenir Light · abcdefghijklmnopqrstuv ABCDEFGHIJKLMNO

ABCDEFGHIJKLMNOPQRSTUVWXYZ
abcdefghijklmnopqrstuvwxyz 1234567890.,:;!?''"""--()[]*&$¢/%#£

# *Souvenir Light Italic · abcdefghijklmnopqrst ABCDEFGHIJKLM*

*ABCDEFGHIJKLMNOPQRSTUVWXYZ*
*abcdefghijklmnopqrstuvwxyz 1234567890.,:;!?''"""--()[]*&$$¢/%#£*

# Souvenir Medium · abcdefghijklmnopqr ABCDEFGHIJKLM

ABCDEFGHIJKLMNOPQRSTUVWXYZ
abcdefghijklmnopqrstuvwxyz 1234567890.,:;!?''"""--()[]*&$$¢/%#£

**Souvenir Demi Italic · abcdefghijklmno ABCDEFGHIJK**

ABCDEFGHIJKLMNOPQRSTUVWXYZ
abcdefghijklmnopqrstuvwxyz 1234567890.,:;!?''""--()[]'&$$¢/%#£

**Souvenir Bold · abcdefghijklmnop ABCDEFGHIJK**

ABCDEFGHIJKLMNOPQRSTUVWXYZ
abcdefghijklmnopqrstuvwxyz 1234567890.,:;!?''""--()[]'&$$¢/%#£

**Thorowgood · abcdefghijklmno ABCDEFGHIJKL**

ABCDEFGHIJKLMNOPQRSTUVWXYZ
abcdefghijklmnopqrstuvwxyz ffflflffl 1234567890.,:;!?"-[]()'&$¢%/£

***Thorowgood Italic · abcdefghij ABCDEFG***

*ABCDEFGHIJKLMNOPQRSTUVWXYZ AMNVWY*
*abcdefghijklmnopqrstuvwxyz fiflfl 1234567890¹²³⁴⁵⁶⁷⁸⁹⁰.,:;!?""-()&*$¢%/*

Times Roman · abcdefghijklmnopqrstuv ABCDEFGHIJKLMNO

ABCDEFGHIJKLMNOPQRSTUVWXYZ
abcdefghijklmnopqrstuvwxyz 1234567890¹²³⁴⁵⁶⁷⁸⁹⁰.,:;!?""'-()[]&*$$¢%/£

*Times Roman Italic · abcdefghijklmnopqrstuvwx ABCDEFGHIJKLMN*

*ABCDEFGHIJKLMNOPQRSTUVWXYZ*
*abcdefghijklmnopqrstuvwxyz 1234567890¹²³⁴⁵⁶⁷⁸⁹⁰.,:;!?""'-()&*$$¢%/£*

**Times Roman Bold · abcdefghijklmnopqrst ABCDEFGHIJKLM**

ABCDEFGHIJKLMNOPQRSTUVWXYZ
abcdefghijklmnopqrstuvwxyz fffiflfflffi 1234567890¹²³⁴⁵⁶⁷⁸⁹⁰.,:;-"!?£&*$¢%/$

***Times Roman Bold Italic · abcdefghijklmnopqrstuv ABCDEFGHIJKLMN***

*ABCDEFGHIJKLMNOPQRSTUVWXYZ*
*abcdefghijklmnopqrstuvwxyz fffifflffiffl 1234567890¹²³⁴⁵⁶⁷⁸⁹⁰.,:;'""!?()-'&$¢£%/*

**Windsor · abcdefghijklmnopqrs ABCDEFGHIJKLMN**

ABCDEFGHIJKLMNOPQRSTUVWXYZ
abcdefghijklmnopqrstuvwxyz 1234567890¹²³⁴⁵⁶⁷⁸⁹⁰.,:;!?""-()[]'&$$¢%/

# Windsor Bold · abcdefghijklmnopqr ABCDEFGHIJKLM

ABCDEFGHIJKLMNOPQRSTUVWXYZ
abcdefghijklmnopqrstuvwxyz 1234567890 .,:;!?"”--—()[]&$¢%

# Windsor Elongated · abcdefghijklmnopqrstuvwxyz ABCDEFGHIJKLMNOPQRSTUVWXYZ 1234

ABCDEFGHIJKLMNOPQRSTUVWXYZ
abcdefghijklmnopqrstuvwxyz 1234567890¹²³⁴⁵⁶⁷⁸⁹⁰ .,:;""!?-()[]`&$¢£%/

# Alt. Gothic No. 2 · abcdefghijklmnopqrstuvwxyz ABCDEFGHIJKLMNOPQRSTUVWXYZ

ABCDEFGHIJKLMNOPQRSTUVWXYZ
abcdefghijklmnopqrstuvwxyz 1234567890¹²³⁴⁵⁶⁷⁸⁹⁰ .,:;!?'"”-...()&*$$s¢°%/*/

# Alt. Gothic No. 2 Italic · abcdefghijklmnopqrstuvwxyz ABCDEFGHIJKLMNOPQRSTUVWXYZ

ABCDEFGHIJKLMNOPQRSTUVWXYZ
abcdefghijklmnopqrstuvwxyz 1234567890 ¹²³⁴⁵⁶⁷⁸⁹⁰ .,:;!?'"”-()*&$s¢%/

# Avant Garde Extra Light · abcdefghijklmnopq ABCDEFGHIJKLMN

ABCDEFGHIJKLMNOPQRSTUVWXYZ    A AA CA © EA FA FR GA HT KA LA LA LL M NT RR RA SS ST ST TH UT N V W
abcdefghijklmnopqrstuvwxyz 1234567890.,.!?"”--()()*&$¢%/#£    ct fi ffi ffl ffl fft N W

# Avant Garde Book · abcdefghijklmnopqrst ABCDEFGHIJKLMNO

ABCDEFGHIJKLMNOPQRSTUVWXYZ    AA ÆÇAŒEAFAŖGAHTKALALALLMMNTØŒRRRASSSTTHUTNVVNW
abcdefghijklmnopqrstuvwxyz    æcç eff fififfiffløœßN v wwy ATaeeimnr
1234567890.,.;"'".!?i¿()()()[]/\\/--/*``¨˜˜$¢$#%³ºс&&£

# Avant Garde Medium · abcdefghijklmnop ABCDEFGHIJKLM

ABCDEFGHIJKLMNOPQRSTUVWXYZ    AA C CA EA FA FR GA HT KA LA LA LA L M NT RR RA SS ST ST TH UT N V W
abcdefghijklmnopqrstuvwxyz 1234567890.,.;!?"”-()()*&$¢%/#£    ce ff fifi ffi ffl fft N v wy

# Avant Garde Bold · abcdefghijklmnop ABCDEFGHIJKLM

ABCDEFGHIJKLMNOPQRSTUVWXYZ AA Æ CA ŒEAFAŖGAHT KA LA LL M MNTØŒ RR RA SS $ ST ST TH UT N V NW
abcdefghijklmnopqrstuvwxyz æce ff fifi ffi ffl ffløœt vv wwy ATaeeimnr
12345678901.,.;'"”!?i¿()()()[]/\\/--/*``¨˜--$¢$%#

# Clearface Gothic Bold · abcdefghijklmnopqrst ABCDEFGHIJKLMNOPQ

ABCDEFGHIJKLMNOPQRSTUVWXYZ ÄÅÆÇÖØŒ
abcdefghijklmnopqrstuvwxyz äåæçöøœ 1234567890.,.;'"!?``¨˜-()&$¢ß

**Clearface Gothic Extra Bold · abcdefghijklmnopq ABCDEFGHIJK**
ABCDEFGHIJKLMNOPQRSTUVWXYZ ÀÄÆÇÖØŒ
abcdefghijklmnopqrstuvwxyz àäæçöøœ 1234567890.,:;"'!?¨˘ˇˆˆ˜-()&$¢ß

**Compacta Bold · abcdefghijklmnopqrstuvwxyz ABCDEFGHIJKLMNOPQRSTUVWXYZ 1234567890**
ABCDEFGHIJKLMNOPQRSTUVWXYZ ÀÄÆÇÖØŒ
abcdefghijklmnopqrstuvwxyz àäæçéénüøœü 1234567890.,:;"'"'!?-¨¨¨¨ß$£ß¢

**Eurostile Bold · abcdefghijklmnopqr ABCDEFGHIJKLMN**
ABCDEFGHIJKLMNOPQRSTUVWXYZ
abcdefghijklmnopqrstuvwxyz 1234567890¹²³⁴⁵⁶⁷⁸⁹⁰ .,-:;"!?()&⁰/₀c$$ᶜ⁰�֥✶

**Eurostile Condensed · abcdefghijklmnopqrstuvwxyz ABCDEFGHIJKLMNOPQRSTUVWXYZ**
ABCDEFGHIJKLMNOPQRSTUVWXYZ
abcdefghijklmnopqrstuvwxyz 1234567890.,:;!?'"'-—()*&$¢%/#

**Eurostile Medium Ext.· abcdefg ABCDEFG**
ABCDEFGHIJKLMNOPQRSTUVWXYZ&
abcdefghijklmnopqrstuvwxyz 1234567890¹²³⁴⁵⁶⁷⁸⁹⁰ .,:;'"'"--()!?P✶*$$$*⁰ᶜ *$%/o¢/£

**Eurostile Bold Ext. · abcdefghijkl ABCDEF**
ABCDEFGHIJKLMNOPQRSTUVWXYZ&
abcdefghijklmnopqrstuvwxyz 1234567890|¹²³⁴⁵⁶⁷⁸⁹⁰| .,:;!?"'"-()*$$$¢ᶜ⁰/o/£

*Eurostile Light Ext. It.· abcdefghijkl ABCDEF*
*ABCDEFGHIJKLMNOPQRSTUVWXYZ aemnr&*
*abcdefghijklmnopqrstuvwxyz 1234567890¹²³⁴⁵⁶⁷⁸⁹⁰ .,:;!?'"-()&✶$$¢%*

Eurostile Normal · abcdefghijklmnopqrs ABCDEFGHIJKLMNO
ABCDEFGHIJKLMNOPQRSTUVWXYZ
abcdefghijklmnopqrstuvwxyz 1234567890|¹²³⁴⁵⁶⁷⁸⁹⁰ .,:;!?""-()&✶*$$¢ᶜ£%/|

**Folio Bold · abcdefghijklmnopqrs ABCDEFGHIJKLMNO**
ABCDEFGHIJKLMNOPQRSTUVWXYZ R
abcdefghijklmnopqrstuvwxyz 1234567890¹²³⁴⁵⁶⁷⁸⁹⁰ .,:;!?'"'"()-'&$¢%/$¢%/

**Folio Extra Bold · abcdefghijklmno ABCDEFGHIJKLM**

ABCDEFGHIJKLMNOPQRSTUVWXYZ
abcdefghijklmnopqrstuvwxyz 1234567890.,:;!?'""''-()'&$¢

**Folio Bold Condensed · abcdefghijklmnopqrstuv ABCDEFGHIJKLMNOPQRSTUV**

ABCDEFGHIJKLMNOPQRSTUVWXYZ
abcdefghijklmnopqrstuvwxyz 1234567890.,:;-'""''"()?!¢$&

**Folio Medium Ext. · abcdefghijklm ABCDEFGHIJK**

ABCDEFGHIJKLMNOPQRSTUVWXYZ  aemnr
abcdefghijklmnopqrstuvwxyz 1234567890.,:;-'""''!?()$¢£%/*&

**Franklin Gothic · abcdefghijklmnopqrs ABCDEFGHIJKLMNO**

ABCDEFGHIJKLMNOPQRSTUVWXYZ
abcdefghijklmnopqrstuvwxyz 1234567890¹²³⁴⁵⁶⁷⁸⁹⁰.,:;!?'""-()&*$$¢°%/

*Franklin Gothic Italic · abcdefghijklmno ABCDEFGHIJKLM*

*ABCDEFGHIJKLMNOPQRSTUVWXYZ*
*abcdefghijklmnopqrstuvwxyz 1234567890 ¹²³⁴⁵⁶⁷⁸⁹⁰.,:;!?'""-()&*$$¢%/*

**Franklin Gothic Extra Condensed · abcdefghijklmnopqrstuvw ABCDEFGHIJKLMNOPQRST**

ABCDEFGHIJKLMNOPQRSTUVWXYZ
abcdefghijklmnopqrstuvwxyz 1234567890 ¹²³⁴⁵⁶⁷⁸⁹⁰.,:;!?'""-()...&$$¢%/

Futura Light • abcdefghijklmnopqrstuvwxyz ABCDEFGHIJKLMNOPQRSTUVWX

ABCDEFGHIJKLMNOPQRSTUVWXYZ
abcdefghijklmnopqrstuvwxyz 1234567890 ¹²³⁴⁵⁶⁷⁸⁹⁰ .,:;!?'''--()*$¢%/£&

Futura Book • abcdefghijklmnopqrstuvwxyz ABCDEFGHIJKLMNOPQRSTU

ABCDEFGHIJKLMNOPQRSTUVWXYZ
abcdefghijklmnopqrstuvwxyz 1234567890 ¹²³⁴⁵⁶⁷⁸⁹⁰ .,:;!?''''''""-()*$¢$¢%/& ff fi fl

Futura Medium • abcdefghijklmnopqrstuvwxyz ABCDEFGHIJKLMNOPQR

ABCDEFGHIJKLMNOPQRSTUVWXYZ
abcdefghijklmnopqrstuvwxyz 1234567890 ¹²³⁴⁵⁶⁷⁸⁹⁰ .,:;!?''''-()...*$$¢%/&

**Futura Demibold · abcdefghijklmnopqrstuv ABCDEFGHIJKLMNOP**

ABCDEFGHIJKLMNOPQRSTUVWXYZ
abcdefghijklmnopqrstuvwxyz 1234567890 ¹²³⁴⁵⁶⁷⁸⁹⁰.,:;!?""''-()...'&$$¢'%/

**Futura Bold Condensed · abcdefghijklmnopqrstuvw ABCDEFGHIJKLMNOPQRS**

ABCDEFGHIJKLMNOPQRSTUVWXYZ
abcdefghijklmnopqrstuvwxyz 1234567890¹²³⁴⁵⁶⁷⁸⁹⁰.,:;!?'""''-()...'$$¢%ˢᶜ

***Futura Ultra Bold Italic · abcdefghijkl ABCDEFGHIJKL***

*ABCDEFGHIJKLMNOPQRSTUVWXYZ&*
*abcdefghijklmnopqrstuvwxyz 1234567890 ¹²³⁴⁵⁶⁷⁸⁹⁰.,:;!?'""''-()...'$$¢%/£*

**Futura Display · abcdefghijklmnopqrstuvwx ABCDEFGHIJKLMNOPQRS**

ABCDEFGHIJKLMNOPQRSTUVWXYZ
abcdefghijklmnopqrstuvwxyz 1234567890¹²³⁴⁵⁶⁷⁸⁹⁰.,:;'""!?-[]'&$£¢%/   ɭ

Gerstner Medium Exp. · abcdefghijklmn ABCDEFGHIJ

ABCDEFGHIJKLMNOPQRSTUVWXYZ ßÆØŒ&&  ¢¢%//¼½¾ ˙ˆ¨˜˘°$ˢ£
abcdefghijklmnopqrstuvwxyz  æcɪøœ 12345678901¹²³⁴⁵⁶⁷⁸⁹⁰¹ .,:;'\'"'"",,!?---—·()[]«»‹›§†...*

Gill Sans · abcdefghijklmnopqrstuvwxyz ABCDEFGHIJKLMNOPQRST

ABCDEFGHIJKLMNOPQRSTUVWXYZ
abcdefghijklmnopqrstuvwxyz ffi1234567890¹²³⁴⁵⁶⁷⁸⁹⁰.,:;!?'·—/()[]&$ˢᶜ£

**Gill Sans Extra Bold · abcdefghijklm ABCDEFGHIJK**

ABCDEFGHIJKLMNOPQRSTUVWXYZ
abcdefghijklmnopqrstuvwxyz 1234567890¹²³⁴⁵⁶⁷⁸⁹⁰.,:;!?''-()[]—&$¢/ˢᶜ£

**Gill Sans Ultra Bold · abcdefghijk ABCDEFGHI**

ABCDEFGHIJKLMNOPQRSTUVWXYZ
abcdefghijklmnopqrstuvwxyz 1234567890¹²³⁴⁵⁶⁷⁸⁹⁰.,:;!?-—/''()[]&$ˢᶜ£

Grotesque No. 9 · abcdefghijklmnopqrstuvw ABCDEFGHIJKLMNOPQRST

ABCDEFGHIJKLMNOPQRSTUVWXYZ
abcdefghijklmnopqrstuvwxyz 1234567890¹²³⁴⁵⁶⁷⁸⁹⁰ .,:;!?'"''-()[]'$¢%&£ˢᶜ%£//

## *Grotesque No. 9 Italic* · *abcdefghijklmnopqrs* *ABCDEFGHIJKLMNOPQR*

**ABCDEFGHIJKLMNOPQRSTUVWXYZ**
**abcdefghijklmnopqrstuvwxyz 1234567890**1234567890**.,:;!?'"''"-()`$¢%$¢%&/**

## *Helvetica Light Italic* · *abcdefghijklmnopqrstuv* *ABCDEFGHIJKLM*

ABCDEFGHIJKLMNOPQRSTUVWXYZ
abcdefghijklmnopqrstuvwxyz 1234567890¹²³⁴⁵⁶⁷⁸⁹⁰.,:;!?'"''-()&*$$£¢%/

## **Helvetica Bold** · **abcdefghijklmnopqrs** **ABCDEFGHIJKL**

**ABCDEFGHIJKLMNOPQRSTUVWXYZ**
**abcdefghijklmnopqrstuvwxyz 1234567890** 1234567890**.,:;!?'"''"-()&$$¢%/ˣ£**

## **Helvetica Demibold Italic** · **abcdefghijklmn** **ABCDEFGHIJKL**

**ABCDEFGHIJKLMNOPQRSTUVWXYZ** *aemnru*
**abcdefghijklmnopqrstuvwxyz 1234567890.,:;!?'""-()₊''''''&£$¢%/**

## **Helvetica Bold Italic** · **abcdefghijklmno** **ABCDEFGHIJKL**

**ABCDEFGHIJKLMNOPQRSTUVWXYZ**
**abcdefghijklmnopqrstuvwxyz 1234567890**1234567890 **.,:;!?'"''-()*&$$¢%/£**

## **Helvetica Extra Bold Ext.** · **abcdef** **ABCD**

**ABCDEFGHIJKLMNOPQRSTUVWXYZÆÇŒØ æçœøı ''''''¿!?**
**abcdefghijklmnopqrstuvwxyz 1234567890 .,:;-''""?!*() «»+'' &ß$$¢%/£**

## Helvetica Regular · abcdefghijklmnopqrstu  ABCDEFGHIJKLM

ABCDEFGHIJKLMNOPQRSTUVWXYZ
abcdefghijklmnopqrstuvwxyz 1234567890¹²³⁴⁵⁶⁷⁸⁹⁰.,:;!?'"''-()&*$$¢%/£

## Helvetica Regular Condensed · abcdefghijklmnopqrstuv ABCDEFGHIJKLMNOP

ABCDEFGHIJKLMNOPQRSTUVWXYZ
abcdefghijklmnopqrstuvwxyz 1234567890 ¹²³⁴⁵⁶⁷⁸⁹⁰.,:;''''!?--·()*$$£¢%/&

## *Helvetica Thin Italic* · *abcdefghijklmnopqrstuvwxyz* *ABCDEFGHIJKLMNO*

*ABCDEFGHIJKLMNOPQRSTUVWXYZ ÆÇŒØ*
*abcdefghijklmnopqrstuvwxyz ıæçœø 1234567890.,:;!?()*''''''''''''- «»+ ¿&ß$$¢%/£*

Kabel Light • abcdefghijklmnopqrstuvwxyz ABCDEFGHIJKLMNOPQRSTUVW
ABCDEFGHIJKLMNOPQRSTUVWXYZ
abcdefghijklmnopqrstuvwxyz 1234567890¹²³⁴⁵⁶⁷⁸⁹⁰.,:;!?" "-( )&*$¢£%/ «»

Kabel Bold • abcdefghijklmnopqrstuvwxyz ABCDEFGHIJKLMNOPQRSTU
ABCDEFGHIJKLMNOPQRSTUVWXYZ
abcdefghijklmnopqrstuvwxyz 1234567890¹²³⁴⁵⁶⁷⁸⁹⁰.,:;!?""-·--·()[]«»˙$ˢ¢£%/&

**Kabel Black • abcdefghijklmnopqrstuv ABCDEFGHIJKLMNO**
**ABCDEFGHIJKLMNOPQRSTUVWXYZ**
**abcdefghijklmnopqrstuvwxyz 1234567890¹²³⁴⁵⁶⁷⁸⁹⁰ .,:;-'!? $ˢ¢ &%/« ··**

News Gothic Condensed • abcdefghijklmnopqrstuvwxyz ABCDEFGHIJKLMNOPQRSTUVWXYZ 1
ABCDEFGHIJKLMNOPQRSTUVWXYZ
abcdefghijklmnopqrstuvwxyz 1234567890¹²³⁴⁵⁶⁷⁸⁹⁰.,:!?"".·()&ˢ$¢%/

Optima • abcdefghijklmnopqrstuvwxyz ABCDEFGHIJKLMNO
ABCDEFGHIJKLMNOPQRSTUVWXYZ
abcdefghijklmnopqrstuvwxyz 1234567890¹²³⁴⁵⁶⁷⁸⁹⁰$¢ᶜ.,:;!?'\"''--()[]*&$ˢ¢ᶜ%/£

*Optima Italic • abcdefghijklmnopqrstuvw ABCDEFGHIJKLMNOPQ*
*ABCDEFGHIJKLMNOPQRSTUVWXYZ*
*abcdefghijklmnopqrstuvwxyz 1234567890¹²³⁴⁵⁶⁷⁸⁹⁰.,:!?'"''-()*&$ˢ$¢ᶜ%/£*

**Optima Semibold • abcdefghijklmnopqr ABCDEFGHIJKLMN**
**ABCDEFGHIJKLMNOPQRSTUVWXYZ**
**abcdefghijklmnopqrstuvwxyz 1234567890¹²³⁴⁵⁶⁷⁸⁹⁰.,:;!?''''-()&*$ˢ£¢ᶜ%/**

**Optima Ultra Bold • abcdefghijklmnop ABCDEFGHIJKLMN**
**ABCDEFGHIJKLMNOPQRSTUVWXYZ**
**abcdefghijklmnopqrstuvwxyz 1234567890.,:;!?"'-[]&%$‡¢**

Olive Antique • abcdefghijklmnopqr ABCDEFGHIJKLMNOPQ
ABCDEFGHIJKLMNOPQRSTUVWXYZ
abcdefghijklmnopqrstuvwxyz 1234567890|¹²³⁴⁵⁶⁷⁸⁹⁰|.,:;'""!?()[]---·-·*&$ˢ£¢ᶜ%/

**Olive Antique Medium** · abcdefghijklmno ABCDEFGHIJKLMN

ABCDEFGHIJKLMNOPQRSTUVWXYZ
abcdefghijklmnopqrstuvwxyz  1234567890¹²³⁴⁵⁶⁷⁸⁹⁰¹   .,:;"""!?--—-()[]*&$$£¢¢%/

**Olive Antique Bold** · abcdefghijklmno ABCDEFGHIJKLMN

ABCDEFGHIJKLMNOPQRSTUVWXYZ
abcdefghijklmnopqrstuvwxyz  1234567890¹²³⁴⁵⁶⁷⁸⁹⁰¹    .,:;"""!?&()[]--—-·*£$$¢¢%/

**Olive Antique Narrow** · abcdefghijklmnopqrs ABCDEFGHIJKLMNOPQRSTUVWX

ABCDEFGHIJKLMNOPQRSTUVWXYZ
abcdefghijklmnopqrstuvwxyz  1234567890¹²³⁴⁵⁶⁷⁸⁹⁰.,:;"""!?----()[]...*&$$£[¢¢%/¹

Peignot Light · abcdefghijklmnopqrstuvwxy ABCDEFGHIJKLMNOPQ

ABCDEFGHIJKLMNOPQRSTUVWXYZ
abcdefghijklmnopqrstuvwxyz  1234567890₁₂₃₄₅₆₇₈₉₀.,:;-'"()!?*&$¢%£/

Peignot Medium · abcdefghijklmnopqrstuvw ABCDEFGHIJKLMNOP

ABCDEFGHIJKLMNOPQRSTUVWXYZ
abcdefghijklmnopqrstuvwxyz 1234567890 ₁₂₃₄₅₆₇₈₉₀.,:;\`´`""!?-·/%¢[]$&

**Peignot Bold** · abcdefghijklmnopqrstu ABCDEFGHIJKLMNOP

ABCDEFGHIJKLMNOPQRSTUVWXYZ
abcdefghijklmnopqrstuvwxyz 1234567890 ₁₂₃₄₅₆₇₈₉₀.,:;\`´`""!?·/%¢()$&

Radiant Medium · abcdefghijklmnopqrstuvwxyz ABCDEFGHIJKLMNOPQRSTUV

ABCDEFGHIJKLMNOPQRSTUVWXYZ
abcdefghijklmnopqrstuvwxyz 1234567890¹²³⁴⁵⁶⁷⁸⁹⁰.,:;!?"""·—-()[]*&$$¢¢%/S

**Radiant Heavy** · abcdefghijklmnopqr ABCDEFGHIJKLMN

ABCDEFGHIJKLMNOPQRSTUVWXYZ
abcdefghijklmnopqrstuvwxyz  1234567890¹²³⁴⁵⁶⁷⁸⁹⁰.,:;!?'""''-()'&$$¢%/

Souvenir Gothic Light Condensed · abcdefghijklmnopqrst ABCDEFGHIJKLMNOPQ

ABCDEFGHIJKLMNOPQRSTUVWXYZ  ÆÇØŒ
abcdefghijklmnopqrstuvwxyz  æçøœ  1234567890¹²³⁴⁵⁶⁷⁸⁹⁰.,:;'""!?¡¿·--°˜ˆ˜~«»()[]*&$$¢¢£ß%/

## Souvenir Gothic Medium · abcdefghijklmn ABCDEFGHIJKLMNOPQ

ABCDEFGHIJKLMNOPQRSTUVWXYZ Æ Ç Ø Œ
abcdefghijklmnopqrstuvwxyz æ ç ø œ 1234567890¹²³⁴⁵⁶⁷⁸⁹⁰.,;:''""!?¡¿--˚¨ˆˇˋ˜˜«»()[]*&$$¢¢£ß%/

## Souvenir Gothic Bold Expanded · abcdef ABCDEFG

ABCDEFGHIJKLMNOPQRSTUVWXYZ Æ Ç Ø Œ                                      $$¢¢£ß%/
abcdefghijklmnopqrstuvwxyz æ ç ø œ   1234567890¹²³⁴⁵⁶⁷⁸⁹⁰.,;:''""!?¡¿--˚¨ˆˇˋ˜˜«»()[]*&

## *Souvenir Gothic Demi Italic · abcdefghijklmn ABCDEFGHIJKL*

*ABCDEFGHIJKLMNOPQRSTUVWXYZ Æ Ç Ø Œ*
*abcdefghijklmnopqrstuvwxyz æ ç ø œ   1234567890¹²³⁴⁵⁶⁷⁸⁹⁰.,;:''""!?¡¿--˚¨ˆˇˋ˜˜«»()[]*&$$¢¢£ß%/*

## Standard Bold Condensed · abcdefghijklmnopqrstuvwxyz ABCDEFGHIJKLMNOPQRSTUVW

ABCDEFGHIJKLMNOPQRSTUVWXYZ
abcdefghijklmnopqrstuvwxyz 1234567890 ¹²³⁴⁵⁶⁷⁸⁹⁰.,;:'""!?-—()*&$¢£%/

## Standard Extra Bold Condensed · abcdefghijklmnopqr ABCDEFGHIJKLMNOPQR

ABCDEFGHIJKLMNOPQRSTUVWXYZ
abcdefghijklmnopqrstuvwxyz 1234567890 ¹²³⁴⁵⁶⁷⁸⁹⁰.,;:'""!?-—()*&$$¢£«»%/

## Standard Ext. · abcdefghijklmnop ABCDEFGHIJKLM

ABCDEFGHIJKLMNOPQRSTUVWXYZ
abcdefghijklmnopqrstuvwxyz 1234567890¹²³⁴⁵⁶⁷⁸⁹⁰.,;:!?'""-—()*$$¢%/&£ÅåØø

## Standard Light Extended · abcdefghijklm ABCDEFGHI

ABCDEFGHIJKLMNOPQRSTUVWXYZ ÅÄÖØ
abcdefghijklmnopqrstuvwxyz åäöø 1234567890¹²³⁴⁵⁶⁷⁸⁹⁰.,;:!?'""-—()*&$$¢%/

## Univers 49 · abcdefghijklmnopqrstuvwxyz ABCDEFGHIJKLMNOPQRSTUVWXYZ 1234567890 ¹²³⁴⁵⁶⁷⁸⁹⁰.,:!?'"-—()|&&£*$$¢¢%/

ABCDEFGHIJKLMNOPQRSTUVWXYZ
abcdefghijklmnopqrstuvwxyz 1234567890 ¹²³⁴⁵⁶⁷⁸⁹⁰.,:!?'"-—()|&&£*$$¢¢%/

## Univers 55 · abcdefghijklmnopqrstuvwxyz ABCDEFGHIJKLMNOP

ABCDEFGHIJKLMNOPQRSTUVWXYZ G
abcdefghijklmnopqrstuvwxyz 12345678901¹²³⁴⁵⁶⁷⁸⁹⁰.,;:!?'"-()*%/£&&

## Univers 57 · abcdefghijklmnopqrstuvwxyz ABCDEFGHIJKLMNOPQRSTUVWXY

ABCDEFGHIJKLMNOPQRSTUVWXYZ
abcdefghijklmnopqrstuvwxyz 12345678901 ¹²³⁴⁵⁶⁷⁸⁹⁰¹.,;:'""!?-—()[]&&*ß$$£¢%/

Univers 53 · abcdefghijklmnopqrs ABCDEFGHIJKLMN

ABCDEFGHIJKLMNOPQRSTUVWXYZ
abcdefghijklmnopqrstuvwxyz 1234567890.:,;!?"-—()*&$¢%/£

**Univers 73 · abcdefghijklmnop ABCDEFGHIJKL**

**ABCDEFGHIJKLMNOPQRSTUVWXYZ**
**abcdefghijklmnopqrstuvwxyz 1234567890** 1234567890 **.,:;!?'"–()&*$\$¢¢&£%/**

*Univers 48 · abcdefghijklmnopqrstuvwxyz ABCDEFGHIJKLMNOPQRSTUVWXYZ 123456789*

*ABCDEFGHIJKLMNOPQRSTUVWXYZ*
*abcdefghijklmnopqrstuvwxyz 1234567890* 1234567890 *.,:;!?''""-–( )*&$¢%/$¢%/*

*Univers 68 · abcdefghijklmnopqrstuvw ABCDEFGHIJKLMNOPQRS*

*ABCDEFGHIJKLMNOPQRSTUVWXYZ G*
*abcdefghijklmnopqrstuvwxyz 1234567890* 1234567890 *.,:;!?'"-()*$\$¢%/£&&*

Venus Light Condensed · abcdefghijklmnopqrstuvwxyz ABCDEFGHIJKLMNOPQRSTUVWXYZ 1234567890

ABCDEFGHIJKLMNOPQRSTUVWXYZ
abcdefghijklmnopqrstuvwxyz 1234567890.,:;'""!?-()*&$¢

**Venus Bold Condensed · abcdefghijklmnopqrstuvwxyz ABCDEFGHIJKLMNOPQRSTUVWXYZ 1234567890**

**ABCDEFGHIJKLMNOPQRSTUVWXYZ**
**abcdefghijklmnopqrstuvwxyz 1234567890** 1234567890 **.,:;'""!?-()*&$\$¢¢£%/**

Venus Light · abcdefghijklmnopqrstuvwxy ABCDEFGHIJKLMNOPQRSTUVW

ABCDEFGHIJKLMNOPQRSTUVWXYZ
abcdefghijklmnopqrstuvwxyz 1234567890 1234567890 .,:;'""""!?-()*&$\$¢£%/

*Venus Medium Italic · abcdefghijklmnopqr ABCDEFGHIJKLMNOPQRS*

*ABCDEFGHIJKLMNOPQRSTUVWXYZ*
*abcdefghijklmnopqrstuvwxyz 1234567890.,:;'""!?-()*&$\$¢£%/*

**Venus Extra Bold · abcdefghijklmnopq ABCDEFGHIJKLMNOP**

**ABCDEFGHIJKLMNOPQRSTUVWXYZ**
**abcdefghijklmnopqrstuvwxyz 1234567890** 1234567890 **.,:;'""!?-()*&$\$¢¢%/%/**

**Venus Extra Bold Extended · abcdef ABCD**

**ABCDEFGHIJKLMNOPQRSTUVWXYZ**
**abcdefghijklmnopqrstuvwxyz 1234567890.,:;"!?()−–&$¢/**

## *Venus Bold Italic* · *abcdefghijklmnopqr* *ABCDEFGHIJKLM*

*ABCDEFGHIJKLMNOPQRSTUVWXYZ*
*abcdefghijklmnopqrstuvwxyz* *1234567890*¹²³⁴⁵⁶⁷⁸⁹⁰*.,:;'""""!?-()*&$*¢£%/*

## Beton Medium Condensed · abcdefghijklmnopqrstuvwx ABCDEFGHIJKLMNOPQRSTU

ABCDEFGHIJKLMNOPQRSTUVWXYZ
abcdefghijklmnopqrstuvwxyz 1234567890 ¹²³⁴⁵⁶⁷⁸⁹⁰.,:;!?"""-[]'&$¢%/$¢%/£ᵍ

## Beton Bold Condensed · abcdefghijklmnopq ABCDEFGHIJKLMNO

ABCDEFGHIJKLMNOPQRSTUVWXYZ
abcdefghijklmnopqrstuvwxyz 1234567890¹²³⁴⁵⁶⁷⁸⁹⁰.,:;!?"""-()'&$¢%/£$¢%/£

## Beton Extra Bold · abcdefghijklmnopABCDEFGHIJKLMN

ABCDEFGHIJKLMNOPQRSTUVWXYZ
abcdefghijklmnopqrstuvwxyz 1234567890 .,:;"""!? -«»()&'£$¢%/

## Craw Clarendon · abcdefghijklmn ABCDEFGHIJK

ABCDEFGHIJKLMNOPQRSTUVWXYZ
abcdefghijklmnopqrstuvwxyz 1234567890¹²³⁴⁵⁶⁷⁸⁹⁰.,:;!?""""--()&*$$¢%/

## Craw Clarendon Condensed · abcdefghijklmnopqrs ABCDEFGHIJKLMNOP

ABCDEFGHIJKLMNOPQRSTUVWXYZ
abcdefghijklmnopqrstuvwxyz 1234567890 ¹²³⁴⁵⁶⁷⁸⁹⁰.,:;!?""""-()&*$$¢%/£

## Fortune Light · abcdefghijklmnopqrs ABCDEFGHIJK

ABCDEFGHIJKLMNOPQRSTUVWXYZ
abcdefghijklmnopqrstuvwxyz 1234567890.,:;'""!?()-'«»&$£%/

## Egyptian Bold Condensed · abcdefghijklmnopqr ABCDEFGHIJKLMNO

ABCDEFGHIJKLMNOPQRSTUVWXYZ
abcdefghijklmnopqrstuvwxyz 1234567890¹²³⁴⁵⁶⁷⁸⁹⁰.,:;'""!?-()'&$£¢%/

## Lubalin Graph Book · abcdefghijklmnopqrs ABCDEFGHIJK

ABCDEFGHIJKLMNOPQRSTUVWXYZ AA ÆÇAÇ ÇŒFAFAGG GHT KAIAIA MM NT ØŒERRASS THU VV WW
abcdefghijklmnopqrstuvwxyz æçeffffifflfløœtvvwwy 1234567890.,:;!?'""--()()*&$¢%#ß£«»¿'``˜¯

## Lubalin Graph Medium · abcdefghijklm ABCDEFGHIJK

ABCDEFGHIJKLMNOPQRSTUVWXYZ AA ÆÇAÇ ÇŒFAFAGG GHT KAIAIA MM NT ØŒERRASS THU VV WW
abcdefghijklmnopqrstuvwxyz æçeffffifflfløœßtvvwwy 1234567890.,:;'""!?¿¡()()'--...'`˜¯«»&$¢£#%/

# Lubalin Graph Demi Bold · abcdefghijklm ABCDEFGHIJ

ABCDEFGHIJKLMNOPQRSTUVWXYZ AAÆCÆCÇEAFGGAHTKAIALAMMNTØŒRSSTHUVVNW
abcdefghijklmnopqrstuvwxyz œçefffiffiffifflfløœtvvwwy 1234567890.,:;""''!?i¿()()---`˙˜ˆ«»&$¢£ß#%/

# Lubalin Graph Bold · abcdefghijklmno ABCDEFGHIJKLM

ABCDEFGHIJKLMNOPQRSTUVWXYZ AAÆCÇACFAGHTKAMMØŒRASSTHVVNW
abcdefghijklmnopqrstuvwxyz œçefffiffiffifflflvvwwyøœ 1234567890.,:;""''!?i¿()()*---«»˙˜ˆ$¢ß£%/#

# Stymie Light · abcdefghijklmnopqrstuv ABCDEFGHIJKLMNOP

ABCDEFGHIJKLMNOPQRSTUVWXYZ A
abcdefghijklmnopqrstuvwxyz 1234567890 1234567890 .,:;'`""()-&?!*$¢%//

# Stymie Medium · abcdefghijklmnopq ABCDEFGHIJKLMN

ABCDEFGHIJKLMNOPQRSTUVWXYZ
abcdefghijklmnopqrstuvwxyz 1234567890 1234567890 .,:;'""()-&?!$$¢%/

# Stymie Medium Condensed · abcdefghijklmnopqrstuvwxyz ABCDEFGHIJKLMNOPQRSTUVWXYZ 1234567890 123456789

ABCDEFGHIJKLMNOPQRSTUVWXYZ
abcdefghijklmnopqrstuvwxyz 1234567890 1234567890 .,:;!?""`-()&$$¢%/$¢¢/

# Stymie Bold · abcdefghijklmnopqrstuv ABCDEFGHIJKLMN

ABCDEFGHIJKLMNOPQRSTUVWXYZ
abcdefghijklmnopqrstuvwxyz 1234567890 1234567890 .,:;!?""''-[]*&$¢%/$$¢%/*£

# Stymie Extra Bold · abcdefghijklmnopqr ABCDEFGHIJKLM

ABCDEFGHIJKLMNOPQRSTUVWXYZ
abcdefghijklmnopqrstuvwxyz 1234567890.,:;!?""-()&*$c£%/

# Brush · abcdefghijklmnopqrstuvwxyz ABCDEFGHIJKLMNOP2RSTUV

ABCDEFGHIJKLMNOP2RSTUVWXYZ Th t th tt
abcdefghijklmnopqrstuvwxyz 1234567890.,:;!?`˜-()...*$$¢%

# Dom Casual · abcdefghijklmnopqrstuvwxyz ABCDEFGHIJKLMNOPQRSTUVWXYZ 123456789

ABCDEFGHIJKLMNOPQRSTUVWXYZ
abcdefghijklmnopqrstuvwxyz 1234567890.,:;!?""-()&*˙˙%/

# Dom Diagonal · abcdefghijklmnopqrstuvwxyz ABCDEFGHIJKLMNOPQRSTUVWXYZ 1234567890.,:;!?""-

ABCDEFGHIJKLMNOPQRSTUVWXYZ
abcdefghijklmnopqrstuvwxyz 1234567890 1234567890 .,:;!?""--()&˙˙£%/

**Flash Bold · abcdefghijklmnopqrstuvwxyz ABCDEFGHIJKLMNOPQRSTUVWX**

ABCDEFGHIJKLMNOPQRSTUVWXYZ
abcdefghijklmnopqrstuvwxyz 1234567890¹²³⁴⁵⁶⁷⁸⁹⁰.,:;!?'""-()´&$$¢¢%/

*Formalscript · abcdefghijklmnopqrstuvwxyz ABCDEFGHIJKLMNOPQRSTUVWXY*

*ABCDEFGHIJKLMNOPQRSTUVWXYZ*
*abcdefghijklmnopqrstuvwxyz 1234567890.,:;!?'""-()´&"%*

*Snell Roundhand · abcdefghijklmnopqrstuvwxyz ABCDEFGHIJKL*

*ABCDEFGHIJKLMNOPQRSTUVWXYZ*
*abcdefghijklmnopqrstuvwxyz æ ð o´c œ ⁿᵈ ʳᵈ st th 1234567890¹²³⁴⁵⁶⁷⁸⁹⁰.,;'""""!?-–-·()/¦.…*&ß§¢¢£%*

*Vivaldi · abcdefghijklmnopqrstuvwxyz ABCDEFGHIJK*

*ABCDEFGHIJKLMNOPQRSTUVWXYZ HCMW*
*abcdefghijklmnopqrstuvwxyz ðghz 1234567890¹²³⁴⁵⁶⁷⁸⁹⁰.;'!?-()*&$£¢%/*

Bookman Open/Swash · abcdefghijklmno ABCDEFGHIJ

ABCDEFGHIJKLMNOPQRSTUVWXYZ  ABD AEFHIJKLM MNPRR UVWXY
abcdefghijklmnopqrstuvwxyz 1234567890¹²³⁴⁵⁶⁷⁸⁹⁰.,:;!?""()*&$¢¢%/  fir y

Cooper Ultrabold Outline/Flair · abcde ABCDE

ABCDEFGHIJKLMNOPQRSTUVWXYZ&  A AA AB D EFGH IJ KKKK L
M MMM N NN N P R RRR R ST T UV V VW W WX X XY Y YZ
abcdefghijklmnopqrstuvwxyz  a c d e f h i j k l m n q r t u v w x y y z
1234567890 .,;:!?'""'-()·$*¢/

Craw Clarendon Outline · abcdefghijkl ABCDEF

ABCDEFGHIJKLMNOPQRSTUVWXYZ&
abcdefghijklmnopqrstuvwxyz 1234567890¹²³⁴⁵⁶⁷⁸⁹⁰.,:;!?""-()[]*$¢¢%/

Egyptian Bold Condensed Outline · abcdefghijklmnopqr ABCDEFGHIJKL

ABCDEFGHIJKLMNOPQRSTUVWXYZ
abcdefghijklmnopqrstuvwxyz 1234567890.,;""!?()&-$$%/¢

Eurostile Bold Outline · abcdefghijklmnopqr ABCDEFGHIJ

ABCDEFGHIJKLMNOPQRSTUVWXYZ
abcdefghijklmnopqrstuvwxyz 1234567890 .,:;!?""-()$$¢%&

# Futura Ultra Bold Outline • abcdefghijklm ABCDEFGHIJ
ABCDEFGHIJKLMNOPQRSTUVWXYZ
abcdefghijklmnopqrstuvwxyz 1234567890 1234567890.,;:"'"""-!?()\*&\$¢%/

# Goudy Heavy Face Condensed Outline • abcdefghij ABCDEFGHIJ
ABCDEFGHIJKLMNOPQRSTUVWXYZ
abcdefghijklmnopqrstuvwxyz f 1234567890.,;:""!?()--&%\$¢

# Helvetica Medium Outline • abcdefghijklmnop ABCDEFGHIJKL
ABCDEFGHIJKLMNOPQRSTUVWXYZ ÆÇŒØ ß
abcdefghijklmnopqrstuvwxyz æçœø 1234567890 .,;:?!()""-""& '""··-^ «»°+¿¡

# Kabel Mite Outline • abcdefghijklmnopqrs ABCDEFGHIJKLMNO
ABCDEFGHIJKLMNOPQRSTUVWXYZ Ä Å Æ Ç Ö Ø Œ
abcdefghijklmnopqrstuvwxyz äåæçöøœü 1234567890.,;:""!?()[]°--&\$s¢†ß£%

# Palatino Semibold Outline • abcdefghijklmno ABCDEFGHIJKL
ABCDEFGHIJKLMNOPQRSTUVWXYZ
abcdefghijklmnopqrstuvwxyz 1234567890 1234567890.,;:!?""--()\*&\$¢%/,

# Serif Gothic Outline • abcdefghijklmnopqrs ABCDEFGHIJKLMNOP
ABCDEFGHIJKLMNOPQRSTUVWXYZ €L
abcdefghijklmnopqrstuvwxyz æfkrstz 1234567890 1234567890 80 80 .,;:!?""--()()[]\*&\$s¢•£%/

# Stymie Outline • abcdefghijklmnopqrst ABCDEFGHIJKLMN
ABCDEFGHIJKLMNOPQRSTUVWXYZ A
abcdefghijklmnopqrstuvwxyz 1234567890 1234567890.,;:°""()-&?!\*\$¢%/

# Univers 65 Outline • abcdefghijklmno ABCDEFGHIJKL
ABCDEFGHIJKLMNOPQRSTUVWXYZ G
abcdefghijklmnopqrstuvwxyz 1234567890 1234567890 1'.,;:!?"-()&\*\$s£¢%/

# Windsor Outline • abcdefghijklmnop ABCDEFGHIJKLM
ABCDEFGHIJKLMNOPQRSTUVWXYZ
abcdefghijklmnopqrstuvwxyz 1234567890 1234567890.,;:!?""-[]()&\*\$¢£%%/

# BETON OPEN · ABCDEFGHIJKLMNOPQRSTUV

ABCDEFGHIJKLMNOPQRSTUVWXYZ
1234567890.,:;!?""''-&()$

# DAVIDA DROP SHADOW · ABCDEFGHIJKLMNOPQRSTUVWXYZ 1

ABCDEFGHIJKLMNOPQRSTUVWXYZ
1234567890 1234567890 .,:;!?""'-&°¢/¢%§°   ‹‹›‹›‐‹››‐›‹‹

# Eurostile Bold Shaded · abcdefghijkl ABCDEFGHI

ABCDEFGHIJKLMNOPQRSTUVWXYZ
abcdefghijklmnopqrstuvwxyz  1234567890 .,:;!?""''()-&$$¢¢%‰

# Helvetica Bold Drop Shadow · abcdefghijklm ABCDEFGH

ABCDEFGHIJKLMNOPQRSTUVWXYZ
abcdefghijklmnopqrstuvwxyz 1234567890 1234567890 .,:;""!?()'-&$$¢¢.¢%‰

# PIONEER · ABCDEFGHIJKLMNOPQRSTUVWXYZ 123456Z

ABCDEFGHIJKLMNOPQRSTUVWXYZ AHJKLMNQRTWY ÆŒØÇ
1234567890.,:;?--()[]""'''...#//°%$¥££&ïﬁ×`˜˜

# PROFILE · ABCDEFGHIJKLMNO

ABCDEFGHIJKLMNOPQRSTUVWXYZ
1234567890 1234567890 .,:;""'''!?()-°&$¢%‰/°'¢.¢/

# *Souvenir Gothic Contour Italic · abcdefghijkl ABCDEFGHI*

*ABCDEFGHIJKLMNOPQRSTUVWXYZ ÆÇØŒ*
*abcdefghijklmnopqrstuvwxyz æçøœ 1234567890 1234567890 .,:;''""!?¡¿--'"""``^^~«»()[]°&$$¢¢£B%/*

# SANS SERIF SHADED · ABCDEFGHIJKLMNOPQRSTUVWXYZ

ABCDEFGHIJKLMNOPQRSTUVWXYZ
1234567890¢ 1234567890 .,:;""!?-°($$¢¢%/%£)ÆŒ&

# Souvenir Open Shadow · abcdefghijklmno ABCDEFGHI

ABCDEFGHIJKLMNOPQRSTUVWXYZ ÁаÆÇÉGÍMNØŒ§¶
abcdefghijklmnopqrstuvwxyz æçhmnøœß ¸ç 1234567890 .,:;?!""()[]-–#&$$¢£`'``°°°•‹%/

# Bodoni Fancy Flair · abcdefghijklmnopABCDEFGHIJKL

ABCDEFGHIJKLMNOPQRSTUVWXYZ aaᴀ̣ᴀᴀᴀABCDeEE·FGHJHHﬁ·JKK·K̲LLmmm
MMMMmᴍnnNNNØ·PQrTRR·RSSSTTUU·VVWWXXYYŻ 1234567890.,:;-!?&'"`'/'()•.¸%‰
abcdefghijklmnopqrstuvwxyz aᴀbᴄᴅeᴅefﬀſħiᴉjkᴋlmnᴩqrſssss–ttᴜᴜᴠWX̲X̲yyŷ̲ẑ·ﬂ

Bookman Bold Swash · abc de fghi jkl mn ABCDEFGHI
ABCDEFGHIJKLM NOPQRSTUVWXYZ A AAGG HKK KL LLM MMN NRR RT VW Y
abc de fghi jkl mnopqr stuvwyz  ff g kr st yy The ef  1234567890.,:;"'"/!?()•-&&.%%$sc

Cooper Black Italic Swash · abcdefghi ABCDEFG
ABCDEFGHIJKLMNOPQRSTUVWXYZ
abcdefghi jklmnopqrstuvwx yz fgr  1234567890.,;;""'"()[]/*•!?-&$sc%., AAFMMNRY

New Caslon Black Swash · abcdefghijklmno ABCDEFG
ABCDEFGHIJKLMNOPQRSTUVWXYZ  A AKKKL M MN NNRRRVWY
abcdefghijklmnopqrstuvwxyz  abf hhkkmnu  1234567890 1234567890 .,:;"'"!?-O&%/s¢"' ·

Celtic Flair · abcdefghijklmnopqrstuvwxyz ABCDEFGHIJKLMNOPQRST
ABCDEFGHIJKLMNOPQRSTUVWXYZ
abcdefghijklmnopqrstuvwxyz  aa 1234567890.,:;"'"7()•&9!-&c

DAVIDA · ABCDEFGHIJKLMNOPQRSTUVWXYZ 1234567890 .,:;!?"
ABCDEFGHIJKLMNOPQRSTUVWXYZ AEF
1234567890 $123456789 .,:;!?""-||-֎֍-'& &8¢% ֎||֍

Engravers Old English · abcdefghijklmnopqrstuvw ABCDEFGHIJKLM
ABCDEFGHIJKLMNOPQRSTUVWXYZ
abcdefghijklmnopqrstuvwxyz 1234567890 1234567890 .,:!?""''-()*$s¢%/£

Fractur German Text · abcdefghijklmnopqrstuv ABCDEFGH
ABCDEFGHIJKLMNOPQRSTUVWXYZ ßü
abcdefghijklmnopqrstuvwxyz äfiflföü 1234567890.,:;!?'"÷()&£/·„

Firenze · abcdefghijklmnopqrstuv ABCDEFGHIJKLMNOP
ABCDEFGHIJKLMNOPQRSTUVWXYZ
abcdefghijklmnopqrstuvwxyz fffiflffiffl 1234567890 7 ...:;!!?'˜"--()§*&8¢%/"£

Fatface · abcdefghijklmnopqrstuvwx ABCDEFGHIJKLMNOPQRSTUVWX
ABCDEFGHIJKLMNOPQRSTUVWXYZ
abcdefghijklmnopqrstuvwxyz fffiflffiffl 1234567890.,:; .,:;!?'"""-()&$s¢%/*£ç

Goudy Medieval · abcdefghijklmnopqrstuvwxyz ABCDEFGHIJKLMNOPQRS
ABCDEFGHIJKLMNOPQRSTUVWXYZ
abcdefghijklmnopqrstuvwxyz 1234567890 1234567890 .,:;!?'"""-()&*$s¢%/

Goudy Old Style Italic Swash · abcde fghijklm_n_opqrst~ ABCDEFGHI
ABCDEFGHIJKLMNOPQR STUVWXYZ   A N Qu&ThY
abcde fghijklm_n_opqrst~uvwxyz ct eff fiffifl fflgmn_qust tvw   1234567890 1234567890.,;'"!?.()'·&&& $$&¢%''///~~

Ringlet · abcdefghijklmnopqrstuvwx ABCDEFGHIJKLMNOPQRS
ABCDEFGHIJKLMNOPQRSTUVWXYZ ÆÆ&&M
abcdefghijklmnopqrstuvwxyz æœhmn 1234567890.,;'"!?-()& $¢£/

Signwriter's Roman · abcdefghijklmnop ABCDEFGHIJKLM
ABCDEFGHIJKLMNOPQRSTUVWXYZ
abcdefghijklmnopqrstuvwxyz 1234567890 .,:;'""!?()-&$

## Souvenir Demi Bold Swash · abcdefghijkl ABCDEFGHIJ
ABCDEFGHIJKLMNOPQRSTUVWXYZ Aa ÆÇegmnØŒST'
abcdefghijklmnopqrstuvwxyz æçhmnøœers₁° 1234567890.,:;'""!?i¿--.**˚˙˘ˆ˜«»[]()&$$¢#£ß%/

Times Roman Bold Swash · abcdefghijklmno ABCDEFGHIJ
ABCDEFGHIJKLMNOPQRSTUVWXYZ  AHKK LMN RVWY
abcdefghijklmnopqrstuvwxyz 1234567890 1234567890.,:;!?'""-()'&$¢%/ˢᶜ%£°○·■·

Uncial · abcdefghijklmnopq ABCDEFGHIJKLMNOPQ
ABCDEFGHIJKLMNOPQRSTUVWXYZ
abcdefghijklmnopqrstuvwxyz abcdefghijklmnopqqrs 1234567890.,:;!?'&-/$

## AD LIB · ABCDEFGHIJKLMNOPQRSTUVWXYZ&
## abcdefghijklmnopqrstuvwxyz
## $1234567890¢ (.,:;!?'""".-–*$¢/£%)

American Typewriter Light · abcdefghijklm ABCDEFGHIJ
ABCDEFGHIJKLMNOPQRSTUVWXYZ ÆÇŒØR
abcdefghijklmnopqrstuvwxyz æ æçeœœø 1234567890.,;'""!?--()[]*&&$$$¢«»˚˜£ß@#%/

American Typewriter Medium · abcdefghij ABCDEFG
ABCDEFGHIJKLMNOPQRSTUVWXYZ ÆÇŒØR
abcdefghijklmnopqrstuvwxyz æ æçeœœøq 1234567890.,;'""!?--()[]*&&$$$¢˚˜«»£ß·@#%/

**American Typewriter Bold Condensed · abcdefghijklm ABCDEFGH**

**ABCDEFGHIJKLMNOPQRSTUVWXYZ ÆÇŒØ**
**abcdefghijklmnopqrstuvwxyz æçœø 1234567890.,:;'""!?--()[]*&&$$¢'""~`^«»£ß@#%/**

Amelia · abcdefghijklmnopqrstuvwxyz ABCDEFGHIJKLMNOPQRSTUVWXYZ

ABCDEFGHIJKLMNOPQRSTUVWXYZ K
abcdefghijklmnopqrstuvwxyz fiœ 1234567890¹²³⁴⁵⁶⁷⁸⁹⁰.,:;'""!?.--()˘&$©&%/

**BABY TEETH · ABCDEFGHIJKLMNOPQRSTUVWXYZ 12345**

**ABCDEFGHIJKLMNOPQRSTUVWXYZ**
**1234567890.,:;¯¨`^‹‹··??()˜$£--/&**

Baker Signet · abcdefghijklmnopqrstuvw ABCDEFGHIJKLMNOPQR

ABCDEFGHIJKLMNOPQRSTUVWXYZ
abcdefghijklmnopqrstuvwxyz 1234567890.,:;'""!?--'£/%&$¢()

Barnum, P.T. · abcdefghijklmnopqrstuvwxyz ABCDEFGHIJKLMNOPQRSTUVWXY

ABCDEFGHIJKLMNOPQRSTUVWXYZ
abcdefghijklmnopqrstuvwxyz ff fi fl ffi ffl 1234567890¹²³⁴⁵⁶⁷⁸⁹⁰.,:;!?''""--—··()[]&*$$¢ᶜ£%/

Bernhard Modern · abcdefghijklmnopqrst ABCDEFGHIJKLMNOPQR

ABCDEFGHIJKLMNOPQRSTUVWXYZ
abcdefghijklmnopqrstuvwxyz 1234567890¹²³⁴⁵⁶⁷⁸⁹⁰.,:;'"!?()-...*&$$¢§%/

Bernhard Fashion · abcdefghijklmnopqrstuvwxyz ABCDEFGHIJKLMNOPQRSTUVW

ABCDEFGHIJKLMNOPQRSTUVWXYZ ÆŒ

abcdefghijklmnopqrstuvwxyz 1234567890.,:;-""!?«»&-[]$

*Calligraph · abcdefghijklmnopqrstuvwxyz ABCDEFGHIJKLMNOP*

*ABCDEFGHIJKLMNOPQRSTUVWXYZ*

*abcdefghijklmnopqrstuvwxyz 1234567890 .,:;!?"-()&»*

Caslon Antique · abcdefghijklmnopqrstuvwxyz ABCDEFGHIJKLMNOPQRS

ABCDEFGHIJKLMNOPQRSTUVWXYZ
abcdefghijklmnopqrstuvwxyz 1234567890¹²³⁴⁵⁶⁷⁸⁹⁰.,:;!?'""-()&*$¢°%/

City Light · abcdefghijklmnopqrstuvwxyz   ABCDEFGHIJKLMNOPQRSTUVW
ABCDEFGHIJKLMNOPQRSTUVWXYZ
abcdefghijklmnopqrstuvwxyz  1234567890¹²³⁴⁵⁶⁷⁸⁹⁰.,:;'"'!?--«»†()[]*&$⁵¢ᶜ£ᵉ%%/

**Dynamo · abcdefghijklmnopqrstuvw  ABCDEFGHIJKLMNOPQR**
**ABCDEFGHIJKLMNOPQRSTUVWXYZ ſ**
**abcdefghijklmnopqrstuvwxyz ãäèéõûû 1234567890..:;'!?ß()˝˝˜˚˜«»-&$£**

**EXPORT · ABCDEFGHIJKLMNOP**
**ABCDEFGHIJKLMNOPQRSTUVWXYZ**
**1234567890 .,:;?!""""()ˌ-$%/**

**FOTO ORBIT · ABCDEFGHIJKLMNOPQRSTUVWXYZ  1234567890¹²³⁴⁵⁶⁷⁸⁹⁰.,:;ᵢ!?"'"""$¢%[ ]˟˟**
**ABCDEFGHIJKLMNOPQRSTUVWXYZ**
**1234567890¹²³⁴⁵⁶⁷⁸⁹⁰ .,:;ᵢ!?"""˟$¢%[ ]& ˟**

**FRANKFURTER · ABCDEFGHIJKLMNOPQRSTUVWXYZ 1**
**ABCDEFGHIJKLMNOPQRSTUVWXYZ**
**1234567890..:;'"?!ˈ˙˙˙˙«»()$/££**

Friz Quadrata · abcdefghijklmnopqrst ABCDEFGHIJKLMNOPQ
ABCDEFGHIJKLMNOPQRSTUVWXYZ ÀÆØ
abcdefghijklmnopqrstuvwxyz çåæø. 1234567890123456789⁰¹²³⁴⁵⁶⁷⁸⁹⁰.,:;'"''""!?--( )«»˟˙ˈˆ˜˜$¢%//&

**Futura Black · abcdefghijklmnopqrs ABCDEFGHIJKLMNO**
**ABCDEFGHIJKLMNOPQRSTUVWXYZ**
**abcdefghijklmnopqrstuvwxyz 1234567890¹²³⁴⁵⁶⁷⁸⁹⁰.,:;!?"""-()&*§ˢ¢ᶜ%/**

Hobo · abcdefghijklmnopqrstuvwxyz ABCDEFGHIJKLMNOPQRSTUVW
ABCDEFGHIJKLMNOPQRSTUVWXYZ
abcdefghijklmnopqrstuvwxyz 1234567890 ¹²³⁴⁵⁶⁷⁸⁹⁰.,:;!?"""-()&*$ˢ¢ᶜ£%/

**Latin Wide · abcdefghi ABCDEF**
**ABCDEFGHIJKLMNOPQRSTUVWXYZ $¢/%**
**abcdefghijklmnopqrstuvwxyz 1234567890.,:;!?"""'-()&***

LIMITED VIEW · ABCDEFGHIJKLMNOPQRS
ABCDEFGHIJKLMNOPQRSTUVWXYZ ÁÄåäÖØ
abdefghijkluparty 1234567890.,;!?"-+¨˜ß&/()÷$¢£%

MOORE COMPUTER · ABCDEFGHIJKLMNOPQRSTUVWXYZ 1234567890
ABCDEFGHIJKLMNOPQRSTUVWXYZ
1234567890.,;!?""--()[]&'$¢£%/:¨:¨¨

Onyx · abcdefghijklmnopqrstuvwxyz ABCDEFGHIJKLMNOPQRSTUVWXYZ 1234567890
ABCDEFGHIJKLMNOPQRSTUVWXYZ
abcdefghijklmnopqrstuvwxyz 1234567890¹²³⁴⁵⁶⁷⁸⁹⁰.,:!?''""-()·&$'¢%/

Parisian · abcdefghijklmnopqrstuvwxyz ABCDEFGHIJKLMNOPQRSTUVWXYZ
ABCDEFGHIJKLMNOPQRSTUVWXYZ
abcdefghijklmnopqrstuvwxyz 1234567890 ¹²³⁴⁵⁶⁷⁸⁹⁰.,:!?''""-()&*$¢¢%/

Peking · abcdefghijklmnopqrstuvwxyz ABCDEFGHIJKLMNOPQRSTUVWXY
ABCDEFGHIJKLMNOPQRSTUVWXYZ
abcdefghijklmnopqrstuvwxyz 1234567890¹²³⁴⁵⁶⁷⁸⁹⁰.,;!?''""-()*$¢¢%/&

Smoke · abcdefghijklmnopqrstuvwxyz ABCDEFGHIJKLMNOPQRSTUVWXYZ 1234
ABCDEFGHIJKLMNOPQRSTUVWXYZ
abcdefghijklmnopqrstuvwxyz 1234567890.,:!?''""-()$¢

STENCIL BOLD · ABCDEFGHIJKLMNOPQRSTUVWXYZ 12
ABCDEFGHIJKLMNOPQRSTUVWXYZ
1234567890¹²³⁴⁵⁶⁷⁸⁹⁰.,:;'""?!()*-&$$¢%/

WEISS INITIAL NO. 2 · ABCDEFGHIJKLMNOPQRSTUVWXYZ 123456
ABCDEFGHIJKLMNOPQRSTUVWXYZ ÆG
1234567890.,:!?'""-...()'$¢&%/

Western · abcdefghijklm ABCDEFG
ABCDEFGHIJKLMNOPQRSTUVWXYZ
abcdefghijklmnopqrstuvwxyz 1234567890.,:!?'""-()&*$¢$¢%*/

# COLOR
## *Chapter 7*

J osef Albers, in his *Interaction of Color,* comments on sensitivity to color in this way: "Just as the knowledge of acoustics does not make one musical—neither on the productive nor the appreciative side—so no color system by itself can develop one's sensitivity for color." Developing an "eye for color" and mastering color usage is a basic necessity for all visual artists. Training in color sensitivity is an evolutionary process, having as much to do with maturation as other factors, but it begins with the formal teaching of color.

The factual aspects of color—its dimensions, the theories of spectrum and systems arrangement, and the physical and psychological phenomenon of sight are the educational springboards to success with color on the intimate level of the professional designer's involvement. One literally cannot proceed successfully into technical or specialized areas of color application or color psychology (all areas affecting the designer) without a thorough working knowledge of the rudiments of what is really, artistically intuitive or not, a realm of science. Admittedly, it is an *inexact* science. It is even more inexact a science when applied to the work of the artist.

Color is by far the most controversial issue we will discuss. Learning to deal with line and shape and with typography are child's play compared with the complexities of color. This applies as much to students of design as to students of the fine arts, for their needs are identical. Color information that relates to painting also relates to designing. It is in advanced training that differences in color exist between the designer and the fine artist. Color is more *defined by technology* for the designer than for the fine artist. The designer is restricted to what effects can be commercially reproduced in the *medium being utilized,* whether that medium is paper, plastic, metal, or other materials. The designer is also restricted to the current technology used in mass reproduction. The designer is faced with vivid differences in the professional use of color. And all too often, the design student is not given the necessary background to help deal with these differences.

Most emphasis in traditional art training is placed on subtractive pigment color theories. Mixed pigment theory offers *basic training* for the designer, but not much else. The designer must function as a professional in the world of commercial printing applications, and that requires specific knowledge and terminology. Indeed, the standard nomenclature used with mixed pigment combinations is totally irrelevant to that used by the printing industry. The red, blue, and yellow primaries of the artist's palette are not the same as the magenta, cyan, and yellow base process colors of the printing spectrum. Names for hues, such as orange, green, violet, are subjective and vague when describing screened percentages in process printing, or even in hue identification for single, solid colors in print.

The professional designer rarely has to depend upon mixing pigment to achieve a result. The main tools used in designing (markers, printed papers, color-key films) are much more convenient than paint, and offer very extensive hue, value, and intensity ranges that accurately reflect the character of printed materials.

For the student designer, color is still a subject where the "bridge" between theory and application is weakest. Only recently, primarily because of heightened interest in photography, film, video, and the advent of the color Xerox as a fine art vehicle, has there been any real interest among artists concerning the technical aspects of color. Without doubt, those students with a strong background in the study of the science and technology of color have a better understanding of the total concept of "color." This background certainly makes for easier comprehension of the reproductive color processes.

We assume that the reader has a basic grounding in fine-art color study. Thus, rather than devote space to a review of color theory that can be found in a hundred different basic texts, we will deal with the designer's application of color and develop a basic understanding of the color system and nomenclature designers use. We will introduce the concept of process color, something the beginning design student most probably has not been exposed to. The designer is also concerned with the psychology of color, in a marketing sense, and we will take a look at this area. In other words, we will leave off basic color study and concentrate on information that is especially pertinent to the designer.

## *Basic Concepts*

There are three basic attributes of color. Hue is the name we give to a spectral combination to distinguish it from others within the entire color spectrum. "Yellow," then, is not *a* color, but a general hue identifier. Value is the lightness and darkness of a hue, or how we perceive it in terms of its light-reflecting abilities. And lastly, intensity, sometimes referred to as chroma, is the strength or carrying power of color. It should be obvious to everyone that some hues are stronger (are more easily perceived) than others.

The artist and the printer use totally different means to achieve color. For the artist, every hue is a "mixture." Whether that mixture is base ingredients that form pigment or a mixture of pigments to form other pigments, the artist blends color to create the effects that are desired. The printer produces color by the blending of pigments also, but the greater part of the printer's involvement is in "blending" color to formulate hue, value, and intensity without *mixing* of pigments. This blending without mixing is called *screen* and *process color* printing.

In four-color process printing, the printer deals with three base hues and black. From these, all other variations can be created. Even in non-process printing, those specially formulated hues the printer uses must be screened to produce value and intensity changes. In printing, paper always stands for white and nothing can be made lighter than the paper. (There are exceptions, of course—where colored paper is used and white ink is applied under screens of another hue.) The printer can either mix ink or screen ink to formulate the effects that are required.

In mixed pigment application, the value of a hue may be changed by the addition of white or black. According to the Munsell system, there are ten value gradients in the black-to-white value scale. Value 0 represents white, and value 10, black. Mixing produces tints or shades of a hue, respectively. In addition, a hue's value may be decreased by mixing with its complement. In all cases, the *physical combination* of pigments is required to achieve results.

In halftone screen printing, an ink is not physically mixed with white or black to achieve a value range distribution. Out of a necessity governed by technical capability and cost management, the printer utilizes screen variations of black printed in concert with a hue to effect shades of that hue. To effect a tint range for a hue, the printer cuts *back* on its full intensity through the use of screen variations. Printer's screens range from 0 to 100 percent, in 10 percent gradients. To achieve the fullest possible range of value gradients, the printer combines screens of hue and black in sequence. (See an illustration of a value scale for a PANTONE®* Color designate in the color insert.) In this example, "0%" to the printer represents the absence of any screen or hue—that is, white paper. Naturally "100%" means a complete, unscreened full coverage of ink. You will see that the "value scale" for the PANTONE Color begins with a 10 percent screen of the hue and then moves progressively toward black and full color coverage. Crossing each other at regular intervals, the screens create a value range for the hue (our example screens only to 70 percent in the black range).

---

*Pantone, Inc.'s standard trademark for color reproduction and color reproduction materials.

In appearance the printed value range is *similar* to that established for mixed pigment by such systems as Munsell—similar, but not the same. Again, the printer does not mix the inks. Instead, the two inks in some combination of screens are printed separately. The eye mixes the inks to formulate the color value. Technically speaking, a screened percentage of a hue is not a true value reduction; it is a *perceptual* value reduction. The ink used to formulate the dot pattern of the screen is the same ink, the same intensity ink, as that used for full coverage. There is simply *less of it* covering a given surface area. The amount of dot (ink) coverage depends upon the screen used. Consequently, a "reduction" in the physical application of ink to a surface will not form the exact same tint range variables as a "reduction" of the actual pigment hue by mixing with white. This holds true for shade variations in a hue as well.

A screened variation of process magenta (see color plate 28) will not produce a full value, "optically correct" "pink." If one wishes to achieve such a "pink" (again, a relative term only), a special mix of process color must be formulated. The following comparison between a 50% screen of magenta and a "pink" such as shown (a mix of screen percentages) points up the differences. Something else becomes apparent when viewing the comparison between the screened down magenta and the mix of process color that approximates the designation of "pink," and this brings us to another new idea.

The intensity of the two areas of color are substantially different. By screening down (applying less) of the magenta on the paper, the printer has weakened the intensity of the ink, or decreased the saturation of the ink by 50 percent. The artist, with a jar full of an equivalent paint hue, could approximate the decrease in the saturation (intensity) achieved by the printer by mixing the pigment with water...this without changing the hue. Once again, the printer *separates* the hue by screening it in minute dots...the artist *extends* the hue by adding water (or some other clear compound). The results are similar intensity changes; but the means of achieving them, like the means of achieving a value reduction, are not the same.

These redefinitions of value and intensity are important distinctions for the designer to understand. What the artist can achieve easily by mixing pigment may be difficult and expensive for the printer to duplicate through the process of printing. This is an especially critical factor when the designer is restricted to one or two flat colors and limited screenwork, or where there is a limitation in the printing technology. Understanding the printing of color will help the designer realize what is possible to achieve in the medium being worked in.

# Color: What's in a Name?

We have already mentioned PANTONE Color and discussed two hues you familiarly conceive of as "red" and "pink." Before we continue with aspects of process color, we will review the concept of color naming.

What is a true "red," "pink," "blue," "orange," or "green"? You may think you know, but your neighbor may have a different idea. We need a system for classifying hues by more specific nomenclature. Pigment systems label hue, value, and intensity in various ways to differentiate between them. Pigment manufacturers have established hue names that relate to the chemical ingredients of their products—"cadmium red," "phthalocyanine and cobalt blue," "alizarine crimson," "lamp black," and the traditional earth tones of "ochre," "umber," and "sienna," only to mention a few. Less technically specific are other classic names for hues that have also evolved—"Chinese white," "Paynes gray," "Prussian blue," "Naples yellow," and many more colors associated with the persons, places, or elements of their origin are probably familiar to you if you have worked with pigment color.

Creators of fashion trends are more capricious in their nomenclature. Everyone is familiar with names like "teal blue," "candy-apple red," "burnt orange," "forest green," "baby blue," "oyster beige," "daffodil yellow," yet some may find it difficult to see these hues in the mind's eye. Constantly we are subjected to idiotic euphemisms, fanciful comparatives such as "cerice," "heliotrope," "taupe," "fuchsia," "russet," "chartreuse," "mocha," "loden," and "olive drab." Color names such as these are coined for pure romance alone and, while they may refer to their inspirational origin, do little to identify the visual character of the hue they represent. The only way such hues are remembered is by repeated exposure. Their real function is to give distinction to and to contemporize already existing color variations, to offer an excuse for modish interpretation, and to help establish a rationale for trading the old for the new. There are no "new" hues. There are only new ways of looking at them. Color has existed in its entire form since light first struck the earth. Man simply finds new and ingenious ways to deal with the phenomenon.

The fashion designer may thrive on innovative color nomenclature. The interior designer and the decorator may value the sense of distinction "nouveau couleur" gives to his or her work. But the graphic designer becomes totally lost in the morass of euphemistic color options. Certainly the graphic designer recognizes and uses trends in color. But there is one major distinction between graphic designers and professional artists in other areas: the graphic designer must deal exclusively with the printing medium. While the graphic designer's work may reflect the current color preferences, the nomenclature used within the profession to refer to that color is pragmatic and will not change significantly until the printing profession itself changes. That is not likely to happen, since an extremely precise and effective system exists for the accurate communication of color effects.

The printer's nomenclature for color, while totally relevant to the work of the graphic designer, is not completely serviceable because of its technical complexity. If the designer had only to talk color with the printer, that system would suffice. However, this is not the case. The designer must talk color a great deal of the time to people outside the realms of art and production, to others in support professions as well as to clients, people who cannot be expected to have printing expertise.

Moreover, not so long ago the color dialogue between designer and printer, and even printer and printer, was haphazard. Before the advent of common color guidelines, many printers developed their own systems for interpreting and specifying color. Consequently, there were a great many sample books of ink "swatches," which anyone working with color had to plow through to verify a color objective. This was confusing enough for the designer, let alone others less experienced with the graphic arts. There was great variation between printers' sample books, and getting what you originally asked for could be a chancy business. Custom mixing of inks was usually required, which was both inefficient and expensive. If the designer found this exasperating, the novice found it impossible!

# *The PANTONE MATCHING SYSTEM*

In 1963, Pantone, Inc., of Moonachie, New Jersey, introduced the first comprehensive color formula system to the graphic arts. With the publication of their PANTONE Matching System Printers Edition (now known as the PANTONE Color Formula Guide), and the PANTONE Color Specifier, a uniform measure for color was finally available and the designer, printer, and ink manufacturer could at last share a common language. The PANTONE MATCHING SYSTEM consists of a full line of color specification books which are coordinated by PANTONE Color Numbers. The system has gained almost total acceptance within the graphic arts industry. The designer and printer both have found the PANTONE MATCHING SYSTEM an invaluable aid in explaining color. The benefits of the system are obvious to anyone at first glance. Instead of struggling to articulate color by the use of subjective nomenclature, or by searching printed color samples to approximate what you are after, the designer simply identifies the hue by a PANTONE Number and refers the printer (or other person) to the PANTONE Manual. For the client who may not understand exactly what a "forest green" is, or for the printer who may look at a "forest green" paint chip and have to guess at the color formulation that makes it up, this is the ideal answer. Each numbered hue carries a formula for accurate mixing. The printer using these references has a reliable system for reproducing the art.

**110**

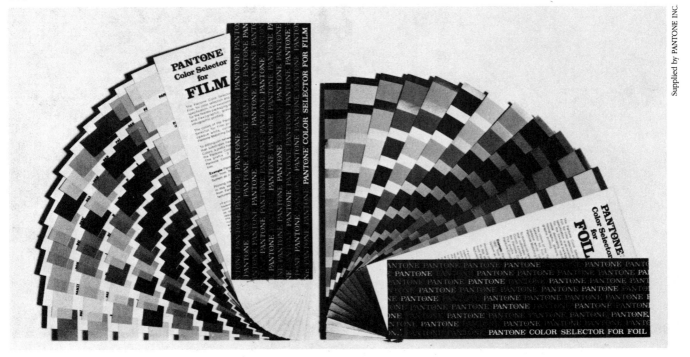

Supplied by PANTONE INC.

Supplied by PANTONE INC.

**111**

**112**

Supplied by PANTONE INC.

Because the PANTONE MATCHING SYSTEM is universally used within the design and printing professions, it is imperative that the student become familiar with it as quickly as possible. The PANTONE Color Formula Guide is available to students at a nominal charge through an "educational package" produced by Pantone, Inc., and can be ordered from them by your professor. This guide will give you easy and repeated access to the range of PANTONE Colors. This system is as necessary to the designer's understanding of color as any of the subtractive pigment systems are to the understanding of basic fine-art color. For information concerning this package, write to: Pantone, Inc., Educational Division, 55 Knickerbocker Road, Moonachie, N.J. 07074.

Although no product or service is recommended above any other in this text, and no association exists between the author and Pantone, Inc., we *will* point out the relevant realities of the profession wherever possible. One of those realities is that the PANTONE MATCHING SYSTEM is almost indispensable to design. At this time it is our state-of-the-art technology. That being the case, those wishing to be designers are well advised to know it.

An excellent way to associate color with the PANTONE MATCHING SYSTEM is to pick out eight or ten of the most commonly used hues (most probably those hues perceived as primary, secondary, or tertiary) and memorize them according to their numbers. Learn to always visually establish hue and number in your mind and refer to a hue by its number in your daily design dialogue. Drop the ambiguities of naming colors "blue" or "orange" or "brown" (a particularly vague reference!). Add new hue/numbers to your mental list as you begin to use other hues in your design work. In this way you can build up a specific color vocabulary without always having to refer to your color guide. By developing this visual memory reference, your ease in discussing color with someone familiar with the PANTONE MATCHING SYSTEM will improve dramatically. Saying "PANTONE 375"—a specific reference; much more specific than saying "yellow-green"—is an accurate way to communicate the particular "yellow-green" you intend. Simply saying "yellow-green" may connote something different in another's mind—perhaps PANTONE 382, also in the "yellow-green" range, but decidedly different than PANTONE 375.

As there are over five hundred individual color designates in the PANTONE MATCHING SYSTEM, you cannot hope to commit all of them to memory, yet you will be surprised at the large numbers of hues that will become familiar friends because of personal color preferences in your work. Following is a list of some of the more commonly specified PANTONE Colors. Find them in a PANTONE Color Formula Guide and see how they relate to your concepts of primary, secondary, and tertiary hues:

| | | |
|---|---|---|
| PANTONE Reflex Blue | PANTONE Rubine Red | PANTONE 116 |
| PANTONE Process Blue | PANTONE Green | PANTONE 151 |
| PANTONE 300 | PANTONE 469 | PANTONE 165 |
| PANTONE Rhodamine Red | PANTONE 375 | PANTONE Purple |
| PANTONE Warm Red | PANTONE 368 | PANTONE 123 |
| PANTONE 485 | PANTONE 100 | PANTONE 266 |

# One Color

"One color printing" is the use of *one color* in solid print (100% coverage) and/or screen application (varying percentage gradients of 1 color) to produce printing materials. One color printing is the simplest, least expensive printing because it requires only one plate-making process, one inking procedure, and no concern with butting or overlapping color to produce other color effects. Any printing utilizing more than one color (2, 3, or 4 or more individual colors) is referred to as multicolor printing. This is to differentiate such printing from process color work which is a completely different (and more complex) application.

There are times when the designer is called upon to work in one color only. This is (as the process implies) simply specifying one hue, screened or unscreened, for the printer to make a printing plate. Although this is the most limiting of all color effects, interesting things can be done by combining a hue with a colored paper. The simplest color usage is a solid print (no screenwork) of a hue. This is called *line color work,* as opposed to printing solid and screened combinations of a hue, which is called *screen halftone work.*

# Multicolor

The PANTONE MATCHING SYSTEM identifies a spectrum range for solid color printing and then expands that range to include all of the possible variables created when solid colors are screened (the PANTONE Color Tint Selector). When more than one solid hue is employed in printing an image, the procedure is referred to as multicolor printing. The simplest usage of multicolor printing is line color work with two hues and no overlap. Overlapping of solid color areas, because of the transparency of printing inks, creates other solid variations of color. As we have already seen, screening solid hues is possible. Each hue in multicolor work requires a different printing plate. If the designer has indicated a two-color job, and specified a PANTONE Color Number for each, all of the color variation for the first hue goes on the first plate, all of the second on the second plate. Combined screen effects are achievable, but only if the screens overlap in the printing. The value scale illustrating the range for the PANTONE Color (see color insert) is a good example of multicolor screen printing. It required a separate plate for black and a separate plate for the PANTONE Color printed in combination to achieve the effects you see.

Multicolor work is used for printing two and three (sometimes four and more) specific solid colors and their screen range variations. It is not employed for full color work. At best (within the realm of practicality), it can only approximate the effects of four-color process printing. If one were to try to achieve the true range of full color necessary for photographic reality in multicolor printing, it would require first identifying every hue variation within a given image, mixing the ink and printing each with its own separate plate . . . a theoretical possibility, but certainly a practical nightmare!

## *Process Color*

*Primary color* is defined as being that color from which all other color can be formulated. Primary color varies from one system to another. In process printing, remember that the printer is *screening* three "primary" colors plus black and superimposing them to produce the full color range of the spectrum. The printer's "primaries" must be scientifically balanced to optically achieve what the artist's pigments achieve by physical mixing. The spectrum of red, blue, and yellow used by the artist is not adequate for the printer. Overprinting of spectrum blue and yellow, because they are complementary, produces black. Spectrum red, overprinting yellow, will still produce red. Red and blue, spectrally exclusive, overprint to produce black. Obviously, the printer's colors must juxtapose and overprint to produce other colors within the spectrum. To understand the printer's problem in this respect, we must consider the concept of color and light, the additive process.

Color is the product of differing wave lengths of light. Without light there is no color. By "adding" these differing wave lengths together, color change can be effected. Sir Isaac Newton was the first to postulate that all color exists in light. By placing a prism in front of a beam of sunlight, he observed the filtered light separate into bands of graduated color, which he termed

"spectrum," the Latin word for sight. Using a second inverted prism, he recombined the spectrum he had created, reproducing the original white light. Most importantly, he discovered that by adding equal proportions of red, blue, and green light, he could also create white light. This fact establishes red, blue, and green as the primary ranges (wave lengths) in the light spectrum, or those ranges from which all other ranges can be produced. Unequal proportions of these three primaries create the following secondary ranges of color: red and blue converge to produce magenta, red and green converge to produce yellow, and blue and green converge to produce cyan.

These secondary light hues, because of their spectral makeup, are correctly balanced for the printer to use as printing "primaries." Magenta is the complement of green. Yellow is the complement of blue. Cyan is the complement of red. Inks formulated to match the spectral characteristics of these light secondaries will combine to produce the equivalent of the light primaries, thereby establishing a complete basic palette which the printer can process to reproduce the full range of spectrum color.

The creation of a wide color range by overprinting of full color inks utilizes the subtractive process. White paper is a source of reflected white light. Each ink, by itself or in combination with others, and according to its spectral characteristics, subtracts some of the light which is reflected from the paper. Yet the additive process of color mixing is often found side by side with the subtractive in full color printing. By examining a strong magnification of a process-printed area, you will notice that large dot areas will overprint to produce color effects, while small dots may group together, separate from one another, to produce visual mixing when seen "en masse."

By formulating his basic palette according to the spectral balance of the light secondaries and by juxtaposing dots of color as well as overprinting of color, the printer utilizes both the additive and subtractive systems in the production of full color printing.

The printer uses the primary palette to reproduce a full color image as follows. A color piece of art that is to be printed must be photographed at least three times. It must be "color separated" through red, green, and blue (light primary) filters. Each primary filter subtracts out certain hues (solid areas as well as percentages found in other hues). Green filters out cyan and yellow (this is the magenta printer). Blue filters out magenta and cyan (this is the yellow printer). Red filters out magenta and yellow (this is the cyan printer). These three exposures are the three color separations from which the printing plates will be made. For the black (which will give the art its value range), a fourth separation is needed. Black is filtered one of two ways: (1)

by an amber filter that allows only gray value to pass through, or (2) by a split-filter process that separates out black by various exposures through each of the three primary filters.

# Color Prejudice and Motivation

Like the camera lens, the eye is only a receiving mechanism. It does not translate visual information. The messages received by our eyes are not color impressions until the brain reacts. Someone totally unfamiliar with the concept of color whose brain had not "seen" color before, would have to learn color as you might learn any unfamiliar subject. While the artist's eye is structurally no different from anyone else's in terms of its receiving capabilities, the artist's brain is more highly developed in its color sensitivity. "Having a good eye for color," a phrase that is often used to comment on a person's intrinsic ability in color usage, really refers to that person's mental level of capability for understanding color.

Over the years exhaustive studies have been conducted on how and why color motivates us for or against things—things in our environment, and personal things we consume and keep around us. Color preferences are far more influential than we realize. In our choice of clothing, color is a more crucial consideration than fabric. In purchasing an automobile, color choice comes second only to the make and model. Color is the first consideration in our carpeting, drapes, furniture, in all our furnishings. Color affects things as basic as our sexual preference . . . blond versus brunette, blue eyes or gray eyes or brown eyes. Color categorizes and directs us both consciously and unconsciously, and categorical distinctions change with trends and periods and vary according to cultural influences. Cultural influences can become clichés that are difficult to abandon . . . and clichés affect the designer.

Christmas and the colors red and green are uniquely American in their relationships to each other. The association has become a visual cliché, along with the jovial fat man in the red hat and suit. Because of this "color attitude" (exclusively fashionable for around 75 years in this country), it is difficult for the designer to move away from these learned color patterns and still convey the psychological potency of the message. To do so and still impart the essence of Christmas with any strength requires considerable creative ability in the management of color's relationship to shape and content. This is an altogether obvious example. Most problems are not so obvious.

Reflect on other cultural symbols that play upon color attitudes. How often have we referred to depression as "a blue mood" or "feeling blue"? Why is a red sports car more of a sports car than a white one? What makes a coward "yellow"? Why do we associate black with death, white with virginity, pink and powder blue with babies? For a long time, black as a hue was not used in food packaging because of its negative associations. The black color barrier in the supermarket was broken a few years ago, and then only timorously in snack-food packaging. Today we seem to have evolved out of our prejudice against black, and it is emerging more frequently as a heavy accent hue on packaging; but it will still be some time before you will see your favorite brand of cereal in a predominantly black box. Certain shades of green are never used with meat and dairy products because they convey an "attitude" of mold and decay . . . intolerable concepts to the hygienically oriented American consumer. Neither feminine hygiene products nor ads for them use intense hues in the red and orange ranges because of current cultural taboos concerning the body. And how many men would buy razor blades in a pink and violet package?

The color of graphic communication is rarely if ever accidental or primarily subject to the whims of fancy. In a project of any importance, considering the possible psychological "color profiles" for the subject you are designing is an obligation the designer cannot ignore. Whether or not to depart from the accepted norm in a particular situation is a judgment that can only be made after weighing the prejudicial barriers you are up against; in other words, is it feasible or even profitable to the creativity of the project to "fight city hall." Breaking ranks with tradition is a natural impulse on the part of every good designer, but the good designer will also be able to turn prejudice and limitation to his or her advantage. This is especially true in the area of color application. Above all else, the designer must seek to sublimate his or her own color preferences. Color can never be a totally subjective medium for the designer, so come to terms with that fact early in your career or you will suffer needless trauma over what you might mistakenly think is a loss of your "design integrity." As far as testing your ability to be objective about color, ask yourself some simple questions: How often do you *repeat* the same color combinations in your design problem solving? Do you look at hue alternatives because you like them, and if so, why do you like them? Have you analyzed what color system best reflects the subject you are communicating? And consider this. How often have you heard the remark "It's a great symbol (ad, graphic, layout, etc.), but the color could be better . . . "? Is this a subjective reaction or an astute reasoning process at work? Most often it is the former!

# *Appropriate Color*

Knowing what is appropriate color is more than understanding the difference between "a silk purse and a sow's ear," but common sense is a large part of designing with color. We have mentioned the word *appropriate* in relation to color more than once: What do we mean by it? If you are designing for Rolls-Royce, your color parameters are sure to be much different than if you are communicating the merits of a rent-a-car company. Selective color choice of this kind in relation to the product or service is outwardly based upon the prejudice and symbolism discussed earlier and upon commonsense reasoning motivated by deeper psychological associations. We have already pointed up a powerful symbol stereotype in our example of Christmas. Perhaps less obvious, commonsense reasoning dictates many areas of appropriate color usage that are also taken for granted. Most people would probably concede that large amounts of intense red or black would not be appropriate for use in hospital graphics and signs. Give yourself a moment and you will undoubtedly think of many more such situations.

The audience you are appealing to is the principle consideration in something as explosively personal as color preference. Levels of sophistication and interest, social economic profiles and environment, all factors that weigh heavily in influencing a person's tastes in color, are constantly in a state of change (sometimes rapid change) depending upon the society you are focusing upon. This change is reflected in the tastes of the consumer, and "adoptive attitudes" in color preference are commonly seen as people change their situations and status in life. Color you preferred when you were young or poor, for instance, might subconsciously be left behind in preference of other color that better reflects the attitudes of your age or of an affluent station in life. One definition of appropriate color, then, is that it is color that is right according to the situation in which you are working...a situation ethic, if you will.

Color motivation is not always an outwardly discoverable manifestation. To help in the emotionally vague areas of color analysis, the designer has a wealth of information concerning the psychological and motivational marketing aspects of color at his or her disposal for reference in problem solving. Conclusions can be drawn from such information that can be used in helping to produce successful communication through design.

Many criteria may be used to categorize color. Bold versus weak, masculine versus feminine, warmth and closeness versus coolness and distance, organic versus man-made, traditional versus contemporary, and many more. When hue combinations that evoke these various attributes are combined with information and symbols relating to ideas being communicated, strong motivational patterns are established. Studies indicate that where color is used that is not normally associated with an object, it tends to *devalue* that object in the eyes of the user. To some people, Christmas "just isn't Christmas" without red and green. Symbolic color identification seems to be most important in situations where the idea must be conveyed immediately. A billboard that may be seen (from a car) for a maximum of 8 seconds must convey the *feeling* of Christmas even before the word message registers in the brain. Thus color is crucial when a visual message is fleeting. The longer the duration of the visual message, however, the less important the need for color patterns that relate to the preconceived ideas about the subject. Christmas may very well be conveyed through any number of color combinations in a department store window, a magazine advertisement, or a package design where the message has ample time to be considered.

Intense color is preferred in situations where the emotional content of the message is high and where there is a strong sense of urgency being conveyed or where the subject relates to the self-expressive side of a person's nature. A classic example of such color usage might be a propaganda poster from communist China, where the total message blend is particularly strident.

Low-key color is more acceptable where the message and image are to be understated. Subtle color is associated with restraint, dignity, exclusivity, and with less forceful circumstances. Color that tends to be darker in value is generally considered more serious. A dark business suit for instance has been proven to "project" more authority than a tan or light-gray one. Darker hues are associated with formality...more official, more important. Banks tend to stay away from hues that might seem frivolous when choosing corporate color schemes, opting instead for more substantial blues, grays, and generally darker values.

Heaviness and lightness in association with a product or image seems to be an important issue. Low-calorie beers do not employ the traditional heavy browns and reds and other hues associated with European products. Menthol cigarette manufacturers neither advertise nor package their products in bright warm color. Within the realm of consumer goods, product and packaging color is especially crucial to the success of the product. In the supermarket, canned goods must look fresh. Red meat must be red or it does not appear wholesome. It is difficult to sell brown eggs to the American market because brown is not a hue associated with dairy products. Male products must appear in "male" colors. Recall the pink and violet razor blade package mentioned as an example earlier. Then we were referring to the negative connotation of those colors with nicks and cuts. But pink and violet have a feminine connotation as well. There is a general association of pastel color with feminine attributes. Cosmetic products reflect this association.

If we ran through a general palette of color from a motivational viewpoint, we would see that there are strong associations, symbolic and cultural, that affect our everyday lives:

1. *Red.* Psychologically, red is the most visible hue. Red is dramatic. It is a life-force hue that is often associated with hysteria, passion, madness, violence, and other deep emotions. Red is also an official hue; it is found in most national flags. A particularly American colloquialism for tedious formality is "red tape"...not blue or green or brown tape. Red is associated with sexuality in our society, with virility, and generally assumes an aggressive, domineering stance. A red sports car is always "more" of a sports car than a sports car of another hue. Because of its advancing nature and its vitality, red is generally favored in both sophisticated and unsophisticated market segments.

2. *Yellow.* Yellow is a paradoxical hue. Traditionally it was considered passive and not a strong attention-getter, but it is used spectacularly in the contemporary marketplace to garner attention. Depending upon its application, yellow can be pointedly masculine or decidedly feminine. It is probably the most often used packaging hue in one context or another. It is an optimistic and expectant hue in its contemporary use, generally associated with warmth, good health, and gaiety. It is the strongest associative hue for almost all food products.

3. *Blue.* Blue is generally a reserved and conservative hue except in its brightest aspect. It is used widely in the contemporary marketplace (like yellow) in product and packaging design because it connotes sensitivity and cleanliness. Like red, there is a strongly official sense to it. Navy blue has long been associated with authority. Blue projects an exclusivity that other hues do not. It traditionally has been thought to soothe and calm, as do other cool range colors, but recent studies indicate that certain variations of pink can also produce dramatic results in curbing aggressive tendencies. Blue is a perennial favorite background hue because it works well with most other colors.

4. *Orange.* Orange, like brown, tends to be associated with organic properties. It is a fertile hue like red, but generally without red's hostile properties. Its intermediate and favorable characteristics tend to give it the same association with food that yellow has. Orange was a popular packaging and advertising hue in the late nineteenth century. It has high recognition as a seasonal (autumnal) hue, and in combination with black projects associations with Halloween, one of our strongest American color stereotypes.

5. *Green.* Green has long been stereotyped as a natural hue. In ancient alchemy, green represented the raw, primordial state. It has wide appeal because it reflects what we view as the balance and normality of our environment. Green also signifies peace, approval, and safety, and like blue it connotes freshness and cleanliness. Like blue, it is a good background hue for warmer, brighter color, its recessive characteristics acting as an effective visual complement.

6. *Violet.* The violet range (including the hue that is commonly called purple) has long been associated with exclusivity and royalty. This association is so strong that it is still used in this context in today's society. It is perhaps the most unstable of all color from a reproduction standpoint, but is used extensively as an accent when implications of power and rank are desired, along with gold and silver in product and package design. Like red, it also has overtones of violence, and it was a common hue in psychedelic graphic statements of the 1960s.

7. *Gold and Silver.* These metallic pigments have always represented wealth and currency. Although overstatement often produces the opposite effect, the stereotype of high value is a very strong one.

8. *The polarity of black and white.* Black is the ultimate formal hue. It is also traditionally associated with death and mourning and with sin and evil. In religious dress, the white mantle crowns or covers the black frock, symbolizing good triumphing over evil. White is associated with purity, health, and cleanliness, and—especially in American society—is a symbolic identifier for medicine, which is still perceived in the mystical sense of goodness. The intermediate values of gray between the two signify the occurrence of age and the conservative aspects that accompany aging.

# LAYOUT
## *Chapter 8*

Layout is, by utilitarian definition, the proportioning and balancing of divergent elements that go into the making of a design. Earlier, we referred to compositional area in terms of boundary and format in the context of shape. Layout, for the graphic designer, is conceptually dealt with in two ways: (1) in packaging and three-dimensional graphic application as format, and (2) in two-dimensional area as the printed page. In the lengthy process of learning layout, the young designer has ample time to develop an aesthetic base upon which to practice the skills of moving elements about to formulate designs. The reasons for and the necessity of developing this aesthetic base is naturally understood by other creative individuals, both in and outside the realm of the graphic arts. But what about other intelligent and competent individuals outside the realm of the creative personality ... individuals that the professional designer must work with on a daily basis and even depend upon for a livelihood? These individuals have little understanding of such complex aesthetics. After all, why should they? Understanding the *designer's* system and justification of aesthetics is not critical to the practice of their professional careers ... at least in their eyes. Yet, these individuals' *patronage* is critical to the *designer's* professional career! Understanding and dealing with "unschooled" attitudes about aesthetics is essential education ... as essential as the learning of the aesthetic base itself.

The danger of developing an elitist attitude about aesthetics in the classroom situation is very real. This can be damaging to the designer's toleration of "real world" circumstances. Very little classroom time is spent in *objectively analyzing people's reactions to* the creative placement of visual elements, to how established preferences affect such reactions, and to just exactly *why* these preferences exist. Nor are designers taught sufficient respect for the logic of noncreative people. It is surprising how many young designers feel "misunderstood" because of their creativity, when, in fact, the *real* reason they have difficulty functioning in harmony with noncreative people is, because of their *own* failure to understand or appreciate anyone else's perspective on a creative situation. This is an *educational flaw* ... certainly not an intelligence deficiency on the part of the creative! It appears later professionally when creative compromise is seen as "selling out." Let's take a look at how this educational deficiency can work against the designer in a "real world" circumstance.

**113 & 114** The layout of a page can be a dynamic statement in figure-ground relationships in which the considerations of "white space" can create tremendous variation in the presentation of an idea. This can be demonstrated best in the rough conceptual sketching phase. This page shows a symmetrical example of one theme idea; page 106 shows an asymmetrical example.

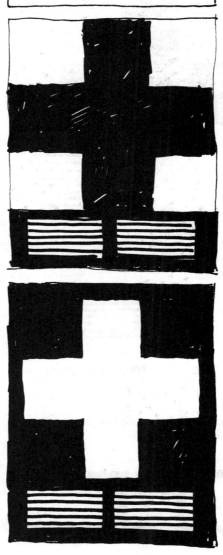

**113**

**114**

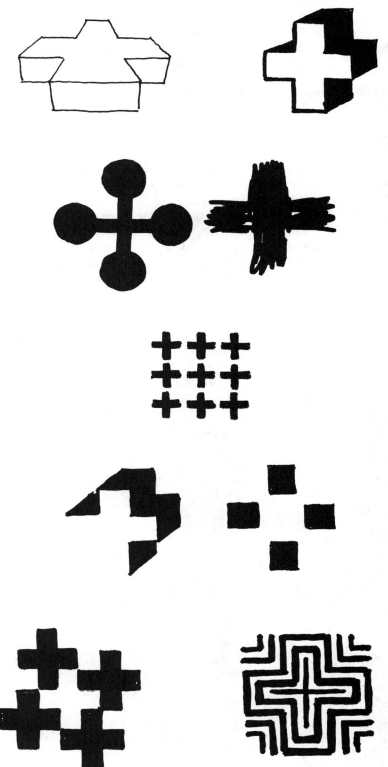

**115** The different visual attitudes of negative-positive or "white space" relationships in our thumbnail sketches are only a narrow group of applications of our subject. The number of possibilities are limited by the time spent in the exploration and in the creative insight of the designer doing the exploring. Even in our narrow application we have produced significant change without even considering a different approach to the presentation of the subject itself! We might very well create new themes by:

(a) projecting our subject into a spacial format
(b) altering the shape configuration of the subject
(c) using other principles such as grouping by similarity and/or proximity
(d) relying upon the prejudice for closure
(e) establishing good continuity through interdependent relationships

# *Understanding the Client's Perspective*

Designer *A* is given an assignment to design and lay out a brochure for businessman *X* that will describe the services he offers his clients. Businessman *X* is eager for a "good" brochure, and designer *A* creates some very nice alternative formats, one of which is very acceptable to businessman *X*. Businessman *X* is very excited to see his ideas coming to fruition. Designer *A* recommends setting the text of the brochure (which was assiduously worked at by both the copywriter and businessman *X* to effectively say what needed to be said) in 6 point light-face type, based on an aesthetic judgment of the type's relationship to the other elements of the composition. Designer *A* sees his responsibility to his idea of creative consistency clearly.

Businessman *X* objects vehemently to this "arty" solution. Businessman *X* demands that the type be set in a minimum of 10 or possibly even 12 point type with the text accented in critical areas by boldface. Designer *A* does as he is told, but feels compromised and possibly embittered because his personal vision of the ultimate solution is bastardized by noncreative input. Businessman *X* is perplexed and even cynically disposed toward designer *A* because he knows what he is trying to accomplish through the communication of his brochure and he cannot understand why designer *A* cannot also understand this: he certainly explained it to designer *A* when he gave him the assignment.

Designer *A* has failed in his assignment because of the following reasons: (1) He has failed to see that the textual information is the *most* critical part of the assignment. This is so because it relates to the practices of business *X*, which is the reason for the brochure in the first place. He has failed to understand that businessman *X*, to whom business *X* is everything, wants the description of what he does and what makes him different than his competition clearly readable and direct. For his own part, businessman *X* is able and willing to use innovative design to distinguish himself from his com-

**116, 117 & 118** Cover ideas and introductory page layout variations for a health care product catalog.

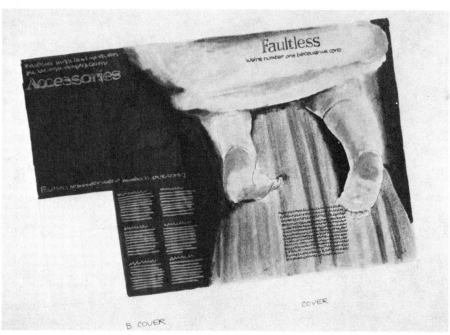

**117**

**118**

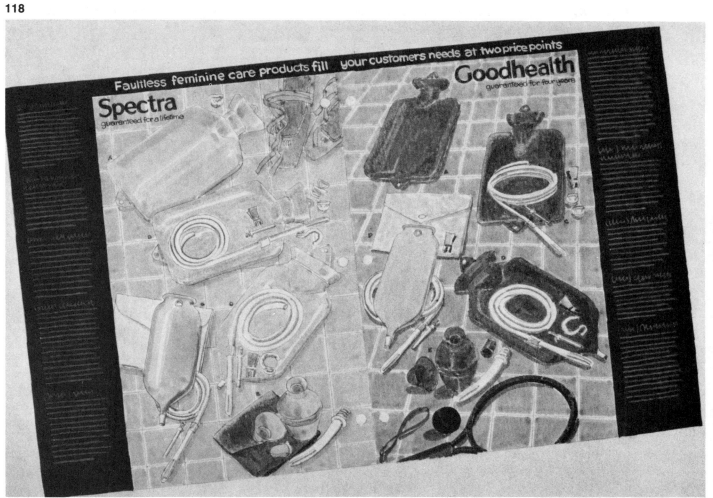

**119** On-premise promotion and support materials for a liquor product.

petition. But, he is not willing to go out on a limb and sacrifice what he feels is the clarity of his message to aesthetic principles that perhaps only he and the designer may appreciate. (2) Designer *A* has failed to judge the extent to which he can sell businessman *X* on creative innovation. Because designer *A* has no empathy for the viewpoint of businessman *X,* he is rigid in his view of the situation and would never be capable of understanding that such a specific aesthetic compromise actually helped improve the *overall* communication concept of the brochure, thereby enhancing the design innovation that *was* achieved!

Clearly, the critical point at which businessman *X* and designer *A* reached their impasse was *not* in conceptual thrust (where businessman *X* was eager for creative input), but in *the layout,* where businessman *X* saw the need for a *practical* solution that would benefit him by meeting his requirements. *The majority of impasses between creative and noncreative viewpoints are not in conceptual creation, but in layout application of the conceptual idea.* Let's repeat that. *The majority of impasses between creative and noncreative viewpoints are not in conceptual creation, but in layout application of the conceptual idea.*

The author himself recently received a brochure *from his own professional society* where the layout of information was so obscured by design devisiveness that it was irritating to read and, consequently, the piece ended up in "the circular file." The example of type working against communication because the designer refuses to understand it first and foremost as a communication vehicle is one educational "mental block" designers seem to have in abundance! There are many others as well. All of them could be eliminated by greater understanding (through education) of the way things really work in the world. Tempering layout with commonsense reasoning is surely not compromising one's artistic integrity! Understanding and appreciating others' sensibilities *(especially since you are designing for them!)* is not being less creative.

By admitting that final judgment on layout is not the *exclusive* realm of the visual designer, the visual designer can come to a fuller, more mature relationship with those whom he or she *must* work with, throughout a career. This is no more or less than other creative people do in the daily exercise of their craft. The copywriter continually compromises on content and phraseology, integrating the client's directives into the basic fabric of the message. The illustrator and photographer are continually under the direction of the art director, and yet it does not diminish their creativity to compromise with the communal integrity of the whole. Why should we, as designers, be exempt from the procedures that govern our associates and, what is worse, be unable to cope with legitimate compromise when we must do so?

110

**120 & 121** Concept presentation boards for products catalog.

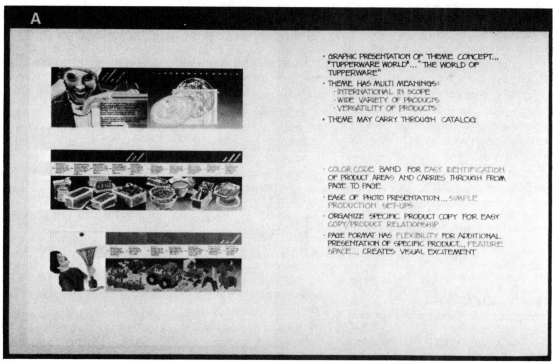

120

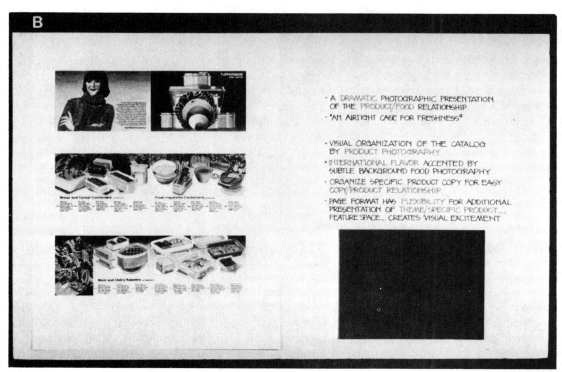

121

So much for the designers and their attitude toward noncreative input. What about the designers' relationships to their co-workers? It is important for the designer to realize that other allied professionals have considerable experience in visually creative work and have some sense of aesthetics (or they would not be very successful at what they do). The good marketing professional is certainly not insensitive to layout. Neither is the writer whose words are such an integral part of *almost all* Graphic Design. By contributing their personal and professional perspective early on in composing layouts, etc., they expand the objectivity of the solution. Collaborative opinion on such crucial aspects of an assignment as copy and layout are quite normal and can help avoid the "myopic" viewpoint toward a subject that all creatives can sometimes get caught up in.

# "Wristwork" Versus "Brainwork"

Although no one has done an actual study, we surely expend at least one-half our design education in the practice of layout development and skills. Once the basic intellectual and aesthetic elements of design study have been absorbed, we apply them through the medium of layout and composition. All designers are rightfully taught to exercise their creativity through these channels. As already discussed, layout artistry is crucial to the professional designer's life. Yet, layout artistry is *not* considered a very "creative" activity by many contemporary designers. Some even look upon it with disdain, and *all* of us seek to avoid situations where someone might (God forbid!) label us "a good layout man." Being "a good layout man" implies one's training and skills are old fashioned, or—couched in less kindly terminology—that one has learned to become "a great pair of hands" or a "wrist." Being a "wrist," as everyone in the profession knows, is the same as being a hack, which of course, is an undesirable professional position. In professional situations "the layout man" is midway down the pyramid in status and dollars. The laurels go to the conceptual "design thinker."

If layout is functionally as important as we assume, why are those who excel at it given a lower place among us? Because the skills of layout and format composition are labor intensive skills, layout *itself* is often (albeit ignorantly) conceived of as more mechanical than cerebral. Modern designers and their discipline have successfully outrun the "commercial art" image of the first half of the century, and, possibly as overreaction, they shy away from activities that connote too close

a link with what now are considered negative, outdated aspects of the job. In the green eyeshade, commercial art of the past, layout artistry was one of the consummate talents of the trade. There is no question that the emphasis on layout was more pragmatic and that design "concepting" was not emphasized to the degree it is in today's professional *and* educational environments. Layout has not suffered (it is neither better nor worse than in the past), but the *image* of layout has!

Designers, with their newer "professional" standard—meaning those concepts and attitudes that have brought us from a trade to a profession—are applying their prejudices to their own situations. We all glorify the concepting process. Unfortunately, too often as the old phrase goes, the baby is thrown out with the bath water. We understand that we cannot be total designers without the capability of expertly practicing *both* aspects of our art. We certainly recognize that the act of laying out elements is as cerebral an activity as conceptual designing and that great design is *still* made or unmade through the medium of layout. However, because of our prejudice against the old mold of commercial art, we pigeonhole a procedural part of our craft, give those who practice it for a livelihood inferior status, and tend, often, to *underplay* our own abilities in this area in favor of emphasizing the conceptual aspects of our talent.

This emphasizing the conceptual over the procedural, which started in the art and design schools and worked its way into the profession, is now affecting education in turn. It is possibly *preprejudicing* you against an activity that *everyone else* associated with the designer values very highly . . . work that is so deeply a part of our creative methodology that we are less than what we ought to be without an essential respect for it. The demand for a reemphasis on traditional learning procedures that has developed in the last few years seems to suggest a swing again in educational philosophy. Perhaps the fortunes of "the layout man" will rise in the near future.

# To Grid or Not To Grid

Few issues have divided the design profession so decisively as has the concept of the grid system. The grid concept proposes designing around a preset and consistently controlled breakup of area, with all variations of layout contained within the framework of that predisposed area. Grid systems, as used by contemporary designers, are planned to solve individual problems of format and layout and are not based on any one standard of proportion. A designer will create a grid to organize

**Plate 1** (right)
Overprinting of primary process inks to show solid print primary and secondary color range.

**Plates 2 and 3**
Side by side comparison of layout and production samples for Pabst Blue Ribbon promotion materials.

PRINTER'S PROCESS TERMINOLOGY
"K" = BLACK
"B" = CYAN
"R" = MAGENTA
"Y" = YELLOW
"S" BEFORE ONE OF THE ABOVE
  LETTERS DESIGNATES SOLID
  (100% PRINT OF HUE).

Plates 4-13

5%Y 5%K

30%Y 40%K

50%Y 60%K

90%Y 50%K

90%Y 80%K

5%R 5%B

40%R 30%B

50%R 90%B

80%R SB

5%B 5%K

50%B 20%K

90%B 50%K

30%R 40%K

50%R 60%K

90%R 90%K

5%Y 5%B

50%Y 60%B

70%Y SB

5%Y 20%R

70%Y 30%R

50%Y SR

5%B 90%Y 10%R

30%B 50%Y 60%R

50%B 50%Y 70%R

80%B 20%Y SR

SB 80%Y 60%R

SB SY 20%R

10%K SY 60%R

70%K 70%Y 80%R

40%K 80%Y 60%B

10%K 20%B SY 40%R

10%K 20%B SY 90%R

40%K 80%B SY 5%R

40%K 80%B 30%Y SR

**14**

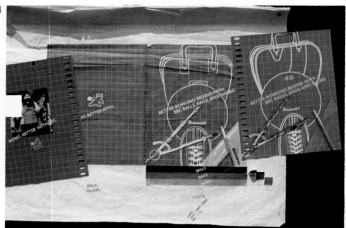

**18**

**15**

**19**

**16**

**20**

**17**

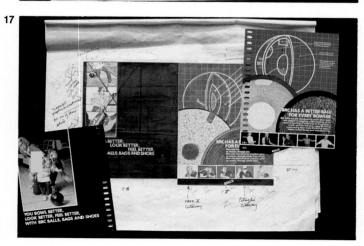

**21**

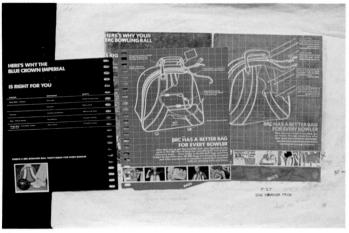

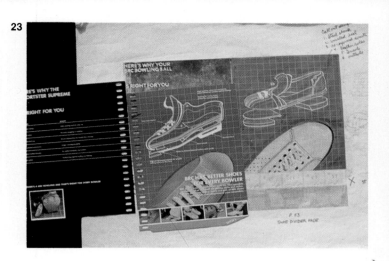

**Plates 14-23**
Actual pages from the Brunswick catalog shown with their layout spreads. These color layouts and other B & W pencil layouts were used to sell the concept to the client and as a guide for the photographer and art director during the shoot itself.

Notice, in this case, how close the original idea sketching is to the final outcome. This is a case where there were very few changes requested by the client, or necessary because of the product situations envisioned by the designer. The designer *knew the client and the product very well.* There were no problems of interpretation and no situations created that were unrealistic for the product.

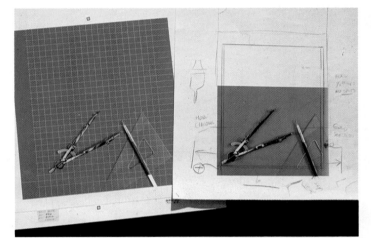

**Plate 24** (left)
A dye transfer variation of the original 8″ × 10″ chrome marked up as a guide for the retoucher to follow. The markings show how to lay in the blue background and the lines of the grid, and how to make the necessary adjustments to the drafting instruments seen next to the finished dye transfer "camera-ready" art.

Notice the substantial variation in the instruments themselves (especially the compass). The "reality" of the photographic image does not work as a vehicle to convey the design intent of the cover. By rearranging the play of light and shadow across the forms and by altering the shapes themselves, a "super-real" situation was created that appeared naturally real. . .and much more attractive than the real image of the photograph.

**Plate 25** (left)
Actual keyline boards for the Brunswick project.

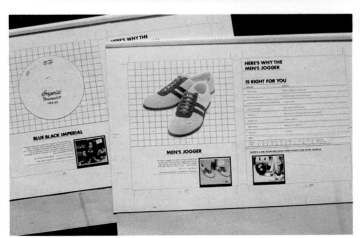

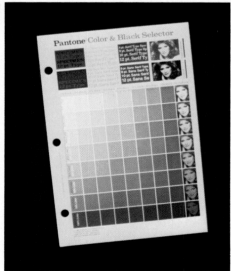

26

27

28

**SOLID MAGENTA**

**50% MAGENTA**

**"PINK"**

**Plates 26 and 27**
Sample loose-leaf pages from
PANTONE® Color and Black Selector
book.

**Plate 28**
Color swatches. (See page 96 for further
explanation)

**Plate 29**
Value relationships of Process Magenta
indicated by screening down the color
from solid print, and by the addition of
black.

**Plates 30–35**
Brochure/mailers done for the International Minerals & Chemical Corporation's Animal Health & Nutrition
Division, Animal Products Group. All
illustrate an extremely creative usage of
typography as an integral part of the
entire design concept.

**29**

**30**

**33**

**31**

**34**

**32**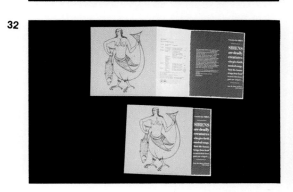

**35**

**36**

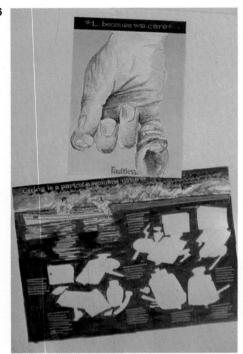

**37**

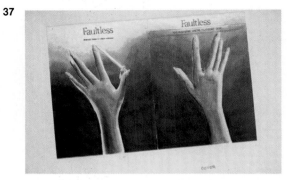

**38**

**39**

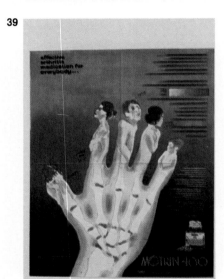

**40**

**Plates 36–38**
Cover ideas and introductory page layout variations for a health care product catalog.

**Plates 39–42**
Poster/mailer roughs for arthritis pain drug shown with finished composite photographic art of each image.

**41**

**42**

elements according to the area they will occupy, establishing the grid proportion based upon the square, rectangle, or other unit related to his or her judgment of how the material should be designed. Consistent proportional application is the essential justification for utilizing a grid system.

Grids are extremely useful where large amounts of typography must be structured into a design format and are generally seen applied to book and magazine publication. Grids are used for signage systems where they help establish a sense of continuity, and to all forms of printed messages from posters to magazine advertisements. A grid system applied to a magazine layout would likely be established on the pica measure and on points in terms of depth rather than on inches. Because typography would be the major consideration, this type of structuring would allow for accurate measure, line by line. Once established, it is a relatively easy matter for the designer to bring together all of the elements—typography, illustration and photography, color application, and so on—into a harmonious order.

In the hands of a talented designer, a grid system applied to material that can obviously benefit from a regimented structure can produce beautiful results, especially when dealing with complex visual elements. Used to cover up a lack of sensitivity to shape and compositional flow, and as a panacea solution to all design problems, the grid can produce unqualified dullness. Controversy rages over the grid as a design tool. The difficulty comes in slavish obedience to the conceptual ideal. Most designers will utilize some type of grid structure when it is apparent that it will aid in the creative solution to a problem. However, many practitioners of the grid concept refuse to consider any other alternative to design problem solving. This is a tragic error in creative concepting that the "commercial art layout man" would probably have been taught to avoid. Creative independence is the most prized possession of the designer. To be a slave of *any* method is tantamount to an admission of mediocrity.

In contrast to the grid methodology, there is designing by intuitive composition, or designing for visual flow. Here, design element *A* coexists successfully with element *C* because of *A*'s and *C*'s relationship to connective element *B*. Thus, intuitive judgment is the common factor in this formula. The fine artist uses exactly the same intuitive judgment in relating the elements of composition.

That most graphic design produced over the last century is a consequence of the intuitive process of visual flow is not *accidental!* This is the classic approach to visual problem solving, and will always be, because designing for visual flow is conceptually broad enough to include all design options in the sum total of the solution . . . as long as they harmonize with the elementary creative equation that has been synonymous with art of all kinds since humans first marked cave walls. A grid system may compensate for a lapse in the designer's sensitivity through its rigid structuring, but visual flow composition will not often tolerate such errors in creative judgment. Every element in a visual flow composition is subject to and dependent upon every other element for a cohesive relationship. This is, of course, its great weakness. Things do not fall into place as they do in a grid system. Visual flow requires those consummate layout skills we spoke of earlier. But its weakness is also its strength. Because it is not tied to a preset system, it holds the promise of innovative spontaneity. It demands more from the designer because the process relies entirely on his or her *total* creative abilities, intuitive and learned, to bring it to a successful conclusion. The delightful sense of accomplishment that accompanies such a design solution is especially gratifying.

We should, however, reemphasize here that *both* perspectives on design problem solving have their application *and* their justifications. Ideally, the student should be taught both . . . and then allowed the freedom to practice either one as the dictates of a problem require.

## *The Copy and the Designer*

The designer's layout is composed, in great part, of words. These words have meaning, and they are meant to communicate through the visual medium. All graphic designers deal with type, whether one word or letter, or a whole book of information. Yet how much do you know about that "other" creative person whose work is so dependent upon the layout you produce . . . the one at the end of the typewriter keyboard instead of the drawing board? How much do you know about how he or she works and thinks to come up with the copy concept so critical to *your* design?

If you are a student, you probably know next to nothing. This is understandable; neither you nor anyone else in your school's department (except a teaching professional) has likely ever come across a writer on a consistent working basis. Many designers who deal in specialized areas such as packaging and corporate identity design have only rare contact with writers; others come into contact with writers more often, or even work as a team member with them on a daily basis. Some designers or educators believe words and copy are just elements that the designer must push around into positions and configurations that work well with

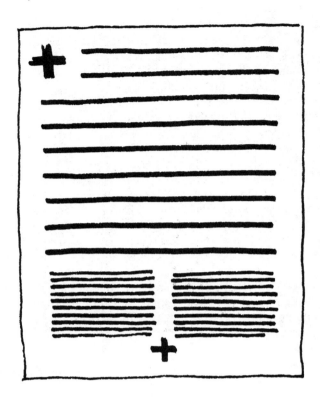

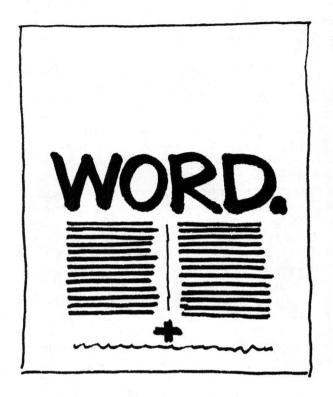

other elements. Such attitudes are rarely espoused by thoughtful "creatives." One can see just how troublesome such attitudes can be when the shoe is on the other foot: try working with a writer who feels layout is absolutely unimportant to the presentation of the textual material and demands that the copy simply be set in type as big as possible!

Understanding that the writer is a "creative friend" with as much at stake as the designer in the problem's ultimate solution is important. Adversary relationships abound in the creative professions, and the primary reason for poor understanding of how and why individuals work the way they do. Since layout is the *common meeting ground* for the designer and writer in *most* design circumstances, we will briefly profile and discuss the copywriter here.

The world of the professional copywriter is structured no differently than that of the professional designer. Copywriters report to copy directors (usually titled "creative directors") just as designers report to art or design directors. They receive information on projects in the same manner and are called upon to digest marketing input and related information prior to creative concepting—just like the designer. The writer spends most of his time at the typewriter doing the

same thing you, the designer, are doing at your drawing board . . . putting down ideas and variations of ideas until he or she is satisfied that enough workable solutions to the problem have been found to warrant discussion. Extrapolating word ideas on a typewriter is creatively no different than extrapolating visual ideas on layout bond. The mind and the talent are employed together in the creative task. Only the mediums are different. Writers use principles of grammar, composition, and creative writing that are not very different from the principles of design. Writers seek to produce the same thing: a sustained, relevant, creative piece of work. They discuss the alternatives with other creatives, including their designers, and with marketing and account service people to determine which directions will be carried further, just as designers do with visual solutions.

The writer is trained, in school and through on-the-job experience, to grasp the central idea of the whole problem. This, unfortunately, tends to be one of the deficiencies in the education and training of the designer. The writer thinks in terms of key idea emphasis. If the copy's essential thrust is not on target with the subject, the ultimate piece will fail as a communication device, so the copywriter *must* develop a perspective on all aspects of an assignment to understand how to com-

**114**

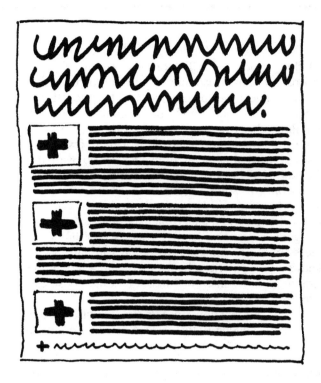

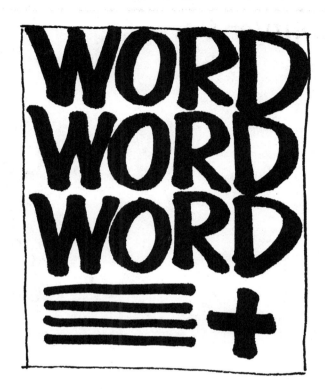

municate that subject to whomever the piece is aimed at. The writer actually has *less* latitude for innovative presentation of his or her material than the designer because words tend to be more literally interpreted than visual elements. It is no wonder, then, that the writer turns to the designer with real concern about the presentation of the written idea. He or she knows full well that the ultimate success or failure of the communication of the idea rests with the designer and the layout. The layout can add to the innovative, character of the copy, or it can detract from it in innumerable ways.

The writer has real cause for concern, and if the opposite were true, if the designer had to depend upon the format of the *writer* for the perception of success or failure of the visual aspects of the assignment, the designer would exhibit the same apprehension. The writer seeks to control the fate of his or her efforts by working closely with the designer so that there will be no "surprises" as the assignment nears completion. If this is accomplished in a positive effort, the designer can benefit from the copywriter's overall perspective on the assignment. Copywriters do not wish to usurp the creative role of the designer anymore than the designer wants the responsibility for producing creative copy! There are always exceptions, but generally, writers and

designers really *want* each other's support on essential ideas and issues.

In the educational environment, too little emphasis is placed on *the content of the message.* Copy concepting, even word/idea association, is usually *not* present in the design classroom. This is a curious circumstance considering that layout is almost always a *mandatory* requirement for communication, advertising, and marketing majors. In some schools even business majors are required to take a course in layout! The argument made by some that the "pure" design environment is removed from involvement with words is simple ignorance. Design professionals cannot afford to scorn the world of verbal communication. Anyone who has put together a proposal for a complex assignment knows better than that! Many design offices have copy creatives on staff or at least close at hand. Anyone involved with the design of intricate corporate communications and annual reports (both of which are done by "pure" design establishments) knows the value of good copy concept. Annual reports are an excellent example of what happens when the designer shows insensitivity to the narrative thrust and specific detail of the verbal message. Anyone on a corporate mailing list knows how unbelievably dull many annual reports are.

# THE STUDIO

*Chapter 9*

In this section we will look at a variety of professional design environments and compare them to each other and in terms of what they have to offer the designer. The student rarely has a perspective on the possibilities that exist in the "real world" of design. Although they may have some idea of their own limitations and what they want ultimately to do with their lives, knowledge of the limitations of the medium comes from two sources only: the working professional who is willing to talk honestly about the day-to-day aspects of design, and from actual experiences on the job. "Paying your dues" is a necessary fact of life in the profession, but learning the hard way can have a lot of negative aspects that can be avoided with a little understanding of how different kinds of design businesses operate.

At the beginning of this text, we discussed the educational challenges that face Graphic Design and how to interpret the guideposts for finding "the right circumstance" for each individual. Here we will apply guideposts for finding the "right" career path. There is great value in knowing your career options and their inherent limitations *before the need arises to cope with them.* "Ivory tower" educators have traditionally steered away from exposing design students to potential "negative" ideas about design careers, taking a head-in-the-sand approach to the whole issue of adjusting to the real working world. Thus by seeking to avoid discussing realities, they hurt their students far more than they help them.

The young designer must understand that it is *crucial* to react positively to your working environment and that *all successful* working environments have positive aspects (or they wouldn't be successful)! *Because one type of design circumstance may be destructive for your talents and personality does not mean that it is destructive for the design profession in general, or that it might not be a valuable and career-sustaining experience for someone with different talents and goal directives.* The thought "Man! I wish someone had told me what it was really going to be like . . . " is an all too common complaint of young designers. Understanding a situation is essential to dealing with it. These chapters are written to eliminate some of the ignorance that leads to unproductive attitudes and bad job experiences—to help you, the student, solidify in your own mind where you might possibly want to work and what you might want to be doing.

# The Studio:
# Analysis and Comparison

Of all design organizations, the studio is the most versatile. Most successful studios are set up to handle all aspects of the graphic arts, from rough concept, through photography, to camera-ready art. The studio will have designers, illustrators, keyliners, photographers, and account service personnel all on staff. Although the vast majority of their work will be done "in-house," they will use freelance creative help when a special skill or style is required, or when all of their regular staff employees are engaged in projects.

The studio is also the most tightly structured of all design organizations. Every hour of working time is accounted for. The time of the creative and production artist is usually logged daily or weekly, and the time sheets are then used to correctly record the number of working hours spent on each assignment. The hourly rate at which a client is charged will vary from job to job, or even on the same job. The design time rate is always more than the production art rate, and many times (especially in the case of illustrators) "special" talents will be billed at a higher rate again. That time which cannot be billed to any account or specific assignment is charged to the studio itself.

Since the art studio's overhead (operating budget) is normally quite high, no studio likes paying for idle time; all try to operate at peak load and efficiency at all times. If there is not enough work generated to keep an employee busy most of the time, that employee quickly becomes a deficit on the studio's books, no matter how talented, and unless the individual is critical to the studio's business image, he or she is simply let go. This is a hard but generally fair system, when you consider the studio's main functions.

As a service organization that revolves around the daily acquisition of new work, with high value put on the ability to present that work quickly and to cater to a client's needs, the studio cannot afford to carry people who are not continually contributing on an hourly, billable basis. Studios are not interested in extremely talented individuals with erratic behavior patterns. They will buy that kind of talent on the outside when they need it. Instead, they want good people who will do competent and attractive work that will please the client on a consistent basis. The studio is not interested in "genius" caliber design, nor do they often get tremendously complex design assignments. Their bread-and-butter profit lies in adequately servicing the daily needs of their clients, no matter how trivial.

Studios are steeped in the hard business of art. Most of them are geared to handle catalogue and two-dimensional design work. Brochures, specialized magazine formats, mailers, booklets, illustration and photography, and promotional displays and promotional packaging are the bulk of a studio workload. Some studios do make a point of going after and getting consumer packaging and corporate communications, but on the average, these are creative luxuries. The emphasis a studio will place on any type of work will depend greatly upon where it is located, or what type of business environment its major clients are involved in. A studio in Detroit, for instance, will be heavily oriented toward illustration and photography simply because the majority of its workload will probably come from the automobile companies. These companies require vast amounts of creative support work of this type in the advertising and merchandising of their products. A studio in Chicago or Cincinnati may be oriented toward design because its clients are packaged-goods companies that require large amounts of promotional packaging, graphics, and merchandising display.

Studios will take work from almost any source, but advertising agencies and large companies seem to be the biggest consistent contributors. For major design assignments, both the agency and the company will seek out designers or design firms that specialize in the areas that concern the immediate problem at hand. The studio has less chance to capture an important design account or assignment, and will generally not employ the same type of design specialist sought by consulting firms. The designers the studio does employ are usually well versed in catalogue and brochure design, rather than in the more marketing- and image-oriented areas of packaging and corporate communications and identity.

It is generally true that illustrators are more highly favored in studio situations than anyone else. It is in this area that the studio can be the most competitive, creatively. There are only two sources to draw upon for illustration: freelance, and the studio. The greater bulk of noneditorial, day-to-day illustration is done by studios. Each studio usually has one or more illustrators whose work they promote on a regular basis. Some studios who depend upon illustration for the bulk of their business, will have a whole stable of "styles" to offer their clients, and will use their "name" talent to obtain entrance to prospective clients.

The other areas in which a studio goes more or less unchallenged are large set and catalogue photography. Work that requires large sets, many set variations, and huge volumes of merchandise is best served in the studio environment.

This is the bare bones outline of the studio business. To better understand the relationship it has with its clients and employees, and the variations in emphasis and operational procedures between studios, let's take a look at three representative situations.

# *Studio* A

Studio *A* is located in one of the largest cities in the country. It occupies an entire floor of a high-rise in a prestigious district. It is furnished smartly, with many unusual touches—but mainly for the publicity and client interest it will arouse, not for the comfort and convenience of employees. It is staffed, on the average, with twenty-five to thirty people, depending upon business trends and the volume of work generated by the studio's sales force.

Studio *A* is owned and operated by one man, Mr. *A,* and the studio bears his name. He is a dynamic and aggressive individual who handles the running of his firm in a totalitarian style reminiscent of an earlier business epoch. Mr. *A* is a somewhat well-known, very successful personality who has worked hard over the years to build his business into one of the more creative studios in the city. First and foremost a promoter, Mr. *A* has expanded his business interests to areas not normally covered by the average studio. He has done this as a speculative venture, as well as a financial check against the always present possibility of a down-turn in the graphics market. He uses these outside interests, and every connection available to him, to promote both himself and his organization.

Studio *A* employs three full-time designers (one of whom is very talented and fairly well-known in the city's graphics community), but it is best known for its illustration and photographic capabilities. Mr. *A* himself is a photographer, and because he understands photography and illustration well, and design hardly at all, studio *A* is heavily oriented toward the two former areas and promotes them on a regular basis.

At studio *A,* the illustrator is king. Mr. *A* has a good-sized stable of illustrators who can handle everything from technical to stylized interpretive and editorial illustration. He has worked diligently to establish and maintain a direct link with certain design schools and consistently hires their illustration graduates. Mr. *A* most frequently trades upon the name of one of his illustrators. Because of the adaptability of this particular illustrator's style, both the illustrator and the studio enjoy a significant popularity, locally and in national markets. This particular illustrator, identified with Mr. *A*'s studio since the beginning of his career, has developed a unique working relationship with Mr. *A.* He is the most highly paid member of Mr. *A*'s organization and,

except for the responsibility of meeting deadlines, works at his own pace and at whatever time he chooses. Mr. *A* and the studio have helped make this illustrator's reputation, and the illustrator has helped make the studio and Mr. *A*'s reputation.

This flexible working relationship, born out of mutual respect rather than friendship, does not apply to the rest of Mr. *A*'s staff. Nor should it. Only a chosen few whose proven superior talents have brought the studio its continued laurels are allowed this freedom. This long-standing policy of creative "flexibility" employed by Mr. *A* has created a pecking order that, at times, has proven detrimental to the studio's morale and work flow. This becomes most obvious when more than one creative personality is involved with any given project.

Most design work done at studio *A* is sales-oriented graphics—the mainstay of studios in general for a long time. Although Mr. *A* promotes himself and his studio as being capable of handling more sophisticated marketing and design problems, his credibility in areas like corporate communications and packaging is extremely thin. Mr. *A* has no marketing people on staff. Since most of the work brought into the studio over the years has been of a collateral nature, Mr. *A* has played to his strong suit with his layout and illustration personnel and has not hired people with impressive backgrounds in disciplines that are necessary to make significant inroads into packaging and corporate communications. What packaging work he receives falls into the sales promotion area.

Mr. *A* has an account staff roughly proportional to his creative talent. They work, as do most design salespersons employed by studios, on a commission basis. Each account within the salesperson's responsibility is run by him or her exclusively. All salespeople are required to keep Mr. *A* informed on the progress of each assignment and must seek ultimate approval from him for all bids or proposals, but in all other matters they bear the responsibility for seeing that the account runs smoothly. They draft and submit all proposals, bring in all assignments, and determine by their job estimates the allowable creative budget for each project under their supervision.

The majority of Mr. *A*'s account people have never worked as designers, photographers, or illustrators at the drawing-board level; indeed, they are not exceptionally creative people. Their backgrounds are strictly business/sales-oriented, and they would probably be as effective selling furniture, automobiles, or life insurance as they are selling design and creative services. While they sometimes sympathize with and share the creative person's problems on a given assignment, they do not truly see things from the creative viewpoint. They are "art salesmen" in the old "commercial art" sense. For all practical purposes, the creative people work for the account staff. The account salesperson represents the studio to the client, and he or she is uniquely placed to decide what the client's needs are. Since creative people rarely see the client, they must depend totally upon the account person's assessment of what the problems and solutions for each assignment are. Unless creative people wish to spend considerable amounts of time on the phone with clients, they must accept the judgments of account people. This is the operational procedure preferred by Mr. A. The strict separation between creative and account responsibilities has been the successful formula for his studio, and very few people are allowed to interfere with that formula.

The daily operation of the studio is overseen by a studio manager who reports directly to Mr. A. This studio manager functions neither as a creative nor as a salesperson. His major responsibilities are seeing that project scheduling runs smoothly and that deadlines are met and time records kept accurately. He is a liaison between the sales force and the creative staff, and is often an arbitrator for the personal conflicts that arise between both. He is the implementer of Mr. A's "fixed position" philosophy, and sees that designers are involved only with design, illustrators only with illustration, and photographers only with photography. He also protects the creative staff from undue harassment from the sales force. The studio manager's position under Mr. A's system is not an enviable one. He makes no important decisions without first consulting Mr. A, but takes the responsibility for seeing that decisions are carried out efficiently. His background, although agency-oriented, is a managerial one. He has not been involved as a creative person.

Because publicly Mr. A *is* the business, and because he and he alone makes all major decisions for the business, if something should happen to him, his studio would suffer an immediate loss in prestige and an inevitable loss of business. Even though Mr. A's talented people would be able to continue producing good work, no single one of them, nor any salesperson, has been given enough decision-making latitude to be familiar with the studio's management policy and thus capable of running it in the same manner it is run presently. Neither is there anyone of sufficient "personality" to keep the place together from a personnel standpoint. With his freewheeling business style, shrewdness, and personal drive, Mr. A has allowed no one into his business organization who might have challenged his judgmental leadership or business abilities. Because of this fact alone, studio A is an unsure place to work.

## SUMMARY OF STUDIO A

Studio A is a well-run, creatively good studio in the areas it is familiar with, and always will be as long as Mr.

A is around. It is an excellent place for an illustrator to build a reputation and, possibly, even a place to stay permanently. For the young designer interested in the design of promotional materials, it is a place to get a great deal of experience and exposure, and to build a good portfolio. Except for his "stars," Mr. A pays his people poorly and offers minimal side benefits. There is no chance for rank advancement in any specialty, as the studio has no management hierarchy. There is little if any chance for gaining experience in any other discipline than the one one is hired for. The creative staff does not become involved in any of the business aspects of the studio, and very rarely comes in contact with the client. Everyone employed at studio A must depend upon the health of Mr. A for their job security and continued livelihood. The chances of the studio continuing at its present size and success rate without Mr. A at its helm are not good.

## Studio B

Studio B is located in a medium-sized city where the industrial economy revolves around three major corporations. The studio is relatively large, forty to fifty people, and has complete facilities to handle all creative work, from concept through finished art, in a number of areas. It is located in its own building in the center of town, near its major client source.

Studio B must share its in-town business with four other major studios, and therefore depends heavily upon out-of-town clients to maintain its financial equilibrium. Because of its earlier successes and the need to seek business outside the immediate environment, studio B has expanded into regional offices in other parts of the country. Although the original business was started by two men, the growth and expansion has necessitated the establishment of a corporate management structure to run the organization. Each office is operated by a General Manager, who in turn is backed up by a Sales Manager and a Creative Director. Each office is independent from every other, in terms of clients, but each shares a common fiscal management and corporate philosophy. The largest office is studio B.

Studio B began as an all-service art studio, but it now sees itself more as a consulting firm and strives to convey that idea to its clients. It is, in reality, a highly creative and adaptable studio that has made some inroads into disciplines traditionally practiced by consulting firms but which continues to do mostly work typical of studio organizations. Because the majority of its clients are packaged-goods companies, studio B is heavily involved in packaging and sales promotional design. Illustration and photography are important aspects of the studio's overall creative capabilities, but they are not the principle source of income that they are to studio *A*.

The majority of individuals running the corporation and its branch offices are former art salespeople or designers who have moved into management positions. There is some personnel exchange between the different offices, and because of this and the corporation's growth and expansion into new design areas, the management base is somewhat flexible. Studio *B* has had three managers in the last ten years. Two of the three have moved up to the position from within studio *B*'s own ranks; one has come from one of the other offices. One of them left the position to help open another office for the corporation in another city.

The General Manager of studio *B* is charged with the overall operation of the business. He coordinates the office fiscal activities with those of the other branch offices, and sees to the general account coverage of the studio. He will help pitch new business if asked by any of the salespeople on his staff and, along with the sales manager, acts as an advisor on any account or studio/client problems. He is not active in sales, although he was once a salesperson with the organization.

The Creative Director at studio *B* is a working designer with the added responsibility of seeing that creative work is assigned and completed on schedule. She also acts in a supervisory capacity overseeing the work done by the designers, illustrators, and photographers under her. She reports directly to the studio's General Manager. If it is deemed necessary, she will accompany the account supervisor on a new client presentation; and after a project has been initiated, she often deals directly with the client by phone or in person to solve some creative problem that has arisen. She works on a fixed salary basis, as do all people not directly involved in sales activity.

The Sales Manager is charged with the responsibility of seeing that the account people under his supervision respond to the client's needs and continue to explore new business leads. He supervises all proposal writing and the submission of job estimates, which he clears for realistic accuracy with the Creative Director. He will only call upon accounts or assist in servicing them at the salesperson's request. His own background as an art director and designer gives him the capacity to aid the client in the critical evaluation of a project. Being able to give a visual interpretation to information received from the client, he is in a better position to aid the Creative Director and the designers who will be charged with the ultimate completion of the assignment. He is also more sympathetic to creative problems that might arise on any given assignment, and is able to offer workable solutions more easily than someone with a non-art background.

The designers employed at the studio work on projects ranging from the design of a violator for a package front, to full-scale promotional or collateral design programs, and occasionally even to new product concepts. This greater variety of work broadens their range of experience as designers and is a benefit to the studio as well as to themselves.

Because they work under the supervision of one creative director, and not the random supervision of various account people, studio *B*'s designers can function easily as a group when the need arises. The lines of authority are clearly drawn, and studio politics are limited by the corporate chain of command. They have a definite and often sympathetic leader in the Creative Director, through whom they can channel their problems and frustrations. Being represented by the Creative Director in management matters, they are free to spend the majority of their time involved in creative design.

## SUMMARY OF STUDIO *B*

Studio *B* is a good place for a designer to work. One can gain experience in several areas and advance upward in the organization. Because studio *B* has offices in other cities, a designer may have the option of transfering if the opportunity arises. The designer's workload is varied at the studio. However, because of the studio's background as a service organization, and because of its lack of marketing expertise and experience, it will never get the large projects usually associated with the consulting firm. It lacks the depth necessary for projects such as corporate identity programs, product development, and other design projects that require marketing input and in-depth design research.

Studio *B*'s illustrators do not occupy the important position they do at studio *A*. Less editorial work flows through studio *B* than through *A*, and the illustrator is more supportive of design projects. Many of the creative individuals at studio *B* serve as both illustrators and designers. Studio *B* is not the place for an illustrator to become a star, yet it offers any young creative talent the opportunity to become involved in a wide range of projects. Within the corporate structure of studio *B*, there is a possible future for everyone working there.

# *Studio* C

Studio *C* is located in a western city on the second floor of an office building in the central business district. It is unlike studio *A* or *B* in one important aspect: all of the people working at studio *C* are self-employed. They solicit their own accounts, bill separately (under the studio *C* name), and are responsible for all work on each of their accounts. They are incorporated for the sake of taxes, rent, and the general convenience of working in proximity to each other and sharing accounts where multiple specializations are necessary.

The studio is made up of two illustrators, one illustrator/designer, two designers, a lettering/layout person, and a keyliner. It's a practical arrangement since all of the individuals in the studio can use each other's services at considerable savings to themselves, instead of going to the outside for supplementary needs. In addition, when one individual calls upon a client and discovers work in an area other than his own, he can recommend one of his associates for the job. This is important both to the client and the studio. The client has only to deal with one source group, and all the artists employed on the job work together, with easy access to each other.

With the variety of people working under the studio *C* name, it benefits from a range of commercial assignments, from national magazine illustration, to keyline production for local agencies, to design and illustration for city service organizations. Because of the collateral "graphic" backgrounds of all the artists associated with the studio, assignments in packaging, products, and long-range corporate design planning are rare. The group, as a whole, is more than satisfied with their success in handling advertising-oriented collateral design assignments, and they use every opportunity to play

their strong suit in soliciting new accounts.

The only salaried employees of studio *C* are a secretary/receptionist and two art assistants. This kind of arrangement works in certain circumstances and with certain personalities. All the individuals at studio *C* are long-established freelance talents. None of them are creative geniuses, but neither are they less than good, sound professionals and businesspeople. They were well acquainted with each other's talents before they formed the studio. Their relationship requires a basic honesty and directness in dealing with each other that is rare in the narcissistic world of the creative arts. Tried by many, it has been achieved by few.

## SUMMARY OF STUDIO *C*

Studio *C* would not be a place to look for a job as a designer or as an illustrator, even if you had accounts of your own. While the group is always interested in expanding the scope of its practice, their shop is closed to outsiders unless they are proven professionals who would contribute to the studio's "sale-ability." For someone wishing to gain general experience by working around a design office, there are definite possibilities for employment. But the only benefit studio *C*'s structure offers to the young designer is a guide for establishing a successful business environment.

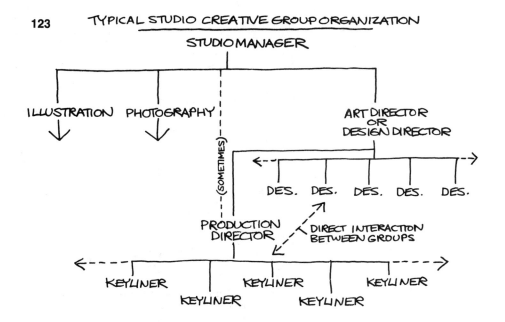

123 TYPICAL STUDIO CREATIVE GROUP ORGANIZATION

# THE CORPORATE DESIGN GROUP

## *Chapter 10*

More than any other design organization, corporate design is in a state of flux. It was the rule and not the exception in the past for the corporation to support, within its structure, complete design and advertising/marketing services. Many companies, depending upon their business interests, still retain such groups, but many more—especially in the consumer products area—have adapted to the changing economy and now rely heavily on outside consultants for design, advertising, and often even marketing services. What has emerged in these evolving corporate structures to replace traditional design function is a highly specialized "managerial design" distinct from other design activities. Managerial design is not exclusively the province of the corporation, but it is within such organizations that it is seen in its most fully developed state. Exposure to it is rare for students, principally because managerial design does not relate directly to traditional teaching methods. This is unfortunate, because this aspect of design offers tremendous possibilities to the individual charting a career path in design.

Corporate design organizations vary tremendously according to the type of products and services their parent companies deal in. For our purposes we will loosely classify these parent companies in two groups: (1) organizations that offer goods and/or services to other companies, and (2) organizations that offer goods and/or services to the consumer. In many instances a company will function in both areas, but usually such organizations will be principally known for their involvement in only one. The thrust of this chapter will be to look at typical design structures from each category. This will also offer a comparison between traditional in-house structures and what we have termed "managerial" corporate design. Both positive and negative aspects of our examples will be discussed, as well as the type of design personality that fits each best.

## *Company Design Group* A

Company design group *A* is an in-house group that fits the category of supplier organizations which offer services or commodities to other companies. Many such organizations offer design services free or at a minimal rate as an incentive in securing a steady source of business for their products. In the past, this was the total function of such groups, and even in today's changed marketplace, it is still the major reason for their existence. This factor drastically affects the nature of these groups and the level of design activity they produce. The design groups of these organizations vary in size and structure according to their parent companies' products and services and in keeping with the design needs these products and services generate.

Company group *A* is a highly creative, though technically limited, source of design expertise. Originally conceived to function around the sales force, the business of servicing the needs of corporation clients is the motivating factor within the group. To this end, a high degree of specialization from managers and designers is mandatory. Group *A* has expanded over the years in keeping with the success of the parent, and regionalized into separately staffed creative subgroups to better serve the national scope of sales. Each unit, headed by a Design Director, acts individually in support of its own sales force. The groups all report to a single marketing/design executive at the main corporate center. In this manner the entire structure is regulated in keeping with the philosophy and practices of the corporation. At one time the design organization was much larger than it is now. The group "peaked" in its growth at a time when the corporation as a whole was looking at its operational process. Company group *A*'s own repeated success in meeting the needs of the sales force added to its strength and influence, but its complexity eventually began to tell against its efficiency.

During an extended austerity move in the late 1960s and early 1970s, company group *A*'s size was cut back severely, new design management was brought in, and a subtle change in philosophy took precedence, a philosophy reflected in the operational procedures of competitive groups in company *A*'s sphere of business. While still acting in its primary capacity as a service for sales, it now began to do two things it had previously not done: (1) to depend upon a steady source of outside talent to meet the increasing demands of the workload, and (2) to solicit design assignments independent from sales-directed requests. The first was a necessity due to its reduction in staff, but the second was a direct reflection of the new management attitude that motivated group *A* to justify its existence, in part, by beginning an attempt to function as an independent profit center for the corporation. The design groups welcomed this new posture. They believed that in proving the viability of the new fee system, they strengthened the parallel justification for evolution to an autonomous design center concept within the protective parent organization that could compete for business with independent design consultants (something all captive supplier design groups believe they can successfully do).

Company group *A*'s revised structure is similar to its old self, only leaner, with fewer regional units. The major design activity is now centered at a main office centrally located in the corporate network. The Design Director of this largest group heads a staff of designers charged with the day-to-day development of projects for the sales force or for corporation clients solicited independently by the design group on a fee basis. The Design Director oversees the general operation of the office and acts as the key liaison with salespeople who service corporate accounts. He works closely with sales in developing new accounts and fixing costs for each assignment that moves through his group. He also assumes responsibility (often along with his Art Director) for presenting and following up on any of the creative work done by staff designers. Although his background is that of a long-time working designer, his prime functions are as a middle-level corporate manager, and he rarely is involved in actual design development.

The person directly responsible for seeing to the project flow and creative output of the staff is the Art Director. A working designer with administrative capabilities, the Art Director reviews each assignment independently or with the Design Director and Salesperson and decides which of his designers is best suited to develop it. He is also charged with seeing that the proper number of hours are utilized for each project and to see that designers receive new work when they are "up" (ready for) a new assignment. About 60 percent of his time is spent actually working at the drawing-board level.

The designers employed at company group *A* work on a variety of projects within the limited scope of the parent corporation's activities. Solicited fee assignments usually relate to the corporation's products, which keeps them similar in nature to the normal sales requested workload. Each designer keeps track of his or her own hours on every assignment, and at the end of the week totals are recorded and handed in to a secretary/bookkeeper. The secretary/bookkeeper keeps a running total of each job and bills out the creative time to the individual client of the design group, or internally to the salesperson's account as the jobs are completed.

The designers themselves rarely if ever come into direct contact with the clients they work for. And usually they have little communication with the salesperson who services the account. They must depend almost entirely upon the Art Director and the Design Director for interpretation of the information concerning the project. Information gathering is not a skill practiced by group *A* designers. It is not demanded by the job, and consequently most of the designers do not have this skill. In part this is a necessary way of working, because the job flow is usually so heavy that the designer has little time to devote to information gathering. Unfortunately, that skill *is* necessary for upward movement within the company, and must be exercised frequently. Most of group *A*'s designers will never be anything other than board-level employees as long as they stay at company *A*.

Because of the nature of its parent corporation's business, its captivity, its structure that facilitates heavy work flow, and its designers who lack versatility and potential as account managers, company group *A*'s attempts to function as an autonomous design force within the larger corporation are doomed to ultimate failure. No company of the group *A* type can compete (either in variety of design expertise or sophistication of marketing input) with the highly individualistic and more freely structured design consulting firms for outside work. It will always be subject to the interests of the sales force, its rightful and ultimate master. In its service role to its parent corporation, and even in its extended role as limited consultant to corporate clients, it performs admirably, but like all organizations it should be aware of its limitations. Company group *A* does not become involved in long-range creative planning or design problem solving. Heavy marketing design is a traditionally weak aspect of their expertise.

## SUMMARY OF COMPANY DESIGN GROUP *A*

All of the varying aspects of company *A*'s design "atmosphere" directly affect the designer and place psychological as well as real boundaries upon his or her ability to develop design solutions. Every structured situation has differing degrees of limitation built in. Environments like company group *A*'s require a certain type of attitude toward design that not all creative personalities are capable of dealing with. A company *A* situation is a marvelous proving ground for the young designer seeking to gain valuable experience in drawing-board skills. It offers a workload of short-term assignments that will enable the young designer to build a strong portfolio of samples in a relatively short space of time. For the more experienced designer who derives satisfaction from heavy drawing-board design, it is an attractive and long-range possibility. Company group *A* offers a friendly, stable career path, reasonably free of politics. Once a niche has been carved, the designer who can meet tight deadlines and work under the particular restrictions imposed by the situation has a comfortable home in which to develop. The relative isolation provided by their office headquarters (being totally removed from the presence of other corporate employees and departments)

enables them to develop a certain amount of freedom and camaraderie more characteristic of the consulting firm environment. They are not subject to corporate dress codes (suit and tie, or equivalent for women) and other traditional regimentation normally requested of company personnel. The corporate benefits are very good and include a profit-sharing plan and the long-term employee is assured of a relatively comfortable retirement income.

# *Company Design Group* B

Company design group *B* is a model of the successful managerial approach to design problem solving. Company *B* produces retail consumer products of a generally high quality. Its public profile is very good, and it strives to keep it that way. The company is divisionalized (as most large companies are) into product brand groups. Each group is administered by a Vice-President/ General Manager. In addition to the product group VP's, there is a Vice-President of Marketing and Advertising who is responsible for all corporate functions within these two spheres. Reporting directly to him is a Director of Marketing under whose jurisdiction falls company design group *B*.

The group itself is managed by a Design Director who is charged with the overall function and coordination of the group. Design Director *B* has an extensive background in corporate communications and packaging and has worked at several other large organizations before coming to his position at company *B*. Although trained as a designer, Design Director *B* has never functioned at the drawing-board level. Instead, he chose early on in his career to pursue a path in the corporate management system. By doing this, he believed he could better utilize his talents to effect changes in design work and attitudes. Design Director *B* is highly intelligent and astute, a skilled manager sensitive to the Machiavellian workings of his corporate environment. To a great degree, he is responsible for the type of organization that company design group *B* has become, and its attitudes and philosophies reflect his. He has effected extensive and excellent change in corporate graphics in his tenure with company *B* by cultivating the right people in the executive hierarchy and by choosing the right people to translate his ideas, both suppliers and employees.

The actual management of the day-to-day design activities generated by company *B*'s extensive product line falls to the design managers who report to Design Director *B*. Their backgrounds vary, some coming from similar corporate design organizations, others from the design supplier and consulting side of the business. They all are university or art/design school graduates, some holding graduate degrees in either business or design. Their major functions are to act as a liaison with management by coordinating projects initiated by the various brand groups, assigning creative tasks of varying size and complexity to outside suppliers, making recommendations on creative directions and concepts to the Design Director and brand or marketing personnel, and following each assignment under their jurisdiction through to a successful conclusion. None of them function at the drawing-board level, yet each is experienced enough that they could if called upon.

They are also the detail people of the corporate design structure. Accurate records of budgets and expenditures are kept by the design managers. Invoices from suppliers must be approved by them before being sent on to accounting for payment. The supplier relies almost exclusively upon them for accurate, up-to-date marketing information and for a realistic appraisal of the parameters of a given project. Under the company *B* group structure, the Design Manager determines the need for support services such as photography, illustration, and special types of sales-promotional design that relate to any project. He or she coordinates and oversees the production of such activity, usually in conjunction with the principle design source for that assignment. Company *B* relies heavily upon photography in the retail presentation and promotion of its products, and the Design Manager quickly becomes adept at using the medium to the product's best advantage.

In all the activities of the Design Manager, judgmental skills are his or her most crucial asset. Without the ability to make corporate policy decisions that relate to design activity, the Design Manager could not successfully function in the company structure. Having the sensitivity to "limits of acceptability" and exercising creative thinking within those limitations requires disciplined effort not generally associated with the creative personality. The Design Manager's skill developments and task levels (like the Design Director's) are of a different dimension than those of the practicing art director or designer involved with drawing-board concepts. Primarily because of these differences, the corporate design manager faces a complex mixture of frustrations that the relatively insulated board level designer of a company *A* group structure does not experience. As the conduit between two worlds which are far removed in their business lifestyles and motivating influences, the Design Manager can face an identity crisis as a result. The managerial design concept is still relatively new

enough that it has not yet become totally ingrained as a traditional business function. Often the design manager is perceived, by his or her own organization, as operating outside the sphere of "critical" company business. Management attitudes about design are changing rapidly, however, and company *B* is characteristic of the forefront of that change.

This aspect of alienation from fellow corporate employees is repeated on the other hand when the Design Manager deals with outside resources. Somewhat distant from the day-to-day design shop and because the Design Manager, after all, acts for the client and distributes information and judges the ultimate efforts of the design team, the Design Manager is perceived as an outsider by the very individuals most closely related to his or her professional interest. A common complaint from design managers is that their function is not fully appreciated by either side. While total understanding and appreciation may be lacking, in actual fact, their role (at company *B* and many other organizations) has proven to be the *most* effective tool for positive change in the design marketing mix of corporate structure.

The managerial design process offers some very tangible benefits to the company involved in design. First of all, it does not have the responsibility for a large internal staff. Most corporate design needs are cyclical and correspond to brand-group's calendar activity. Under the design manager system, talent is purchased only when needed, and the problem of keeping employees busy is not an important factor. As with company *B,* the most managerial design activity is typically carried out by a small number of individuals in comparison with in-house studio situations. The company can literally shop around for the talent it wishes, and it is not committed to long-term situations with individuals of limited expertise. Creative variety is easily attainable.

Because administrative and planning functions are the major components of the Design Manager's job, a skilled individual offers company *B* a more attractive middle-management profile, a person better suited to the needs of the marketing group, and provides the company with an "upward mobility" potential not present in the more specialized creative individual.

## SUMMARY OF COMPANY DESIGN GROUP *B*

For the design student with a broad range of interests who shows a flair for organization and administration, and who is not totally committed to being a practicing designer, or for the intelligent and creatively perceptive individual who is not particularly strong in drawing-board creativity, the design manager concept can be a rewarding alternative. Individuals with strong verbal skills who can deal well with shifting attitudes and alliances and who can handle the inevitable compromises that typify all forms of group activity will succeed in this emerging aspect of the design environment. Interest in the broader perspective of product or corporate development, enjoyment of long-range, evolutionary problem solving, commitment to being a team player (that is, functioning at optimum in give-and-take circumstances), and accepting the regularity and predictability of the corporate environment are facets of behavior one must readily adhere to.

Designers who pride themselves on their individuality and intensity of commitment to the creative aspects of the profession would do well to avoid corporate design situations of the *B* type. Likewise, designers with a limited range of interests who enjoy skill task involvement and cherish a craftsman's approach to the art would be totally lost in such a circumstance. Company *A* design environments are better suited to people who wish a corporate career.

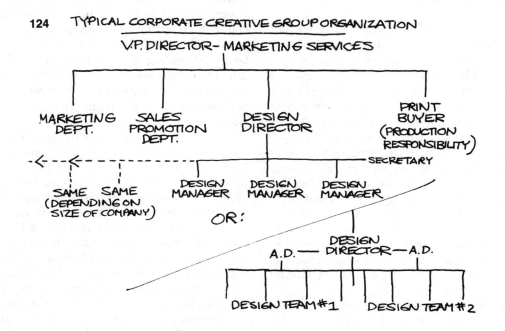

# THE CONSULTING FIRM

## Chapter 11

Deeply ingrained attitudes prevail in design, as in any profession. Traditionally, the design consulting firm has been viewed as the ultimate haven for the "purist" designer—the individual who wishes to be totally involved in the classic aspects of the profession. There is no question that the design firm environment offers the greatest freedom to the designer. Freedom of expression, freedom from regimentation, even a relative amount of freedom in terms of potential, for the small environment of the consulting office allows for and even encourages multidimensional activities among the people involved with it.

Much can be said in deference to the consulting office, but it has its drawbacks too. Consulting offices reflect the attitudes of the principles who run them, and those attitudes are usually quite individualistic. The structures around which these offices are organized are, perhaps, the most varied of any situation in design, again reflecting the individualism of their owners, and it is difficult to generalize when discussing them. What commonalities they share are due more to the business interests they serve than to any other factor. We will discuss three distinctly different consulting office environments that, while not representing hard classifications, do offer fair models of the typical consulting firms to be found today.

## Design Consulting Firm A

Design consulting firm A is a medium-sized (13 person) office in a large southern city. A partnership, it has a prestigious reputation as a highly ethical and creative shop. It has been in business 18 years under its present management, a medium age for a design firm that has not undergone any major management upheaval. Consulting firm A existed before with many of the same individuals, but under a radically different management, philosophy, and structure. Indeed, many of the present firm's clients were clients of the older organization who switched their business loyalties to the new group that emerged. Such radical mutations are not uncommon in consulting practice.

Consulting firm A is not run by any single person but is an association of equal senior partners who all share responsibility for the maintenance and fiscal success of the firm. Each of the partners deals with a range of accounts on an individual basis, representing the interests of the firm through their personal involvement with the clients. Each partner has been in the design business for a long time, and each has established a modest reputation in his or her own right. Members of the old firm in their younger years, when the changeover occurred, they moved together into shared ownership of the present business structure. Because of their long business intimacy, they have come to rely upon each other for feedback and support, creating a unique bond between them. As business grew due to their success, they added to their staff as demand required, and a stable working unit emerged that functions around the needs of the accounts sustained by the office. They have been careful to avoid overstaffing, and this conservative approach has created a secure employment situation and gained them much personal loyalty from their creative staff.

The partners vary in talents and interests, and also in their age range—the youngest, about 44; the oldest, over 60. They all share a concept about their firm that is somewhat unique in the design consulting business, one which they are seeking, with only partial success, to implement. Because they all evolved into business ownership, they are committed to seeing their firm outlive them by cultivating talent with management potential. Their intent is to bring new partners into the senior circle as business dictates, or as elder partners retire, similar to the practices employed by legal firms.

The majority of the partners' time, when not calling on accounts, is spent working at the drawing-board right alongside their employees. One of them, not particularly strong in board-level concepts, has channeled his energies into developing new accounts and maintaining a high profile for the business by involving himself heavily in professional organizations and conferences. He, and consequently the firm, is at the center of peer group activity, both nationally and internationally. This has created unique circumstances and friendships for the group over the years.

Of the entire firm, only four people are not working designers: one partner, a marketing director, a secretary/receptionist, and an executive secretary/bookkeeper. They have no sales or account service people as such. The senior creative people in the firm operate in a dual capacity. As working designers, they function as project supervisors under the loose direction of the partners, and in turn, they supervise junior creative staff and keyline/production personnel through the completion of a given project. In addition to their internal duties, they are also called upon to act as client liaisons, often making presentations with one or more of the senior partners and/or with the marketing director. Following through with client meetings and coordinating the inevitable material-gathering and paperwork that accompanies all project activity is also part of their job.

The office environment of design consulting group A is moderately elaborate. The creative staff (including the partners) share a large open space attractively partitioned off into working areas. A main conference room and reception area screens off the working space and allows for relative privacy. Often clients will visit the firm's office for meetings or for a "tour" through the space with one of the senior partners. The office is usually open to groups of students who wish to see a professional workplace, and the partners make a practice of being available to interview all individuals looking for employment. Because of these and other "public" activities, the office is tastefully decorated with an impressive array of furniture, art, and samples of the design work done by the firm.

Most of the staff are experienced designers who have come to consulting firm A from similar firms, not from different design environments such as studios or company groups. This fact tends to heighten the purist attitude that often permeates consulting office staffs. This subtle attitude can work both positively and negatively on the office output, depending on the reactions of the managers. At consulting firm A it sometimes goes both ways, depending upon the assignment and circumstance.

In the past, the firm has been weak in the marketing support offered their clients. The partners recognized this deficit and sought to strengthen their position by adding a Marketing Director to their senior staff. Her input has greatly influenced the relevance of the work done by the firm. The Marketing Director functions as a project information coordinator on large-scale assignments and is involved with the marketing rationale for all activity within the firm. She works individually with project supervisors and junior designers to interpret client input, and is present at all project creative review sessions. She has considerable background in corporate marketing.

Consulting firm A specializes in no particular area of graphic design. It prefers to go after all types of jobs it feels it can handle (considering the versatility of its senior staff) and will offer more general graphic design service to its steady accounts than most other firms of its kind. Consequently, the designers have a wide range of assignments that tend to keep their interest high and challenge their capabilities. Within a short span of time, a designer might be involved in a number of assignments ranging from packaging redesign, to annual reports and brochures, to corporate identity projects and even product and exhibit graphics.

Anyone inspecting consulting firm A's offices will not fail to observe the positive, casual atmosphere in which business is conducted. A tradition has been established of bringing in sweet rolls every morning, and coffee is brewing all day long. When the workload is heavy and longer hours are required to meet a pressing deadline, everyone stays to help out, not just the individuals responsible for the immediate work on the project. The attitude is that it is an *office* deadline and the *office* will suffer if it is not met. Small "perks" (incentives) are enjoyed by the staff. In the summer months an optional program of working longer hours during the week enables individuals to build up credit for taking time off periodically for long weekends. Substantial Christmas bonuses are given. Such benefits add up to an enjoyable working environment. Since most people spend more time on the job than off it, the ambience of the office environment is an important aspect to consider.

Consulting firm *A*'s junior designers are worked hard at the drawing-board level. They are usually involved in two or three projects during any work week and divide their time according to the dictates of the senior staff. The firm makes a practice of hiring young talent fresh out of school whenever possible. To this end, the partners have engaged for some years in a student training program at the design school of a major university. Each semester, two top students from the school work at the firm for a specified number of weeks. They function as miscellaneous help for the design team, performing tasks from fabricating comprehensives to elementary drafting and keyline assembly. Consulting firm *A*, one of several firms involved in this program in their immediate area, is strongly committed to this positive cooperation between education and commerce.

As is true of many consulting firms, consulting firm *A* does not pay their talent exceptionally well. The principles feel that the opportunity they offer should offset the "temporary" drawback of limited income. Unfortunately, not all the firm's employees have the potential to ascend to partnership status. Few provisions (such as those offered by company design groups) have been made for long-term employees who do not rise within the organization. Raises are not given automatically to everyone, and their size and frequency depends to some extent on just how well the organization is doing at any given time. Even though there has been a conscious effort to democratize the workings of the firm, the natural division between "the bosses" and "the workers" present in every business situation is aggravated by the lower pay and hazy retirement and profit-sharing provisions.

Since the partners have functioned together so well for so long and have worked all aspects of their accounts, it is difficult for them to delegate major account responsibility to nonpartners. This is a serious shortcoming and creates a psychological wall between the partners and the rest of the staff that works against the very system of power transition they so eagerly seek to effect. Again, it is a reflection on the individuality of

the consulting business as a whole and the men and women who run it. Consulting practice functions on uniquely personal talents that vary tremendously with each person involved in it. In effect, one is selling one's self. Designers, especially highly successful ones who work hard to develop business over the years, understandably find it difficult and sometimes impossible to minimize their personal talents and egos in relation to their firm's business interests. For the partners of consulting firm *A*, the need to sustain the firm through new talent is recognized (not so of many such organizations), but the means to that end have still to be completely and successfully utilized.

## SUMMARY OF DESIGN CONSULTING FIRM *A*

To succeed at consulting firm *A*, one needs first of all to be a creative self-starter. The partners are so involved in their own drawing-board assignments that there is little time for the continuous direction of others. All information and creative concept review is done during specified meeting times, and designers, junior and senior alike, are left to their own devices after that. Not all designers can produce under such a free system; they need more elaborate and specific guidance and input from others, especially if they are at the junior level. The way to get ahead at consulting firm *A* is to take charge of and carry through on assignments at the concept stage by oneself.

Information-gathering skills are critical for successful tenure at the firm, and an understanding of the rudiments of marketing is a necessity. Closely associated with information gathering is the verbalizing of concept ideas. Personnel at consulting firm *A* must present their ideas to other staff and the partners regularly and in a convincing manner to effect any progress on an assignment. They must also be ready to present their reasoning for a concept in front of a client. This requires a reasonably self-assured attitude and an ease with the interpersonal relationships that are everyday aspects of the business environment.

At consulting firm *A* the "renaissance man" concept of creative involvement is more highly valued than a talent for extreme specialization within a given area. No one is expected to do everything well, but having an understanding of the different design processes and being able to contribute relevant input when asked is most beneficial to the firm's operation. For talented, intellectually stimulated individuals with a high degree of verbal skills, who are willing to work hard to advance the interests of the firm as a whole before their own, the environment is ideal. Gaining the professional respect of the partners and showing the ability to develop new account areas—diplomatically, where partners' protective management instincts are not threatened—is the key to rapid advancement to principle status. Admittedly, this combination of talent and positive aggressiveness is rare, but no better career opportunity exists for those who think they can achieve this end. Consulting firm A is a good model of many consulting firms in the real world.

# Design Consulting Firm B

In most respects, consulting firm B is exactly opposite from consulting firm A. It is a small "shop" located in a western city and employs a total staff of only six people. The firm has been in existence for over fifteen years and has been owned and managed by one man since its inception. The firm bears his name and specializes in corporate identity and packaging design. Mr. B is a highly educated, sometimes brilliant marketing thinker with a strong background in design management. He is a self-styled maverick in the way he conducts himself and his business, but his conduct is justified by a fairly consistent and impressive track record in design problem solving. Mr. B is a showman cut from the old-style mold—a personality type not unique in the consulting spectrum—who supports the theory that a client is buying a design personality as much as a design solution.

The firm consists of Mr. B, two designers, a keyline/production artist, a secretary/receptionist, and a bookkeeper. Mr. B handles all the accounts and new business contacts. The majority of his time is spent in coordinating these activities. Much of the firm's business comes from companies that are out of state. This requires a great deal of traveling on Mr. B's part, and he is out of the office more than he is in. The daily office activities revolve more around the designers and support staff and the responsibility for daily design function and limited client servicing (phone contact with out-of-town clients and in-town meetings dealing with project specifics).

The majority of Mr. B's business is gotten from relentless and skillful marketing and design selling. While old clients hire him on the strength of past performance, most potential accounts have never heard of him. Mr. B does not pursue a national reputation in design publications, and—unlike the principles of consulting firm A—Mr. B takes no part in national design activities that would reflect any publicity or prestige on his firm. Indeed, Mr. B looks askance at most designers (somewhat justifiably) as being generally bad business people who often do not succeed in selling themselves and their talents and who have little understanding of

marketing. This is the principle reason that his creative staff is not heavily involved with client contacts.

Mr. B is a natural loner and has found it difficult to share his business to any great extent with others. If the firm continues under its present structure, it will most likely not succeed beyond the involvement of Mr. B. Mr B believes that his employees should live up to his own personal standards and finds few individuals willing or able to do so. Consequently (even though he would like to), he has not yet found anyone he considers worthy of "inheriting" his business interests.

Since Mr. B's clients are buying *him,* they do not have any clear-cut profile of the personalities of the designers who are solving their creative problems. This is generally true of contemporary consulting practice. Rarely do individual designers receive the "publicity" that is their due, as the designer or illustrator in a studio might acquire. One of Mr. B's designers does accompany him on the presentation of creative solutions, but more in the capacity of assistant in the actual presenting of the material rather than as a participating expert. Most of the effective traveling the designers do is location environment and/or in-store situation studies that relate to the project being worked upon. Mr. B believes strongly that his designers should be fluent with each client's background and product profile before they engage in any creative development. These "tactics of familiarity" generate a high degree of relevancy in the work by Mr. B's firm. Rarely does any work miss the mark in terms of concept appropriateness or directional emphasis.

Mr. B does not like to share the creative development stage with his clients. He makes a practice of thrashing out all creative options within the intimacy of the staff environment and rigorously pursues every avenue until each is exhausted and the one "right" solution emerges. That solution is then presented to the client along with the highly developed marketing rationale that has evolved as the framework for it. This has been a very successful way of working for Mr. B, mainly because most of his presentations are made directly to top management, who rarely have any art or design training but who do understand and appreciate the formidable marketing rationale with which Mr. B justifies the creative endeavor. This is totally in keeping with Mr. B's style of business delivery. Top management is, after all, buying an expert in Mr. B. How the solution is arrived at is his responsibility. In those circumstances where Mr. B deals with middle-management advertising/sales promotion or design buyers he does modify his design development procedures to include some client input in the rough conceptual stages, but the internal process of designing down to a right solution does not change, and the amount of middle-level management input is carefully controlled and used only as a weathervane for top management attitudes. This system has a decided benefit for Mr. *B*'s designers in that the only person they have to sell their concepts to is Mr. *B*. Admittedly Mr. *B* is no easy sell, yet his is a sophisticated attitude well used to, and encouraging of, unusual and creative concepting as long as it dovetails with or increases the strength of emerging marketing positions.

All designers start out working on a major assignment. Under Mr *B*'s office structure, the designer whose creative concept evolves as the right solution then takes charge of the project and coordinates the efforts of all other individuals through to finish (presentation of keyline art to the client). Usually, if Mr. *B*'s system is functioning smoothly, the final keyline art is delivered at the time the concept is presented to the client. Under this presentation approach, Mr. *B* never presents the chosen concept in any other than a finished manner. In all cases, a limited silk-screen edition of the design solution will be printed. With packaging, work is shown in multiples of 50 to 100 or so units; for other graphics such as corporate identity or corporate communications, samples of applications to all surfaces are produced. This method gives the client the reassuring experience of seeing the project or product physically "there," and if approved, ready to go to production as an actuality. This technique is amazingly effective in selling a concept, and Mr. *B* has learned, over the years, how to employ the method to its fullest potential.

Mr. *B* makes a practice of hiring the best, most experienced talent he can find and afford. Consequently, the firm's designers are well schooled in the profession and in consulting work before they come to Mr. *B*. The intimacy of the small office creates a constant cross pollination of ideas and work habits that are beneficial to the designers. Because they are used to being thrown together to work on assignments, there is usually cheerful cooperation in balancing out the workload that is not always seen in other consulting offices. One never knows at the outset who the project responsibility will go to, and to insure cooperation on the receiving end, one must be ready and willing on the giving end.

Mr. *B* takes a somewhat stern fatherly approach to handling his designers and staff and is sincerely concerned with their welfare, but he does not really understand the basic creative personality as well as one who has been in design so long might. This creates management problems for him. He is a hard taskmaster, he pays his people adequately in relation to the cost of living in his area of the country, but he offers none of the long-term incentives (profit sharing, bonuses, etc.) found with many similar organizations. Merit raises are rarely given without being asked for, and there is no uniform policy toward annual cost of living increases.

In the design profession and especially in de-sign consulting, the "nomad syndrome" is a critical factor in the working environment. Employee turnover rate in Graphic Design is quite high in comparison with other professions. Designers drift from job to job with a disconcerting regularity, giving the most ambiguous reasons as if their internal clocks are set for periodic change. Mr. *B*'s environment suffers from this malaise more than most, and it has undoubtedly contributed to his skepticism concerning designers' ability to commit to long-term goals. Because of this skepticism and the constant trauma of turnover, due for the most part to designers' dissatisfaction with their relationship with Mr. *B*, he has avoided committing his firm to a fixed plan of long-term benefits. This, of course, aggravates any problems in relationships.

## SUMMARY OF DESIGN CONSULTING FIRM *B*

Because of the specialized nature of Mr. *B*'s workload and the rarefied design problems he strives to bring to the firm, designing at consulting firm *B* is generally a creative experience involving relatively long-range problem solving. Deadlines, while inviolate, are set up well in advance, allowing more than adequate working time to complete assignments. There is no day-to-day pressure with impossible workloads and quick assignment turnovers that might inhibit the creativity of the design solutions. On the contrary, Mr *B* is totally concerned with establishing enough time for the most creative answers to emerge, and he relentlessly pursues such solutions. Designers with a strong sense of self and a rugged individuality may do well working for Mr. *B*. A firm grasp of marketing is essential for any success with him, however, and to win his respect (necessary for any long-term gain in his employment) one must be willing to push oneself to the limit and beyond, both in professional and private life, to achieve constantly higher goals. As a temporary work experience, no better situation could be found for gaining exposure to top drawer creative assignments and for building an impressive and in-depth understanding of the marketing/design mix and the systematic approach to problem solving. Many of Mr. *B*'s "graduates" have gone on to key positions in the design profession and have used the positive experiences of working with him to further their careers.

Overly sensitive individuals looking for personally relevant ways to express their talents and creative drives will gain nothing but exposure to "the other side" of the design business in Mr. *B*'s employment. Tell-tale signs of the Mr. *B* personality and business profile (easy enough to spot in interview situations) should be well heeded by such persons.

Designers weak in drawing-board-level skills need have no concern with weighing the pros and cons of employment in Mr. *B*'s firm, simply because Mr. *B* would never hire them. Mr. *B*'s needs are pragmatic. He needs people to get the work done in the sophisticated vein he demands. He considers himself to be the only management-oriented individual necessary to his firm at the present, and does not see the profit in hiring multi-skilled talent. Mr. *B*'s preference for the specialist is a common prejudice in the consulting field, one born of necessity and maintained by the particular brand of individualist ego involvement mentioned earlier in the chapter. This attitude of the consulting business probably will never change. If one is to work in an environment of this type, an understanding and tolerance of the situation is mandatory.

# *Design Consulting Firm* C

Firms in New York City are characteristically unique in their attitudes about design and in their approaches to problem solving. Most pursue business on a national, and even international, scale and enjoy a peculiar sort of prestige associated with the cosmopolitan lifestyle of the city, considered by many to be the world's most exciting. New Yorkers traditionally have had a rather myopic view of activity west of the Hudson River. This can be either an engaging affectation or an irksome provincialism depending upon how it is encountered. Be assured of one thing, residents of the "big apple" always (like the ancient Roman citizen) make their environmental status known!

Consulting firm *C* is a large Manhattan-based organization typical of the New York design establishment. It is owned and operated by three individuals, all native New Yorkers with differing backgrounds. The founder and president of the firm is a designer with considerable experience in board-level concept development. As his business grew, he brought a specialist in business management into the firm on a partnership basis, and their extremely successful collaboration led to adding a third, a long-time associate with a background in corporate design management. This combination produced a wide range of complementary talents and helped make their organization an extremely effective and objective one in terms of design and business development.

Consulting firm *C* employs a total of 23 people in varying capacities. Twelve are involved in board-level design activity (including keyline/production people). The 3 partners handle all account service, new business solicitation, and client contact work. Since many of the firm's clients are outside the Manhattan me-

troplex, the two designer-partners are on the road much of the time.

The internal design staff is supervised by a Design Director who also works at the drawingboard level. In addition to overseeing the daily workload of the office, he coordinates outside activities that relate to the projects such as photography, special design, or keyline/production effects and services. Design Director *C* rarely has personal contact with clients and only occasionally accompanies one or more of the partners in the presentation of work. The partners, being designers themselves, have a great deal of input in each assignment and are more than aware of all factors of every job in the works. All work is systematically reviewed during and at the end of each project, collectively or individually by them. The Design Director functions as a presenter of concept development and finished presentation materials to the partners rather than to the clients.

Like consulting firm *B,* the firm's image is exclusively represented by the personalities of the controlling partners. The physical office space itself is divided so that clients or visitors cannot see work of any type in progress, and the partners make a practice of never allowing outsiders into the "inner sanctum" of design development. There are good reasons for this. Consulting firm *C* works on many sensitive assignments, particularly in the area of new product development. In some instances they have been asked by clients to sign a statement that binds them to complete secrecy before engaging in a design project. In essence, they are protecting themselves as well as their client's work from inquisitive eyes. Such projects are always put away at night where even the janitorial staff cannot see them. This is neither unusual nor extreme behavior when working in a field where the competitive edge is the key to success.

Even though the firm is insular in nature and identified totally with the three principals, the designers and general staff are treated with a great degree of respect and allowed considerable creative input in the running of the business. Salaries are good, even by New York standards, and "perks" such as profit sharing and bonuses are enjoyed by everyone in the firm. Many of the firm's employees have been with it for a long time (by design business standards) and have reached a point where they simply cannot afford to leave. Upward mobility (at this time) is limited, as the partners have no need of additional executive talent; however, should the need for it arise or if any employee were to make a unique place for him or herself within the organization, none of the principals would be averse to rewarding that individual with high pay or a percentage of the business above and beyond profit sharing.

Until recently, consulting firm *C*'s business has been primarily in the areas of packaging and corporate communications. At the request of some long-term clients and in an attempt to diversify their business interests, the partners have broadened their creative base to include sales promotion and point-of-purchase display. They have done this in a very astute way that offers the greatest chance for profit at the least risk. Through shrewd investment of profits they have established a large corporate bank balance. Instead of attempting to add staff to their group that are knowledgeable in these newer areas of interest (staff which might prove to be a deficit if business turns bad), they have opted to identify and "buy into" an existing firm specializing in sales promotion and display design. The arrangement has proved to be ideal.

The sales promotion firm (of long-standing reputation and well respected within the profession), owned by one man, needed working capital; firm *C* needed sales promotion expertise. An agreement was struck. Consulting firm *C* owns its own brownstone (an early investment), and it proceeded to rent space to its new associate. The two groups are basically one in terms of proximity, yet they each retain their own identities and individual leadership as well as their own client lists. The interchange of business possibilities has created new clients for both firms: each sells the other as an "auxiliary arm" to prospective clients.

The interchange of ideas between the designers of each group works to the advantage of both. Many times, when a deadline crunch is on and extra talent or hands to get the job done are needed, one group may "borrow" design time from the other on a credit basis, providing there are designers "up" for new assignments at the time. Because the two disciplines are so different, many times a designer will bring unique thinking to an assignment that might otherwise be ignored in normal in-house concept development.

The majority of consulting firm *C*'s people are commuters and do not live in the city itself. The office working hours are flexible and have to be, considering the trauma of New York commuter service (never very good). The office is officially open for business at 9 A.M. and closes at 4:30 P.M., but all designers who have been with the organization a certain amount of time are given keys; they come early or stay late as they choose and as the needs of the project they are involved with dictate. Couches and lounges within the partners' offices and in the reception area open into beds, and there are washroom and shower facilities for those working too late for the average two-hour trip to the suburbs.

## SUMMARY OF DESIGN CONSULTING FIRM *C*

Consulting firm *C* is a good place for the designer with a renaissance approach to problem solving, who enjoys working on a varied menu of design assignments at the board level. Being able to take direction from a number of people while sorting out the relevant information and contributing personal input is a confusing but necessary ability to have for success in the firm *C* environment. Because it is an insulated environment with little client contact for board-level people, the design firm looks for specific rather than general talent when they hire, even though a prospective employee will probably develop into multiskilled drawing-board activity. People with administrative as well as design skills may enjoy working at consulting firm *C*, but in all practicality their administrative skills may never be used under the present office system. The individual who finds an insular environment frustrating would be wise to seek employment elsewhere.

The firm is an excellent proving ground for the young designer seeking to build a varied portfolio, but unlike consulting firm *A*, the principals prefer to hire individuals whose talents are proven by previous exposure within the consulting business. The feeling of camaraderie is quite high at the firm and is encouraged by the partners. Salary expectations and earning potential for on-the-board employees is good, and the firm is a fine place to stay put in a secure position. Consulting firm *C* has continued to grow consistently and has plenty of capital to work with. No one has been let go because of a lack of business, even in the hardest of times. This is careful management at work. This is also an important fact to be aware of when considering employment at any design firm. Overstaffing is an easy habit to fall into when the workload is heavy, and many firms have loaded up on talent (with the best of intentions and reasons) only to find it necessary to unload individuals when business takes a downturn. It is *always* better to be slightly overworked and continually busy than to be sitting around with nothing to do trying to find ways to justify your salary. Talk to people, inside a firm if possible, and take time to check on a firm's business practices from outside individuals who know before you make any decisions.

Living in New York is truly a two-edged sword for someone not native to the environment. If one is unwilling to make the necessary sacrifices—the commuting, the trauma of inner-city life—no firm in the area is an attractive situation. On the other hand, New York can be a spark for the creative person, a lifestyle that cannot be had anywhere else. Like the city itself, a New York design firm is fast-paced and relatively unforgiving of mistakes—or more precisely, it has less time for them, for no one should forget that New York business operates in "the big league," where winners win and losers fall by the wayside. The firm, again like the city, can absorb and handle (even encourage) flamboyant personal style in their employees because the partners themselves are flamboyant. Many idiosyncrasies that would not be tolerated in Kiokuk, Iowa, are readily accepted here. Providing, of course, one has the talent to justify them.

For the designer with the right combination of personality and talents—talents that complement the activities and personalities of the partners—short- or long-term possibilities both exist. From the short-term perspective, consulting firm *C* can be a springboard almost anywhere. The old, often used cliché that "one cannot always go *to* New York and be a success, but one can always go *from* New York and be a success" is (like all clichés) at least partially true!

125

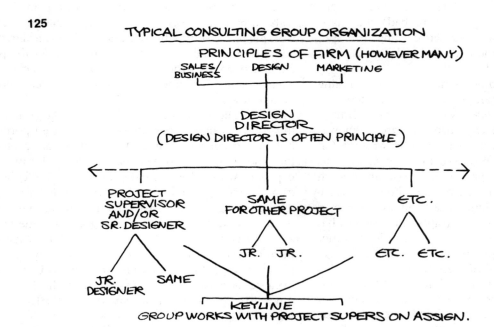

TYPICAL CONSULTING GROUP ORGANIZATION

# THE ADVERTISING AGENCY

## *Chapter 12*

For the designer, the advertising agency experience is critically different from all other creative environments. This is true for one overriding reason: the nature of the creative product. Agencies deal in ideas, strictly speaking. Agencies profit by ideas and they are run by "idea" people. Idea people deal in words (the classic medium for presenting ideas) and word people (for better or worse) are *usually* people who write words: copywriters. . . .

At the beginning of this text, we discussed at some length the criticism most often leveled at designers: their lack of ability and training to express their ideas through the written and spoken word. That fewer designers succeed in advertising agency jobs is a fact. That agencies can and *do* benefit from greater exposure to *properly* trained design talent is also a fact! To understand this, one has only to look at the creatively excellent agency environments and their products. They meld together words and pictures to form harmonic communication experiences. Most often the idea is the word. Sometimes the idea is the picture. Often the image becomes stronger than the word. When the "tail wags the dog" successfully and repeatedly, *it does so because of visual people who have learned the ability of conveying and selling their creative thoughts before the fact, through multiple mediums of communication.*

In the agency environment, art and copy are a developmental team, a unit that gauges the merits of an idea and translates it into the many facets necessary to communicate the message. This calls for special talents and skills. In the usual design situation the designer or art director is rarely teamed on a daily basis with the writer. In the agency, however, the art director or designer rarely works alone. In traditional design solutions are often personal statements and individual efforts. In the agency, the team creative concept is the standard order of fare. Special problems arise swiftly in such relationships . . . often exaggerated by ego involvement, and many times irreconcilable. Any visual creative must learn to adapt to the circumstances and learn to handle or work around them in innovative ways.

Many design curricula avoid dealing with the *real* nature of visual communication as applied to advertising. This is done for various reasons, often because design professors steeped in the traditions of "classic" design thinking simply are at a loss to deal with so virile and complicated a medium, also because the timely nature of the mediums of print and video require knowledge and attitudes that are *absolutely* up-to-date for relevant teaching. Negative attitudes toward advertising are often reflected by academics in design curricula, especially. Advertising tends to polarize. What is average and ordinary in advertising is usually considered bad (perhaps rightfully so) because of the intensity of the medium and its impact on the average American. The crucial problem with *avoiding* the issues presented by the aspects of the medium is simple. The ranks of advertising *are* staffed by art directors and designers. These art directors and designers did not come from law and business schools, from economics or history curricula, they came to the advertising profession *trained as designers*. If university curricula avoid dealing with advertising design in a relevant manner, designers unprepared for the realities of the agency environment will find it increasingly difficult to deal with and succeed in that creative area. It takes no genius to understand that the way to improve the quality of the medium is to produce creative individuals with sufficient background and training to take control of the world they commit themselves and their talents to.

# *Advertising Agency* A

As one of the largest in the world, advertising agency *A* has a total creative staff (in its main office) of over three hundred individuals. This includes executive creative people, writers, art directors, producers, and layout and production people (for both video and print). The creative branch of the agency is divided into divisions, each headed by a Vice-President, Group Creative Director who has overall responsibility for the creative output for one group of the agency's accounts.

Reporting directly to each V.P. Group Creative Director are a number of Creative Directors (group leaders) responsible for the creative assignments for specific accounts. In agency *A*, Creative Directors are usually always writers. The agency's founder was a writer and the traditional leadership roles have usually been assumed by copywriters. The Creative Director is responsible for his or her teams of writers and art directors, and directs the thrust of theme concept development. Although concept thinking and basic directions are often established by the "CD," only occasionally will he or she do any specific writing on a project. As a liaison with the account executives serving each account, the CD ties together concept and marketing for presentation to the client. He or she will often accompany account service people for presentations or will see that a writer or artist from his group who has worked directly on the assignment goes instead.

At agency *A* a Creative Director may be responsible for as many as six to eight art director/writer teams depending upon the size of his or her account responsibilities. Often one "super" account (such as an automotive product) will require a creative director and many teams of artists and writers of its own. In presenting concepts to new clients or when a push is on for a new concept direction for an existing account, the Creative Director may have all of his or her teams working on one account, but generally the group's workload is distributed evenly, with those people responsible for the initial concepting on a problem carrying through on all the aspects of that account's creative development. In a sense, the Creative Director's function in an advertising agency is the same as that of the company Design Director: as overseer of the creative product and coordinator of account creative activities. The team concept applies at the director's level as well as at lower echelons of responsibility. The Creative Director shares decision making on his accounts with an Executive Art Director. The "exec AD" is most involved with the visual theme development of campaigns for the accounts and often will be a direct contributor to the "brainstorming" (idea sessions) used to set the parameters of each campaign. He or she is the direct advisor for art personnel in the group and is usually the final arbiter in terms of the quality of visual material. The exec AD will work at the board level, often in support of ideas arising from a team effort with the Creative Director or other members of the group. When assistance is sought by an Art Director working on an assignment, the exec AD will offer guidance, reassign available people to help out, or jump in and bring his own expertise to the problem. Of the two team leaders, the exec AD spends more time involved at the board level designing than the CD does writing.

At agency *A* all creative alternatives for major campaigns are reviewed by committee and an approved direction is indicated before the work is seen by the client. This creative review committee, the "CRC," is made up of account representatives, the senior V.P. of all creative services, and the V.P. Group Creative Director. The presentation of the entire spectrum of work on the campaign for the committee's review is done by the Creative Director and a team or teams developing the concepts. Once a concept has the approval of agency management it is presented to the client by members of the creative team and the account service representatives. The client either accepts or rejects the agency's recommendations. If the recommendation is accepted, the Creative Director assigns teams to implement and flesh out the bare-bones directions presented to the client, and the real work on the campaign begins.

Refined scripts and storyboards are developed by art director/writer teams for television production (sometimes the initial boards presented to the client go through to production unchanged). Copy lines and visuals for print campaigns and collateral and sales-promotional materials will also be developed for production at this time. Specific scripts and visuals in each of the areas of media concentration are submitted to the client for final approval, and production then begins.

For the Art Director, production can be one of the most exciting and rewarding experiences in the agency process. In video and film work, the Art Director assists the producer and others in getting his team's ideas—from storyboard and script—on camera and onto prime-time TV. With print ads and collateral materials, the Art Director selects and directs photography and/or illustration sources and shapes the visual personality of the printed piece. At agency *A*, the clients and accounts are large and so are the budgets. The scope of the concepts usually offers the production team interesting and specialized problems to grapple with or take them on location for film or still photography, sometimes to exotic and interesting places. Rarely does an Art Director object to spending three or four days on location, even in the most mundane of environments.

As the visual member of a team, Art Directors rough out the concepts to theirs and the team members' satisfaction, but generally they do not carry the idea to a finished comp state. An AD's thinking time is usually too precious to devote the large block necessary to nail down the image in simulated finished form. Much of the time such tight comp work is unnecessary and keyline art is developed and photography or illustration is contracted directly from the Art Director's sketches. When tight comprehensives or skilled rendering is necessary, the Art Director will turn to layout and illustration specialists within the group or will buy such services from an art studio. If the AD is a skilled draftsperson or has a graphic style that is well suited to storyboarding, he or she may develop sketches for use in creative review committee sessions and these storyboards may even eventually reach the client, but more than likely they will be redone by the agency illustrators. In some instances when an account is basically visual (billboards or collateral and print design with minimal copy) the Art Director is directly involved with the client on a regular basis, and much time is taken up in contact work.

Because the agency Art Director *must* be versatile to succeed, he or she is well respected by their creative peers and by top management. Consequently, the Art Director, on the average, makes more money than the Designer with an equivalant amount of experience. The Art Director's chances of promotion are greater and come more rapidly than the Designer's, and unlike the Designer, the Art Director may advance both in responsibility and position status *without having to*

*ever leave the drawing board.* At advertising agency *A*, all art creatives up to and including V.P. Executive ADs function as creative designers and team members. Ideal ADs have the following qualities: they are good at concepting, verbally as well as visually; are able to present an idea convincingly to a fellow creative as well as to noncreatives and clients; are capable of directing others and organizing assignments to achieve maximum creative results; must have a working knowledge of multiple-media communication processes; are able to sketch and/or draw skillfully enough to capture the essentials of an image. Not all Art Directors have these qualities, yet enough do that the Art Director's self-image is deservedly high.

Not all aspects of advertising agencies are as attractive as those discussed above, however. The pressures upon the traditionally trained designer (who is taught to think in terms of solving the intricacies of design detailing) to learn to cultivate the overall view of the problem can be frustrating. Yet, it is the problem solving capability that is most prized by the agency system. The lack of this capability limits the designer's growth potential in agency organizations. The tendency to "overdesign" an idea is a criticism often leveled at art directors and designers by their writer brethren. Overworking is seen as a negative, diluting the spontaneity of the idea. To paraphrase the words of the late Leo Burnett, a giant of American advertising and founder of one of the world's largest agencies: *A good art director is one who can make big ideas, which are usually simple ones, look as though they had not been art directed at all.* Certainly, the designer's judgment comes into play later on, when a creative solution is being structured and finalized. Then, attention to aesthetic specifics can spectacularly affect the final product. At the beginning thinking stages, however, overdevelopment can be the death of the concept. Remember, in an advertising agency a total concept is rarely the product of one individual. Many hands and minds will contribute to the final product. Overworking the original, source idea may also inhibit another person's contribution to the idea. The art director/designer who has a tendency to "nitpick" every step of the way, rather than where it counts, may not last long on staff.

Many agencies cultivate the "odd-ball syndrome" with their creative people . . . not consciously, but they do. That is, many agencies tend to measure the creativity of an individual in terms of how different or unique they appear in dress and behavior. Thus the agency's careful practice of not inhibiting creative temperament can backfire, and superficial eccentricities can sometimes grab the spotlight briefly for certain people. Ultimately, however, if the "talent" wearing the ripped sweatshirt—who works barefooted, wears sunglasses in the dark, and ties a Doberman to the leg of the desk to insure creative privacy—does not produce, he or she is out! This is an inequity difficult to deal with for many "conservative" but definitely talented artists and writers. Too many creatives entering agencies try to consciously develop eccentricities and compete in the game-playing, often losing their own creative integrity and ultimately their effectiveness as a creative talent. The prima donna personality, at times an asset in selling an idea, is often overvalued in a profession where style and delivery are crucial to success.

## SUMMARY OF AGENCY *A*

Agency *A,* like most large, multifaceted organizations of its type, offers a fast-paced, creatively "free" environment with a great variety of work experiences and constantly changing sets of problems to solve. The latitude for personal expression is as great or greater in agency *A* as in any other type of creative organization (studio, company, consulting firm, etc.), and the chances for "star status" and meteoric rise in both salary and position are typical of the agency business, which is vastly superior to other creative environments in this respect. On the other hand, under such a system you are only as good as your last concept or execution, and loyalties and privileges shift and change quickly and constantly. Last year's hero might very well be looking for a job today and vice versa. Power and consistency are the keys to success. The former is often gained by the latter and sustained by judicial political alliance. Often such Machiavellian activity works against successful creative development, but the flamboyant nature of the creative personality tends to feed the system rather than starve it, and in great part cause the very problems we are discussing. Many creative people thrive in such seemingly hostile environments—that such environments are so successful and so common proves the point—but not *all* agency situations are rampant with political maneuvering. As in any other profession, the higher the stakes at issue, the greater the consequences, the traumas, and the rewards.

For the art director/designer who can adapt to agency work and develop the capacity for excellence, the rewards are there in terms of salary and "perks" (benefits). The spectrum of work done by agencies, at its worst, is sadly deficient in every aspect of creativity, is cheap and small in concept and content, and eminently questionable in value. At its best, the work in video and film, in print, and collateral, is *the* most stimulating and creatively rewarding experience a designer could wish for within the realm of graphic communications. The potential for both exists and changes in every situation with the strengths and weaknesses and the comings and goings of the creative people who make up the business.

# *Advertising Agency* B

The small "boutique" agency, or marketing services agency, is considerably different in philosophy and structure from the large international communication organization characterized by agency *A.* Advertising agency *B* is typical of this second category. In a suburban area of a large midwestern city, advertising/marketing agency *B* is relatively small by agency standards, employing a staff of only ten people. Even though the firm is structured along traditional agency lines in terms of management profile, strictly speaking it is less an advertising agency than a marketing/design services agency. While the firm does handle all aspects of print advertising and sales promotion writing and design, it also actively solicits and involves itself in other endeavors not usually associated with the "traditional" advertising agency. The firm views packaging and display design as intimately related to print and promotion activity. It successfully sells itself to its predominantly corporate clients as a total problem solver, eminently capable of handling all aspects of corporate communications.

The agency is owned and managed by two principals, one of whom is a designer with an excellent background in "classic" graphic design. Consequently, the output of the office tends to be of a high design quality, usually quite sophisticated in concept. Because both partners have creative backgrounds (the other as a writer), there is much concern with hiring and keeping the best talent, people who can contribute to the image of the firm. The firm is small enough to function as a kind of large family, and the partners make a practice of offering excellent salaries and side-benefits to people they feel are valuable members of their organization.

Because of the intimate scale of the staff, job definitions are often flexible and usually always overlap. In a comparable-size consulting office, job structure is much more regimented simply because of the product being produced. The team involvement characteristic of the large agency is in effect at agency *B*. All the personnel, from the secretary—who also functions as a production coordinator—up to the principals, have a greater feel for and involvement in the day-to-day function of the office. The creative and account sides of the agency's business are not clear-cut as in larger agency-*A* situations. The writer/art director teams who develop and present are well equipped to deal with accounts in general and even prefer to do so on a regular basis rather than give them up to others who might be less familiar with the people or problems. This account ability of staffers frees up a considerable amount of time for the principals to develop new accounts, with confidence that the store is being well tended in their absence.

With the accent more on design factors (in the traditional sense) than in more typical agencies, the daily creative working process is more like that of a consulting office environment. The atmosphere is easy and self-contained. There is less emphasis on creative review sessions simply because everyone is more or less familiar with every job that comes through the office and follows its development closely.

The problems inherent in large-agency creative staffing are not present in agency *B,* because the partners do not allow them to happen, and because the staff is too small to divide into factions that would compete against each other. What is positive about agency *B* is that it is new and growing, not primarily in size, but in billing. Most of the employees have been with the group since its inception. By being in "at the creation," everyone benefits from the growing prosperity in a way that employees of older, more established firms do not. Profit sharing is a reality at agency *B,* and all the creative involvement and effort toward the firm's output pays off dramatically at the end of the year. At its stage of development, the firm is really made or broken by the contributions of its employees. Everyone's cooperation is critical, and the partners realize this.

Working hours are flexibly built around the 9 to 5 standard, but a good deal of overtime is put in by almost everyone, given the usual tight deadlines built into most projects. The nature of the creative work done by agency *B* does not allow for the extended periods of development that are more typical of the traditional design consulting office. Turnaround time on the average project is measured in terms of weeks (sometimes days), not months. Being able to think and act—and react—quickly, creatively, and accurately is crucial for the firm's continued success. This often produces stress factors similar to the large-agency situation, factors that are not so common in a consulting situation.

Budgets established for creative work are larger than those usually fixed for most graphic design assignments, but they are a far cry from the huge sums associated with agency-*A* firms. On the average, there is a great deal more money spent by corporations for advertising, promotional materials, and display than for other areas of graphic design. There is also more money to be made by the organizations who specialize in these areas. The margin of profit is higher. Agency *B* can afford to pay its people more generously than a consulting office of similar size and means because of this. In this respect, agency *B* is the perfect blend of two worlds. The designer who wishes total involvement in graphics can work at agency *B,* enjoy the benefits of a small office, and gain valuable exposure to writers and other creative, nonvisual people without suffering from the mania found in large agencies.

Because agency *B* is not "corporate" in size and really lives on a project-to-project basis, like all small design organizations lacking the benefit of multiple retainer contracts, job security is a concern for every employee including the principals. The agency cannot afford to make continued errors or perform badly for a client. One person's error may be compensated for in the complex structure of a large organization, where there is group responsibility for major tasks. At agency *B,* one person's error may be magnified with disastrous results, as each person has major responsibilities on each and every project. Corporations only occasionally succumb completely from bad management. Small businesses do with alarming regularity.

At agency *B,* the designers are the true coordinators of any given project. They are the only people totally qualified to supervise the production of final art, direct the complexities of photography and/or illustration, select and specify paper and typography, and check the printing production as well as work intimately with team writers and clients. The daily internal workings of a project revolve more around art preparation than around copy development, and the Art Director is the center-spring of this clockwork movement. In more traditional design environments where the drawing-board designers are less involved in management aspects of assignments, much of this everyday responsibility would be assumed by a project director. This, of course, severely limits a creative's ability to control the range and scope of any given assignment.

## SUMMARY OF AGENCY *B*

For the creative individual who wishes a design career with multiple involvements and responsibilities, the agency *B* situation has much to offer. Classic Graphic Design skills are necessary, yet so is a sophisticated grasp of communication techniques and the ability to "group-think" and work with nonvisual people just as the art director/designer of the large agency does. No one in an agency-*B* situation can crawl into a hole and produce a masterpiece. Individual solutions are rare, and much more client input is offered and used than in the typical design office.

On the other hand, team involvement is tempered by the intimacy of the office itself, which engenders respect for each person's right of creative domain, and in which each staff person is known by and must work with every other. Politics are minimal, pay is good, but working hours are often long and deadlines tight. Advancement in terms of personnel responsibilities is more or less nonexistent; everyone functions in a different capacity with no more than two or three jobs overlapping responsibilities *within* the same area. Unless the agency grows significantly in size, the situation will remain similar. There are not likely to be any "departments," in the structural sense of the word, within the firm, and individuals eager to exercise classic managerial skills would have little opportunity to do so.

## An Overview

Let us reiterate a few key points made at the beginning of Part III in light of what has just been read. To begin with, the design environments discussed in Part III are models of existing businesses. Presented in the most impartial light possible, in great part they *do* represent the general attitudes, philosophies, business procedures, and demeanors of firms in their respective categories. Of course, *every* situation is unique, and the old adage "being in the right place at the right time" is very true. Any situation is as bad or as good as you make it, and any situation can change; so in this sense, no environment is typical of any other.

The emerging designer's challenge is to pick a career path that complements his or her real interests, and to understand that simply wanting to be a "designer" is too vague a viewpoint to live with for long after your academic career. Remember that design, like law or medicine or any other profession, is a complex and multifaceted experience. Law students and medical students explore their professional options during their undergraduate careers and, usually by the time they graduate, have a fixed idea of exactly the specialty they wish to be involved in, and of the environment it represents. There is absolutely no reason why design should not be approached in the same enlightened manner. A great part of this responsibility falls upon your own shoulders and not upon your instructors', who will, because of their *own* chosen career paths, have a somewhat limited perspective on the matter. Reading and experiencing first-hand (wherever possible), listening to design "gossip" (again wherever possible), and seeking out information from as many different types of designers and design personalities as you can, in as many different places as you can, are all ways to increase your knowledge of your chosen profession. Make it a point to learn about the not-so-attractive aspects of different situations. This will be difficult because professionals will be reluctant to tell you their problems; but by knowing and understanding the *reasons* for the less pleasant realities of work situations will help you avoid disillusionment that might turn you off to an otherwise exciting possibility.

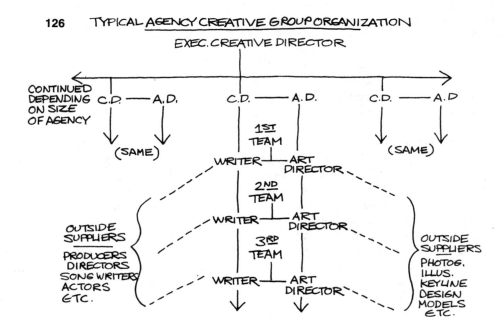

**126**  TYPICAL AGENCY CREATIVE GROUP ORGANIZATION

# THE DESIGNER'S TOOLS
## *Chapter 13*

Like most professional designers, an "office" in the beginning years of this author's career often meant five or so crowded square feet of totally public "bull-pen" space. Professional "perks" usually come with time, and perhaps the satisfaction of a comfortable office and the rewards of creative work are all the more appreciated in the light of those crowded, hectic offices one remembers from the past. The encouraging news for design students is that the rewards are there ... eventually, if you want them ... whether they be your own firm, a large office and a "command" position in a design company, a quiet, private world doing your own thing as a board designer, or whatever you consider the full rewards of a mature career in design. But as much as one's circumstances change as a career comes to its peak—as much as *you* change; your design talents and approaches change; your situation, environs, and office certainly change—one element remains constant: your *tools*, those things that help you in your designing, change *very little* in that same amount of time.

This is a pretty rare situation for highly technical, "avante garde" professions. Computer professionals are constantly changing to improved hardware and software tools. Certainly many of the sciences are not working with the same tools they were ten years ago. Photography equipment is *always* changing. Typewriters steadily improve, and the writer advances technologically. But designers? Their tools change very little. One reason is that we do not use a lot of automatic aids. There are a few: automatic pencil sharpeners, balanced light sources, color-keys. But by and large designers are not too accepting of new gimmicks. A cutting blade is still a cutting blade. Your favorite eraser is still usually an old-fashioned eraser. A glue pot is a glue pot. A straight-edge may be steel, but it is still a straight-edge; and triangles and T-squares and drawing boards are basically the same as they have always been—hand-operated, subject to as much grime and misuse as ever!

A designer's hands are the best set of tools we will ever have, and we tend (rightfully so) to stick with tried-and-true extensions for these "best of tools." Color now flows out of our fingertips through markers instead of chalks, but markers have changed so little in the last fifteen years since their introduction that few if any of us can accurately describe the differences. Aerosol spray glue will no longer cripple your genes, but good old "one-coat" (rubber cement) is still on everybody's taboret. Keyliners have discovered waxers, but like markers they will surely stay relatively unchanged for years.

Transfer type (mentioned in Chapter 3) and "Greek" type have been around and basically unimproved almost as long as markers; they have their uses, but nothing has the grace and style of careful type indication when it's properly learned, and that seems older than time! The only recent radical technological advancement in design is computer-assisted design, and as of this date that has very limited usefulness for the graphic designer.

## The Technology Trap

When it comes right down to it, we really do not *need* a lot of fancy tools for designing, and even less for conceptual thinking. There is a danger in having too many mechanical aids, *especially* for the student designer. The more *time* you take to learn to operate machines *to save yourself time,* the less *time* you have to learn and practice the skills you need to operate with your hands.

Let's take an example a student is most familiar with: the stat machine. Stat machines are wonderful tools for certain aspects of the graphic process. Keyliners rely heavily upon them in the production of final art, and without them production art processes would be set back fifty years. But designers are *not* keyliners—not in the professional world, except at the very lowest apprenticeships or in one-man design situations. Yes, stat machines are wonderful tools, but they cannot create a concept or a drawing; they cannot sketch an artistic comprehensive more beautiful than can a well-schooled pair of hands. Learning to operate them and then using them as a replacement for hand skills is *time consuming* for the student and takes away from the *time* for developing drawing and rendering skills unique to graphic design.

Another case in point: many schools are lucky enough to have computer typesetting available for student use. As a device in the learning of modern typographic techniques, such machines are a fascinating enterprise. Yet these machines are also *time consuming* to learn and operate. The benefit of *understanding* the function of the computer typesetter's importance *in terms of broadening your base of experience in design-related areas* is unquestionable. What is destructive about students using computer typesetting equipment is when *time* and machinery are utilized to *create an effect* that is of questionable benefit to the student's talent and portfolio: that of giving portfolio work the illusory look of finished and printed material. If finished and printed material was the determining factor in judging the talents of a designer, such a portfolio might have some relevance, but this is not the case! *The "experience factor" in judging whether to employ young designers fresh from school is insignificant.* What value does a cosmetic portfolio have for the young designer seeking a job when employers are *most intersted in the prospective employee's ability to reason, conceptualize, draw/think, and render* with those best of tools: the designer's hands and their extensions, the old-fashioned, simple tools of our art.

A neat mechanical portfolio does exhibit the student's ability in terms of craftsmanship, a necessary skill, but it is no indication of conceptual creativity. Even the seasoned designer seeking employment (from whom considerable printed samples are expected) is questioned as to concepting and layout skills, an indication of just how important such talents are.

The question of whether a student should devote any substantial time to learning the skills of typesetting is answered by this simple fact: The instances are so rare that it is safe to say professional designers *never* set their own type. We may do it as a hobby for our own enjoyment, but we certainly don't do it commercially.

There is so little time in most schools—two or at best, three years—to master the skills that make the designer's art. That time would be better employed building a philosophy in which to ground your art and seeking as much additional schooling in business and marketing as possible. Once again, *knowing* about graphics art's processes is the important thing; anything beyond that (unless for personal pleasure) is detrimental to the education of the designer. More and more educators are coming to realize the overkill potential of "labor saving" machinery and going back to basics. Future generations of designers will undoubtedly learn to command sophisticated machinery, initiating, with the press of a button, an entire automated sequence of production art, including typesetting, perhaps from a console on Mars! But for you, now, an eraser is still . . . an eraser. Learn to use the simple tools; they will be your constant partner at the drawing board.

As in every circumstance, of course, balance is the key issue here—balance of craft and technology. With too much technology we become simply technicians. With too little we are left behind. Without enough schooling in the traditions of our craft, we are less than our potential and do not deserve to be a member of the artistic family.

## Reduction and Enlargement Cameras

Of all the mechanical equipment available to the designer, the "lucy" probably ranks higher than any other in use and value. "Lucy" is the generic name for a number of different reducing and enlarging cameras that project a traceable image upon a surface (either a ground glass or an easelboard) from transparent or opaque subjects. Many times I have seen an ingenious student struggling with an overhead projector in a darkened room, trying to find a quicker way to enlarge or transfer an image! The lucy is really just a sophisticated and much more manageable way to solve that problem. A designer used to having a lucy around is loath to work without one, especially under a time crunch.

Like the stat camera, the lucy can be misused, serving as a crutch for individuals who have not perfected their drawing skills. The argument often made that the lucy is a justifiable instrument for designers who can't draw does not hold water. Everyone can *learn* to draw to at least some degree. Drawing is one of the more teachable of the art disciplines, and there should be no such thing as an artist who can't draw. Hard work and study may not produce a master draftsman, but it certainly will develop the capacity to capture an image in an adequate manner, and continued practice improves the skill.

Assuming you avoid making it a crutch, the lucy does offer advantages other equipment does not. It produces instant results, it runs on cheap electric current, and requires little skill to operate. It is an invaluable aid in sizing and resizing layout elements, for transfering images rapidly to most any size by simple tracing, and for outlining and sketching-in realistic imagery from photography that would otherwise take considerable time to render effectively.

Illustrators have utilized the lucy for years in all these capacities and for making quick underlays for their drawings and paintings. Say you wish to increase the size of your rendering of a symbol you have just designed; there are several options available to you. The most elaborate is to "grid" the image and then reproportion it by hand on a larger grid. The expensive choice is to stat the image up to the required size and go through the time-consuming process of developing and drying the image, and then use it for nothing more than an underlay to draw from. The cheapest and fastest option is to throw the art under the lucy, crank the bellows up or down, focus, and sit down to trace the resized image to the surface you wish to work on. In a time crunch, running back and forth to the lucy is easy; running back and forth to the stat machine is not!

By comparison with the stat machine and the computer typesetter, the lucy is a cheap investment. If your design department has one, in this case it is definitely worth the *time* to learn its use.

Last but not least among handy mechanical tools is the color key process. Perhaps the most widely used device, both by professionals *and* student designers, the color key system of making transparent colored cells (usually of type) is considered by nearly everyone to be an invaluable aid in producing "tight" comprehensive art, especially for packaging design. This too is an arguable point: the color key process is *time* consuming—not in learning to use, but in actually operating. More important, it is not a terribly attractive way to build comprehensives, especially when more than one layer of material must be utilized to get the effects you desire. Cut cells tend to cancel the value and intensity of the colors underlying them. The glossy surface of the cells (especially when cut into small pieces) are an unattractive interruption to the surface of the layout. Most important of all, students and designers who depend upon the color key, and the transfer type used to create the image, do so because they have not perfected the ability to indicate typography by hand, something the "old-fashioned" layout man was supremely capable of doing. Once such skills have been learned, not only is it easier and quicker to simply take a brush or a pen and render the characters, but it is also a much more artistically competent and beautiful way to finish an image. Even the smallest of type can be "Greeked" by hand by the skilled artisan. There are several large and well-known design firms specializing in packaging that *only* build comprehensives by hand (unless silk-screened multiples are required). Obviously, such skills are highly prized.

Unfortunately, hand calligraphy is a dying art in design schooling, because few students emerging from their educations exhibit these skills. Evidently, many faculty feel such skills are outdated. However, if painting students are still taught the basic skills of modeling and painting *even while they are being prepared to reject them,* why should the designer not be taught in the same manner? A great painter does not become so by avoiding the classic skills of his or her craft. The skills *are* learned, even when they are contemptuously cast aside!

# PAPER
## *Chapter 14*

Paper affects the outcome of any design project which uses it: as a cost factor—it often exceeds one quarter of the total cost of the job—in terms of the visual effect achieved, and in the practical use and handling of the finished product. The designer has literally thousands of paper samples, in kit, brochure, and book form, which display and describe every paper produced for printing. This material is readily available from paper brokers and supply houses, whose salespeople deal directly with designers on a regular basis. The designer will usually have an idea in mind of the type of paper a graphic should be printed on. Stock samples are requested from a paper salesperson, and the designer either uses the actual paper in producing roughs for the client or includes samples for the client to see along with his design solutions.

In many instances the designer is responsible for the production aspects of the assignment as well as the creative ones: ordering the paper, estimating and buying the printing, and seeing that the job is delivered on time. Obviously, the more designers know about paper, and the papermaking process, the easier their jobs become.

## *A Brief History of Papermaking*

Over the centuries humanity has recorded its thoughts and actions upon stone, clay tablets, wooden boards, impressionable surfaces of plants, wax, the skins of animals, papyrus, and parchments with varying degrees of success. None of these methods, however, has been as important to the preservation of ideas as paper, and just as these materials and methods gave way to the superior qualities of paper, so paper, in the closing years of the twentieth century, is giving way to the computer memory banks of an increasingly technology-oriented society. How much longer the graphic designer will work with and conceptualize in terms of paper is a matter for considerable debate, but until such a revolution is realized in total, printed paper is the quintessential graphic end-product.

Paper, which has been made since its invention from some four hundred different fibrous raw materials, is manufactured by reducing the fibers to pulp and then pressing the pulp into sheets. The Chinese invented the papermaking process around the year 95 A.D.; they took fibrous inner bark from trees, reduced it to pulp, and formed it into sheets by floating it in water and letting it settle and dry. Papermaking came to Europe by way of the Arabian Saracens who conquered Spain in the eighth century. From Spain, papermaking spread northward to Germany and the low countries.

European paper, manufactured by hand, was a laborious and costly process until a Frenchman named Nicholas Louis Robert solved the mechanical problems of producing paper in continuous sheet form. His solution was to use an endless screen wire band passing between two squeezing rolls. Robert was an employee of St. Leger Didot, a member of the famed French printing and publishing family, and owner of a papermaking mill at Essonne, France. His French patent was transferred to Didot, who in turn, through family ties, took out English patents on the process.

A well-known firm of wholesale stationers in England, Henry and Sealey Fourdrinier, was persuaded by Didot and family to finance the patents. The Fourdriniers called upon the skills of a talented machinist, Bryan Donkin, who took Robert's basic idea and improved upon it so much that a new British patent was secured in 1807. Although a mechanical triumph, the combined venture of Robert, Didot, and the Fourdriniers was a financial disaster, and the only one to enjoy a considerable profit from the device was Donkin, by manufacturing and selling it on his own. The principles of the Fourdrinier machine have not changed over the years. The only improvements have been in speed and capacity. The Fourdrinier name is used even today in reference to papermaking machines.

Although the most significant advance in the art of papermaking was accomplished by the British, they were among the last Europeans to make their own

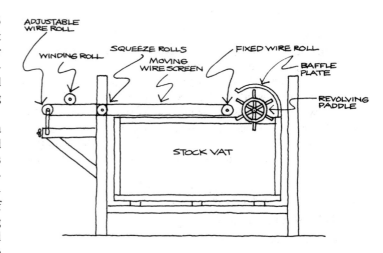

**127**   First paper machine of Louis Robert

paper. The papermaking industry was not established in England until 1688, only two years before the first mill was set up in America. The Dutch and the Germans who settled in Pennsylvania, with a much older papermaking heritage, developed the art of papermaking in the colonies. William Bradford, an English emigrant and Philadelphia publisher restricted because of his reliance on European sources for paper, went into partnership with William Rittenhouse, a Rhenish German from a long line of papermakers. Bradford and Rittenhouse, along with three other backers, erected a mill at Germantown, Pennsylvania, and began to manufacture the first American paper in 1690.

The Rittenhouse family soon came into complete control of the enterprise, and additional mills were erected in the area by successive generations of the family. Other mills in competition with the Ritten-

**128**   The Donkin Paper Machine

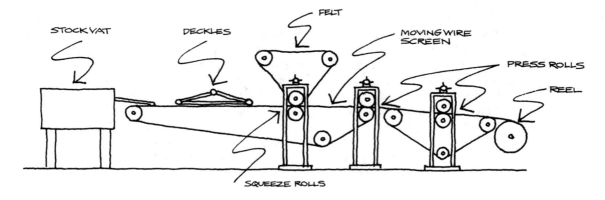

house family soon began to dot the surrounding countryside, and a Pennsylvania industry took root. The establishment of paper mills in Massachusetts and Connecticut followed soon after.

The first machine-made paper produced in this country is generally credited to Thomas Gilpin, one of two brothers who owned and operated a mill near Wilmington, Delaware. Gilpin's machine was simply a cylinder, making paper continuously in endless lengths instead of sheets, and was first introduced into his mill in 1817.

## THE WATERMARK

Papermakers identified their product by an imprint called a "watermark." The watermark first appeared in European paper in 1498. Watermarks are made by placing a wire pattern in the wet paper pulp before the sheet is formed. This thins out the pulp and produces a design that is seen when the sheet is held up to light. The watermarking of paper is a way of insuring against counterfeiting for currency, stamps, and negotiable materials, as well as a way of identifying or individualizing a custom-made paperstock. Watermarks indicate a superior paper product, and are not found on common milled stock and papers for general use (other than stationery).

# *Papermaking Methods*

## HAND PROCESS

Early European papers were made entirely from cotton and linen rags. Even today much of the best papers available are "rag" papers or papers with a high "rag" content. The oldest practice was to take the cotton and linen rags and allow them to ferment and partially decay in a warm, damp environment and then to reduce the fermentation to a pulpy mash of fibers. A later development was to place the rags in a vat together with water, and then beat the mix with hammers or large pestles to form a mash. In time, hand beating was replaced by beaters mechanically operated by waterwheel power.

When sufficiently pulped, the mash was dipped out of the vat by a vatman and placed in a mold resembling a large sieve. A thin frame of wood called a "deckle" was placed on the mold to retain the pulp and regulate the size of the sheet. The excess water drained through the sieve. By shaking the deckle and sieve, the pulp was distributed evenly over its surface. The deckle was then removed and the pulp sheet was turned out of

the mold onto a felt mat by a special worker called a "coucher." The pile of six to eight sheets on their felt mats was put into a frame and pressed to remove excess water. The felts were then removed, and the sheets or "plys" of material were put into another press and heavy pressure was applied to bond them together. The bonded sheets were then hung up to dry. The smoothness of the paper was determined by how heavily it was pressed, and the color was given by the color of the original rags used.

The low availability of rags in the American colonies was the greatest drawback to widescale paper production. Advertisements urging families to save rags and cloth scraps were common. Prizes were offered by associations like the American Philosophical Society to families that saved the greatest number of scraps, and legislation was even tried to compel people to save rags. All of these methods were to no avail, however, for colonialists had few rags of any type to throw or give away. Because of the small supply of available usable materials, the paper industry everywhere was conducted on a small scale.

## MACHINE PROCESS

Today, rags are used only for the most expensive specialty and custom papers. Wood is the most widely used raw material. In many instances paper made from wood cellulose has a degree of "rag" content, and "100% rag" papers are usually always promoted as such. Where wood is scarce or not available, other fiber sources such as vegetable fiber, jute, bamboo, esparto (a variety of grass), and hemp are used. Pulp is obtained from many sources in many different ways, but in general two main methods account for most papermaking fibers.

1. *Mechanical Pulping.* This process has changed little from that used in the first commercial groundwood mill in America in 1867. Logs are forced against a revolving grindstone which reduces them to fiber. The original grindstones used were natural sandstone, carefully quarried and shaped for the task. In the modern process, where rotary speeds may reach as high as 4000 horsepower, artificial monolithic stones of cement are used. The high speed of the grinding action coupled with the pressure against the wood generates considerable heat. To absorb this and carry the pulp away from the surface of the stone, water is injected during the process. The amount of water injected determines whether the pulp is "cold ground" or "hot ground." Cold ground pulp is more uniform in character and of a finer texture. Hot ground pulp is coarse, parts with water more freely, and is the source of one of the most abundantly used paperstuffs, common newsprint stock.

Pulp is collected in a pit under the grinder and forced through coarse screens that take out knots and large splinters. Once through the coarse screens, the fibers pass over a sand settler which removes stone particles that might have broken from the stone. Finer screens then cull out smaller particles that might cause imperfections or defects in the paper. The screened pulp is then partially separated from the water and collected in tanks where it remains until ready for use.

All types of woods may be made into ground-wood pulp, but because the pulp is not bleached, lighter woods such as jack and white pine, gum woods, southern pines, birch, and poplar are the most common. Groundwood pulp gives a high commercial yield and is very economical, but the impurities within the wood cause a certain amount of discoloration and the papers produced in this method are not high in tensile strength. As mentioned above, newsprint is the most common product of groundwood pulp, but a variety of other papers are also produced such as tissue, wallpaper, cheap book and magazine papers, and wallboard, along with pressed and molded paper used for constructing egg containers, etc. Groundwood products are of temporary value because they age and yellow quickly when exposed to light. Groundwood pulp is also used as a base to which minerals and adhesives are added to produce a paperstuff which is more resistant to weathering and light. By steaming the wood and removing much of the soluble material before it is pulped, a longer and stronger fiber is produced, but doing so creates a darker coloration to the fiber.

2. *Chemical Pulping.* The chemical-pulping process removes most of the resins, gums, and other components of the wood and leaves cellulose fiber. Papers that are made from purified cellulose fiber are more durable than groundwood pulp papers. The chemical processes involve reducing wood to pulp by cooking it in large tanks lined with acid-resistant brick. These tanks are called "digesters." There are three chemical cooking processes: (1) the soda process, (2) the sulfite process, and (3) the sulfate process.

The Soda Process: The soda process is the oldest of the three methods. Developed in England in 1851, it uses caustic soda as a reducing agent. When used to cook long-fibered coniferous woods, it produces pulp which makes strong durable paper. Most soda fiber, however, is produced by using hardwoods which have short fibers without much tensile strength. When short, soda-processed fiber is mixed with long fiber pulp, the soda fiber aids in producing a smooth and consistently uniform paper sheet.

The Sulfite Process: Experimentation with sulfurous acid as a reducing agent for wood was done shortly after the Civil War in America, and the process

was improved in Sweden, and finally used extensively in England about 1880. The cooking "liquor" for the sulfite process is a combination of calcium bisulfite and sulfur dioxide that is made by burning sulfur to form the sulfur dioxide, and absorbing it in water.

The sulfur liquor has a lower solvent power than soda, and the presence of bark and knots in the wood tends to cause more impurities in the wood pulp than in the alkaline processes. The woods most commonly used in this process are long-fibered evergreens like spruce, hemlock, balsam, and the true firs. Sulfite pulp bleaches well and produces a durable paperstock.

The Sulfate Process: The sulfate process is an alkaline method similar to that used with soda. It was developed in Germany in 1883 as a cheaper alternative to cooking with soda ash. The process (sodium sulfate reduced to sodium sulfide and caustic soda) produces a dark-colored fiber which makes stronger paper than other fibers. It is referred to as the "kraft" process (from the German word for "strength"), and we call the paper produced from such pulp "kraft paper." Fir, spruce, southern pine, and gumwood are commonly used, but excellent pulp for book papers can be made from hardwoods. The versatility of this process has

**129** Sketch of a section of a vertical digester showing inlets, pump & piping

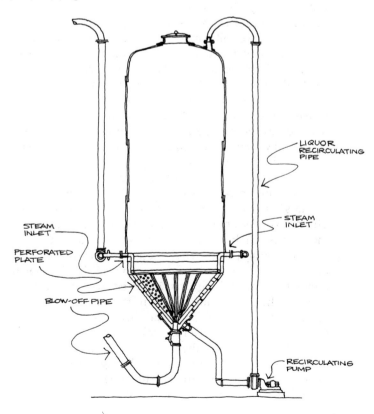

LIQUOR RECIRCULATING PIPE

STEAM INLET

STEAM INLET

PERFORATED PLATE

BLOW-OFF PIPE

RECIRCULATING PUMP

made it more important than either the soda or sulfite processes, and more fiber is produced by it than by any other process.

## Bleaching

None of the methods used for producing fiber reduce out all the impurities and yield a completely pure cellulose lacking the coloration necessary to make a paper with a high degree of whiteness. Bleaching is an additional process that accomplishes this end. Many of the papers we use in daily living do not require whiteness (such as common kraft), and papers such as newsprint can be produced without bleaching by combining only light woods to produce pulp.

Writing papers and stock used for printing do require varying degrees of brightness and whiteness, and numerous stages of bleaching are necessary to produce a strong pulp of the highest whiteness. Chemicals like chlorine and chlorine dioxide are used along with treatments of caustic soda and water in the modern bleaching process.

## Stock Preparation

Stock preparation is the preparation of pulp before it is made into paper. The process involves repulping and pulp blending, the addition of chemicals and fillers, and the mechanical treatments of beating and refining.

Almost all papers are made from fibers which have been put through a beating or refining process. Beating fibers achieves the following results: (1) it swells the fiber; (2) it increases the fiber's flexibility; (3) it creates internal fibrillation (the breaking up of the internal bonds of the fiber); (4) it cuts the fibers; and (5) it increases the surface area of the fiber and creates fibrils (individual strands that spread out from the main body of the fiber).

The beating of fiber is a practice as old as the papermaking process itself. The Chinese used stone mortars set into the ground to beat and separate fibers. The Arabs beat linen with manually operated trip hammers. In Spain, by 1150, stamping mills were in use operated by waterpower. The first application of the modern principles of beating were employed by the Dutch about 1680. An oblong tank was used, rounded at both ends, with a revolving wooden roll fitted with iron knives over a stone or metal bedplate. As the roll turned, the fibrous material was cut and separated between the knives and the bedplate. Today, this type of beating is done in a large tub employing this same basic principle. The pulp is circulated by a revolving roll and passed between steel bars which crush and cut the fi-

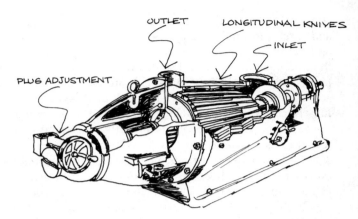

**130**    Sketch of a modern Jordan refiner showing cut-away view of internal mechanics

bers. This beating machine is known by the name "Hollander" after its country of origin.

The amount of beating done will depend upon the kind of paper being manufactured and upon the fiber that is used. A wide diversity in paper types can be produced out of the same fiber simply by controlling the beating time.

Refining has replaced the beating process in many situations, as a faster and more efficient way to prepare fiber. The shortcomings of the Hollander beating method, which requires considerable floor space, much power consumption, and is subject to wear, led to the development of refining as a preparation for fiber. There are three basic types of refiners, of which the conical Jordan refiner is the most common. Refiners are used extensively in high-speed production mills.

The Jordan refiner, developed in 1858, consists of a conical plug, covered with longitudinal knives, which fits into a conical shell also lined with cutting edges. Moving the plug in and out adjusts the cutting action of the knives. The stock enters from an opening in the small end of the shell and passes in a circular motion around the plug. It is then discharged at the larger end by the centrifugal action of the plug.

Fillers and sizing agents are added to the beating or refining process to give the pulp water repellency and improve the smoothness, opacity, and affinity for ink. Fillers increase a paper's weight more than add to its bulk. The most common filler is clay, the next most, calcium carbonate (precipitated chalk). Calcium sulfate, talc, and titanium dioxide are other fillers that are used. Sizing is done with various agents such as rosin, animal glues, starch, and sodium silicate.

The coloring of the "stock solution" (as it is

called at this point in the papermaking process) is done with soluble dyes of three types: (1) acid dyes, which give even, lightfast (permanent) colors of a medium intensity; (2) basic dyes, which give brilliant color with greater depth but are not as lightfast; and (3) direct dyes, which take well to unsized fibers but do not impart strong color brilliance.

Resins formed from formaldehyde mixtures added to the stock give it "wet strength." Such resins attach themselves to the fiber and keep papers from coming apart when wetted during usage. Photographic, blueprint, filter, and tea-bag papers are all examples of papers with high wet strength factors. Outdoor posters, bag papers, building papers, wrappers for foods, paper towels, napkins, and tissues are all given increased wet strength. The effectiveness of a paper's wet strength is often expressed in a percentage related to its dry strength. A wet strength of 35 percent is considered good; 50 percent (half the paper's dry strength) is excellent.

# The Papermaking Machine

A Fourdrinier paper machine is really many machines in one, each designed for a particular purpose, all working together, synchronized to produce a single continuous sheet of paper. Although using the same essential parts, paper machines are constructed to individual specifications and vary in design according to the builder. The machine consists of three basic sections: (1) the "wet end," or paper-forming section; (2) the press section, where water is removed through pressing action; and (3) the drying section, where moisture content is reduced and controlled.

## THE WET END

As the stock passes through the Jordan machine to a machine chest, a device known as a "consistency regulator" dilutes it with water to hold it at the desired consistency. From the machine chest the stock is pumped to a regulating box that controls the amount of stock flowing to the paper machine. This regulates the weight of the paper. More water is added to the solid content of the stock, and it passes to the headbox at the wet end of the fourdrinier. An apron of rubberized cloth carries the stock underneath vertical "slices" of solid brass which create a uniform flow of stock over the surface of a woven, endless wire screen belt.

The weave of the screen belt varies according to the type of paper being made. The finer the wire belt used, the higher the grade of the paper. Excess water drains through the mesh. The screen vibrates to disperse the direction of the fibers across as well as along the direction the screen is moving. The direction of the fibers creates the grain of the paper. Rubber straps, the "deckles," rest on the edges of the screen and are moved along on flanged pulleys. The deckles keep the stock from flowing off the sides of the screen, and create an uneven edge to the paper that, when left untrimmed on the finished product, we refer to as "deckle-edged paper."

The screen passes over a series of suction boxes which remove much of the excess water and under a "dandy roll," consisting of a cylindrical frame covered with woven wire or parallel, evenly spaced wires that compress and imprint the top surface of the fibers. The texture of the dandy roll determines whether the paper is "wove" (from the woven wire pattern), or "laid" (from the parallel lined wire) stock. The dandy roll is also used to imprint the watermark in the surface of the paper. After the dandy roll, additional moisture is removed by the remaining suction boxes, and the sheet passes on to the pressing section.

**131** The wet end

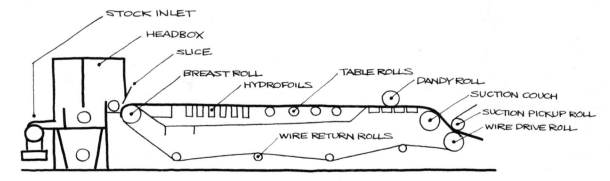

## THE PRESS SECTION

As the paper starts into the pressing section, it still contains about 80 to 85 percent of its moisture content and can support its own weight for only a short distance. At this point, it is picked up by wool felt bands and carried through a series of presses, each consisting of two rollers that eliminate more water and compact and level the paper by removing wire and felt marks from the surface. The last press rollers are made of rubber (top) and metal (lower), and the paper travels through them without the aid of the felt blankets.

## THE DRYING SECTION

The purpose of the drying section is to remove the excess of water that cannot be taken out by the pressing action. The water at this point is about 70 percent of the paper's weight. The dryer consists of steam-heated, cast-iron drums with polished surfaces. They are set in tiers, and the paper web is held in place and guided through them by a continuous strip of cotton/asbestos. The cotton/asbestos band holds the paper firmly in place against the dryers as it moves through the system. In the drying section, roughly 50 percent of the water is eliminated from the paper, or about two pounds of water for every one pound of paper that is produced.

The drying section is usually covered by a hood, and the moisture-laden air produced by the humidifying action of the hot rollers against the wet paper web is drawn off and warm, dry air is pumped in in a continuous action.

**132**   The Press Section

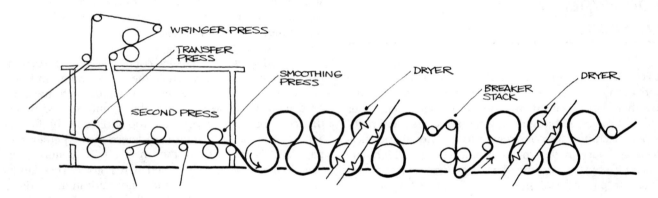

**133**   The Drying Section

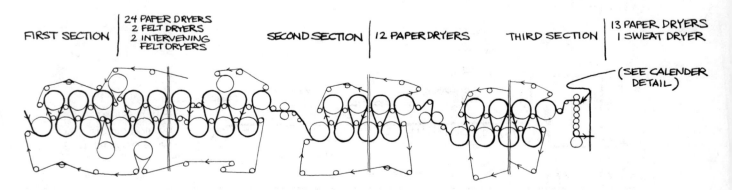

# Paper Finishing

At about 5 percent moisture level, the paper passes to large rolls of cast iron called calenders which are stacked vertically and driven by friction from a larger bottom roll. The paper is fed in at the top of the calender stack and works its way down through each roll where it is then wound into a large roll. A paper machine may have more than one calender roll stack, but the progression through each stack is uniform. The calender action is designed to compact the sheet and give the surface a better finish. From the large roll, called a "mill roll," the paper is rewound and passed through a series of slitter knives which trim the edges and cut the paper into measured widths which are, in turn, wound into smaller rolls. Paper cut and trimmed to specified widths and wound into rolls ready for use is called "roll stock." Another process, similar in nature, uses a revolving drum set with a knife to cut the roll stock into sheet form and stack it in the desired number of sheets.

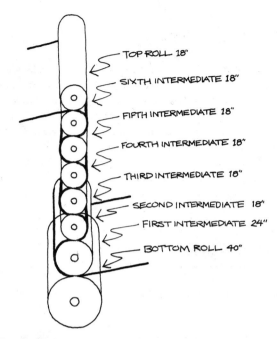

**134**  Typical Calender Stack (Paper feed shown in heavy line)

# Coated Papers

Much of the commercial printing done today is on coated paper. Coated stock reproduces much finer halftone screens than regular stock, with greater color fidelity. Coatings range from dull to high gloss, and a paper may be coated on one or both sides, depending on how it is to be used.

The coating process involves taking a base paper stock and covering it with a mixture of pigments (clay, chalk, zinc oxide, etc.) and adhesives (casein, glue, starch, etc.) applied by rollers, air-brush coaters, and trailing blades. Coatings are applied in two different ways. The earliest method to be developed, called conventional coating (still used today for the best coated stocks) requires transfering the raw stock paper to a special plant where the coating is applied. The second method, called machine coating, is done as a part of the papermaking process itself, at the same speed.

In America, coated papers began appearing about 1824. Early coating was done by hand until a machine was developed about 1852 to coat paper in a continuous web process not unlike that used for paper manufacturing.

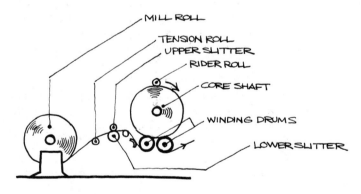

**135**  Two Drum Winder

# *Paper Weight*

Printing papers are identified by their "basis weight." Basis weight is the pound weight of a ream (500 sheets) of a paper cut to the basic size for that particular grade of stock. Basic size varies from stock to stock; for example, book paper is cut 25 inches × 38 inches, newsprint stock, 24 × 36. A ream of book stock paper weighing 70 lbs is referred to as "70 lb book stock." In addition to its basic size, each grade of paper comes in a wide variety of sizes and weights.

# *Paper Grades*

The most common grades or classifications of paper are:

1. Bond stock—Basic size of 12 × 22 and a weight range of 13 to 40 lbs. These are papers most commonly used for business forms and letter stock.
2. Text stock—Basic size of 25 × 38 with a weight range of 50 to 100 lbs. Text stock is an expensive form of book stock. Sometimes deckle-edged and watermarked, it is used for quality book paper. Text is one of the most commonly used paper grades for collateral graphics (booklets, brochures, etc.).
3. Book stock—Basic size of 25 × 38 with a weight range of 30 to 120 lbs. Most commonly used for trade and text books.
4. Offset stock—Basic size of 25 × 38 with a weight range of 40 to 100 lbs. Offset stock is a specially prepared, moisture-resistant paper, similar to book stock, suitable for offset printing technology.
5. Coated stock—Basic size of 25 × 38 with a weight range of 40 to 100 lbs. As mentioned above, coated paper is used for high-quality printing where fine screenwork is desirable.
6. Cover stock—Basic size of 20 × 26 with a weight range of 40 to 100 lbs. As the name implies, cover stocks are heavier varieties of text and coated papers as well as many special finished papers which are utilized as covers for booklets, brochures, annual reports, and all types of graphic design.
7. Newsprint stock—Basic size of 24 × 36 with a weight range of 28 to 35 lbs. 32 lb newsprint is the most commonly used weight.
8. Bristol Board—Basic size of 22½ × 28½ with a weight range of 67 to 160 lbs. Bristol board stocks are used where a stiff, inexpensive paper is desired, most commonly as index cards, post cards, file dividers, and cheaper types of mounting and mat boards.

Other stock grades include rotogravure newsprint, cardboard, parchment tag board, kraft papers, and various art paper grades such as tracing paper, layout bond, vellum, illustration and mat boards, and fine art printing, drawing, and watercolor papers of all types.

# *Paper Finishes*

All paper stock has a degree of smoothness according to how it is finished. It can be used as it is right off the dryers, or it can be calendered and, additionally, supercalendered. The characteristic smoothness of uncalendered, calendered, and supercalendered stocks vary tremendously. Uncoated book paper finishes can be classified in order of increasing smoothness in the following manner:

1. Antique finish—This finishing approximates the rough surface quality of early printing papers. It is run through the machine on long nap felt and is given no additional finishing at the end of the papermaking process. Subcategories of antique finishing are as follows: (a) Eggshell finish—a relatively rough surface resembling the surface of an eggshell produced with special felts. (b) Text finish—smoother than eggshell, text finishes have a large variety of surface treatments and are used extensively for offset lithography. (c) Vellum finish—a fine-grained textured surface reflecting the characteristics of classic vellum made from the skins of animals.
2. Machine finish—Any other finish that is obtainable on the machine without calendering or supercalendering is referred to as machine-finished stock.
3. English finish—English finish is a low-gloss, high-clay-content surface obtained through special calendering in the drying section of the papermaking machinery.

# *Supercalendering*

Supercalendering, as mentioned, is a further process in finishing the surface of a paperstock. The process is accomplished with the same type of vertical roller stack as in regular calendering with the difference that the rolls are alternately steel and cotton or compressed paper. Supercalendering is done for both coated and uncoated papers.

Referred to as "super" or "SC," supercalendered stock is smoother and less bulky and opaque than

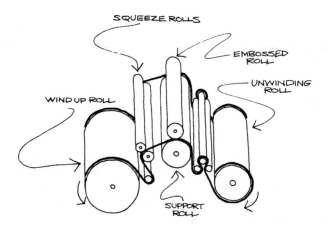

**136** Embossing Machine (Paper feed shown in heavy line)

grain. When wetted, a paper will expand more readily across the grain than along it. Observe sometime a large sheet of paper that has been subjected to a change in humidity, and you will see its tendency to "ruffle" on its two cross-grain sides. Grain direction is an important consideration in the ordering, cutting, and printing of paper. In book papers and collateral design pieces where page format is utilized, paper is cut so that the grain runs parallel to the fold or binding. This insures good lay and flexibility in turning pages. Sheet-fed offset printing requires paper with "long grain" (grain running parallel to the width of the press). This is to reduce the chance of register problems in the printing process itself caused by variations in the stress characteristics of the paperstock.

English-finished paper. It is steam treated and polished by the friction of the steel and cotton or paper rollers through which it tracks. It is commonly used for magazines, books, and booklets where less bulk is desirable.

## *Embossing*

Embossing a paper is producing raised impressions or relief designs and images on the surface of the stock after the paper has been dried. An embossing machine consists of a series of rollers through which the paper is passed, and is similar in principle to the calendering process. One roll is utilized to impress the pattern into the surface of the stock. Common embossing patterns are linen, tweed, and pebble grain.

## *Grain*

All paper made on a machine has grain. Grain refers to the directional orientation of the pulp fibers as they settle on the moving wire screen at the wet end of the papermaking process. The grain flow is along the length of the sheet and with the movement of the screen. Grain affects paper in several ways. Paper folds easily with the grain; against (across) the grain, it has a tendency to crack and roughen. The general tension or stiffness of a paper sheet is greater with the grain. Rolling or flexing a sheet of paper is done much more easily across the

## *Choosing a Paperstock for Use*

Because of the many paper samples available, the designer sometimes finds it difficult to decide which to use. Several factors should be kept in mind when ordering for each job.

Color and brightness in a stock can affect the character of the images being reproduced. Type reads better against a soft white tone, while process color is more accurate on a neutral white stock. A "brilliant" stock (papers treated with artificial brighteners) increase the contrast of printed images and give a crispness that is not otherwise attainable. The opacity of a paper sheet can be a critical factor where printing is done on both sides. Papers with fillers tend to be more opaque. The thickness, or pound weight, of the stock can be a factor here also. The smoothness and gloss of a stock will affect the images. Solid areas of tone or color and halftones appear "rougher" as stock smoothness decreases. A clay coat stock, for example, produces a finely detailed image, and gives a "glossy," expensive look. As mentioned in the chapter on typography, some types reproduce better on one stock than on another (Baskerville being a case in point). Paper/ink relationships will affect images, and ink absorption and diffusion of imagery should be considered by the designer.

Cost is always a factor when considering a paper for use. As mentioned at the beginning of the chapter, paper commonly represents a quarter of the total job cost. It is always wise for the designer to have two or three alternative paper samples at hand of similar type, in case the stock he prefers is not available or proves to be impractical, from a cost standpoint, for the job.

# PRINTING
## *Chapter 15*

The previous chapter devoted considerable space to the various aspects of paper production. This was done principally because designers know less about papermaking than about other processes connected with the design profession. Paper is no less important to design than printing, yet knowledge of printing procedure is much more prevalent among designers and design students, no doubt because designers are directly involved with the process of printing and not with papermaking.

Since the printing process is much more familiar to most design students, we will not devote space here to a lengthy discussion of the mechanical aspects of the many different printing methods. Instead, we will take a slightly different look at printing production, *from the designer's viewpoint,* and discuss those problems and processes most commonly encountered by the professional designer when dealing with print production. Although this is a decidedly different view than is taken by most other texts dealing with aspects of design and graphic arts, it is, nonetheless, a relevant one in light of the emphasis and span of material covered by this volume. At the same time, it is highly recommended that the student find information on printing technology as a reference while reading this chapter. Much excellent reading is available on this subject in your college library.

As a rule, designers do not haunt the corridors of printing establishments. We are far too busy with our own profession to devote the loving attention to detail necessary to become experts in the art of printing. Printing is a very old, terribly complex medium, best left to the specialist. The designer's main obligation is to know how to communicate his or her desires accurately to the printer and to learn the necessary terminology to do that. Recall the model catalogue used as an example earlier in this book. Where it applies, we will continue our discussion of the catalogue and the print production problems faced by its art and production directors. We will discuss printing in nontechnical language that a novice will easily understand, and we will introduce the useful printing terms that are a part of the designer's vocabulary. Of necessity we will, of course, oversimplify this information. Understand this at the beginning ... and, as we have recommended, fill in with independent reading where you feel the need for more technical information.

As a clue to looking for this type of information, consider the following. The art library is generally the last place to look for detailed material on printing. The best bet is to seek out the printing library in the College of Graphic Arts and Technology (if your school has one) or find that section in your main campus library. The best source books on typography (and paper as well) can be found there, too.

# *Lithography*

If you are involved with collateral and corporate design (brochures, catalogues, posters, annual reports, and various other publications), you are likely to be almost totally concerned with lithography production. Over the years, lithography has become the most efficient and usually the cheapest method of printing for these types of materials.

Lithography (or "litho") is the planographic method of reproduction. This means simply that it is the process in which the printing area is flush with the surface of the plate. This is opposite from letterpress printing which contacts the paper from "raised" areas: areas left at the original plate level after the rest of the surface has been etched away to a deeper level. The litho process is based on the proposition that oil (grease) and water do not mix. A visit to the lithography area in the printmaking department of your art school will show you the original lithographic process. There, lithography is practiced in the traditional mode of, literally, drawing on stone.

Watching a fine art lithographer work, you would see the following process for creating a printable image on the lithostone. The artist either draws the image directly on the stone with a litho crayon or produces a drawing on paper he or she can transfer to the stone. The stone is treated chemically, fixing the greasy properties of the drawn line to the stone. Water is then applied to the stone and it is inked, the ink sticking only to the greasy image areas, and the stone is ready to print the image on paper.

In modern commercial printing, thin zinc and aluminum sheets, which can be curved to fit high-speed rotary presses, now take the imagery once applied to stone. The most commonly used method of lithographic printing is the offset process. This requires transferring the image from the printing plate onto an intermediate surface (a blanket cylinder) before applying it to paper. This "offsetting" of the image to a second surface allows for greater image control and faster production than in the older direct (plate to paper) transfer process.

Our catalogue was produced by the offset lithographic method. In our earlier use of the catalogue example, we mentioned that the job was printed on a "smaller proof press" because of the limited quantity being run. "Small" is a relative term, however. This "smaller" proof press is an immense and complex mechanism requiring auxiliary machinery and considerable manpower to operate.

In direct printing from plates to paper, the plate image is "backwards" so as to produce a "right reading" print. In offset lithography the plates themselves are "right reading," thereby transferring a "backwards" image to the intermediate blanket which, in turn, lays it "right reading" on the paper. If we were to look at plates from our job, we would see a right reading image of our catalogue on a thin metal sheet. There would be four of these sheets, one for each of the process color cylinders: yellow, magenta, and cyan, and black. The printing plates (the thin sheets of metal) are wrapped around cylinders on the press. Each process color cylinder sits next to dampening and inking rollers. The blanket cylinder (the intermediate receiving surface) sits next to the plate cylinder. The paper is guided through the press by the impression and sheet transfer cylinders, the former bringing the paper into contact with the blanket cylinder.

All offset production presses have stations at which the above procedures are performed. If it is a two-color press, it takes two stations. Process color presses have a minimum of four stations. Today, it is becoming increasingly common to see presses with five and even six stations ... presses that will facilitate the run of a "private" color (such as mentioned in our section on producing the job) and/or a varnish station, a procedure often used to seal the printed surface from fingermarking and scuffing when touched as well as to heighten the gloss effect of the printing.

## APPROVING THE OFFSET JOB "ON PRESS"

When designers go "on press," they do not usually come into direct contact with the production press or working crew in the pressroom, unless the proofing table is adjacent to the press itself. In many modern printing plants, after the "cook's tour" of the facilities has been made, viewing the work coming off the press for approval is done in a viewing room or booth. In this area are balanced lights to standardized conditions used throughout the printing industry for judging printing color effects. These controlled conditions allow for accurate judgment of the process mix, and this is where decisions are made concerning whether to "hit the red harder" or "back off on the cyan," and so on, to achieve the desired results.

In the viewing room at the printer efforts were made by the printer and the art and production directors to stabilize the blue background of our catalogue as it printed from spread to spread. This was no small task and required considerable fine "tuning" the press at each of its stations until the right mix of process inks flowed uniformly over all the background area.

## PROOFING

Proofing is generally the same for most printing processes. Before the art director even goes "on press," he or she sees what the job looks like through a facsimile printing. The facsimile printing is part of proofing the job. Done essentially for the art director and other design people, the rule with facsimiles is "what you see is what you get." And unless corrections are indicated on the facsimile, that is generally the case.

There are four commonly used methods of proofing for review. Most experienced art directors are very familiar with all four. Two of the methods are usually used for process work. The other two are less expensive means of proofing for nonprocess runs such as two-color design.

The most expensive but most accurate (in terms of mimicking the final printed product) is the progressive method. Usually referred to as "progs," paper progressives are actually printings of the image in each process color by itself, and in an additional progression from yellow to yellow and magenta in combination, to yellow and magenta and cyan, and finally to a complete mix including black for the full four-color effect. The paper used is usually the same stock that will be used for the actual printing. Stapled together, these progs are a systematic analysis of the process mix, and by looking at them carefully the art director and printer can determine what any problems are and note changes accordingly.

Another, more common method of producing a facsimile is a single-image proof that approximates the final effect of the printed piece. This method uses each film separation (the film for each color plate) to develop and lay down a process hue, one on top of another, just as in the printing process itself. There are two types of single-image proofs. The "transfer key" employs transparent film (the same you might use in the color-key process to formulate tight comprehensives) in a subtractive method of process image building. If you will remember from Chapter 2, on the comprehensive, we mentioned "a process similar to silk-screening" that used layers of transfer material to achieve a finished look for package design comprehensives. This is very nearly the same method used by the printer to formulate the production proof. The drawback to this method is that special effects in color (such as a fifth "private" hue) cannot be approximated because one is limited to the specific type of color-key films that are available. Suppose a fifth silver hue is wanted; since there is no

silver color-key film, the method is inadequate to produce the effect of the final printing.

A variation of single-image proofing eliminates this problem by using powdered dyes instead of color films to achieve the result. This method is an additive process. Simply stated, instead of developing a color-key image from each film separation, a very thin layer of transparent film is applied to a high-quality paperstock. The layer of film is tacky in the image area and nonadhesive over the rest of the surface. The powdered color is then dusted over the surface of the film and it adheres in varying proportion to the tacky area (which, of course, duplicates the density of the film separation for that particular process hue). Each of the process hues, in turn, is applied in the same manner: a film layer is dusted with powdered color to the density levels of the film separation from which the tacky surface is generated, and then covered with the next film layer, when the process is repeated for the next hue. The powdered color is transparent and gives the same effects as the process inks used in the final printing. After the last layer has been dusted with color, a final covering of film is applied to protect the surface from damage. The tacky surface of the film layers can grip and hold any powdered color that can be formulated, allowing for the addition of "private" custom color effects. Our catalogue was proofed utilizing this method.

The third method of color proofing is the color-key method. As stated earlier, it is a simpler, more economical method usually reserved for nonprocess production. This method is only slightly more complicated (because of the use of screen effects) then producing color-key cells for comprehensive development. Cells are laid over each other, one for each hue used in the production of the design image. This approximates, in film, the general distribution of color from plate to plate, but it does not give an accurate color identification. The skilled art director can detect any deviations from the original keyline by observing the films individually as well as together in their combined relationships. This process is used to proof process work, but it is becoming less popular because of the film's inherent inability to accurately reflect the final process paper image.

The last, simplest and most economical method of proofing, used mostly for one- or two-color jobs) is the blue line, or silver print. In this procedure, the art director receives a paper print in variations of blue (or silver) that approximate ink laydowns (solid prints, screen, and combination screen variations) as they will actually occur in the final production run. No attempt is made to reproduce a color effect. The densities of blue or silver represent hues. Critical evaluations are made concerning screen percentages and fits, and general layout relationships are checked against the keyline for errors.

## "SHEET-FED" VERSUS "WEB"

A final word on the lithographic process: the two most commonly used litho systems are the sheet-fed and web methods. The sheet-fed method, as its name implies, works from stacked sheets of cut paper, drawing them into the press one at a time to be delivered through the inking process. Considerably slower than the web process, sheet-fed lithography lends itself to the printing of general collateral materials: catalogues, mailers, posters (except those printed by direct lithography), packaging, annual reports, and other items where quality is an important factor in the image development.

The web offset method uses paper that is fed into the press from giant reels. This method allows for extremely fast printing where efficiency and time are more critical factors than quality. The continuous paper feed is cut down after the printing has taken place at the other end of the press. Web offset is used in the production of newspapers, inserts, books, and magazines, where long runs are required. Shorter runs are printed on coldset presses, longer runs on heatset presses, in which the application of heat to the inked surface speeds up the drying process.

# Letterpress

The letterpress, the original method of printing from moveable type, was first employed in Germany over five hundred years ago. Letterpress printing produces an extremely good image when used correctly, and it is still the only method where the actual type meets the surface of the paper. A relief method of printing, cast metal type or plates on which the printing surface is raised from the background area—cut or etched away by chemicals—are inked by rollers, and the plate then prints the image. Although expensive compared to offset lithography, the letterpress is still economical for original jobs in which last-minute changes must be made. There are three types of presses in letterpress printing: (1) the platen press, (2) the flatbed cylinder press, and (3) the rotary press. The first two reproduce from flat printing plates; the third prints from a cylinder of curved plates. Many newspapers are printed from rotary letterpress plates, when the tremendous speeds o. web offset are not required. The true beauty of typographic form can still be best observed from the crispness of the letterpress process, and the character of black and white halftones is undeniably improved. One need only look at older books or illustrations produced by letterpress to appreciate the difference.

Letterpress printing is also accomplished by sheet and web-fed presses. The platen and flatbed cylinder presses print from sheets and are used for short jobs such as letterheads and business cards, announcements, and small brochures. Larger variations of these presses will accommodate general printing and even some packaging, although letterpress is not a common medium for package printing. Cylinder letterpress printing of magazines and newspapers employs the web (rollstock) method. Except in magazine and newspaper reproduction, letterpress is a small production process compared with the tremendous size and complexity of lithographic machinery. Letterpress accounts for a much smaller share of general printing, and the designer will come into contact with it infrequently unless involved in publication design.

# Gravure

Gravure is the recessed or intaglio printing process. If we had needed to run upwards of a million copies of our catalogue, gravure would have been the method used, both from the cost and quality standpoints. For exceptionally long runs which require consistency of ink application and richness of surface, gravure is the cheapest of all printing methods, even though the process of preparing gravure cylinders is the most expensive of all major printing mediums.

Designers heavily involved in packaging design are generally familiar with gravure printing. Many labels, bags, and even boxes are printed by gravure presses. The cylinders are made of metal heavily coated in copper and contain thousands of recessed areas corresponding to the value distribution of the image for the process hue they are transferring to the paper— larger, deeper recesses for heavier ink coverage, smaller, shallower recesses for lighter coverage. Ink fills these recesses as the cylinder rotates through an ink tray. Excess ink is wiped away from the cylinder by a flexible steel knife edge called a "doctor blade." A companion impression cylinder presses the passing paper to the freshly wiped copper, and the ink is deposited to the paper as the plate cylinder turns. As in other rotary printing systems, there is a different color station on the press for each process hue.

Every image in gravure printing is screened because the recessed holes need to contain the ink. There are no solid print areas. Since gravure screens usually contain 150 lines per inch, it is very difficult to detect such screens with the naked eye. And because the ink has a tendency to spread slightly after laydown, the effect of the gravure-screened color is much the same as the solid-print color of other processes. If, however, one were to put a magnifying glass to a type character printed in gravure, the sawtooth edge of the dot process would be noticeable. This is a characteristic of gravure printing.

The speed of a gravure press is very slow in comparison with offset lithography, and the mechanical process of gravure is considerably less involved. Designers who work exclusively in collateral materials seldom come into contact with the gravure process unless their creations are run in the Sunday supplements, which are often gravure printings, or they are creating ads that will be run in magazine publications that are printed in gravure. Decorative patterning of wallpaper, plywood, and Formica laminates are usually run gravure. Although there are no particularly complicated circumstances that must be designed to when using the gravure process, because of the necessary breakup of areas into dot patterns, it is wise to stay away from extremely small and delicate type which may tend to fracture in the printing process.

## Screen Printing

In three-dimensional display and limited-run poster and display banner work, screen printing is often the most effective and inexpensive reproduction method. It is widely used to print on three-dimensional objects such as glass bottles and plastic containers. Product graphics and signage for consumer goods often use screen printing because it is adaptable to curved as well as flat surfaces.

The cost advantage lies in the "make-ready" (preparation) time. The screens used to print are much easier and cheaper to fabricate than in other production processes. Everyone involved with the arts is somewhat familiar with what is traditionally known as "the silkscreen" process. Although commercial screening is not done with silk, the process is very similar. The majority of commercial work is done with photomechanical screen processing which allows for effects that cannot be achieved by traditional handcutting methods.

Screen printing inks are opaque and color blending cannot be achieved by overprinting. A new screen must be cut for each hue variation in a design. Exactly because of the opacity of the pigment, rich and brilliant color effects are possible that are difficult to accomplish in other mediums.

For designers, one disadvantage of the medium is the lack of a really effective way to proof screen printing short of doing the actual printing itself. Because of this, the art director must make doubly certain that the printer understands the artwork completely before the process of developing the screens begins.

## Flexography

Many designers will never have to be concerned with flexography, but in packaging design flexography is often the only viable medium for reproduction. Flexography is the process for the high-speed printing of paper bags, poly bags and film, foil, and similar materials. Chances are, when you pick up a loaf of bread, a poly bag of sugar, a bag of kitty litter, a roll of toilet tissue or paper towels, or a transparent package of spaghetti in the supermarket, you are looking at a flexographic-printed graphic design.

Flexographic printing is similar to letterpress in that it is printing from a raised surface. The difference is that it is printing from a rubber block rather than from a metal or plastic plate. It also utilizes thin liquid inks that dry very quickly.

Contrary to other printing mediums where there are relatively few restrictions placed on the designer in terms of what can and cannot be done, flexography has very specific requirements if successful printing is to be performed. It is difficult in the flexographic process to lay down large areas of solid ink that are to be accompanied by delicate or finely detailed designs. The pressure exerted on the rubber plate to hold the solid area would distort small typography or intricate linework. It is difficult as well to hold a register (the printer's term for keeping proper alignments between plates upon the press during a printing run) in flexography, and the designer must allow for a certain amount of shrinkage at the platemaking stage. Also, when the plates are mounted on the cylinders for printing, stretching will occur (usually in one direction) and a fractional amount of distortion will be present. Thin serifs have a tendency to disappear from distortion of typography, and there is also a fill-in factor when dealing with small point sizes. It is generally considered unsafe to use type any smaller than 6 point, and for situations where type is coming out of a dark ground it is best to stay away from light faces completely. Because of the thinness of the ink, most color must be "backed up" (underlaid) with white when working with transparent films (such as a bread wrap) to achieve any kind of richness and opacity. This also can create register problems when working with involved illustrations or typographic designs.

Even with all these pitfalls, it is possible to create interesting design images in the flexographic medium if the proper care is given to the preparation of the art the printer will use. Also, many of these complications can be avoided by working closely with an experienced "flexo" printer who really knows the process.

So far we have looked at major areas of printing most designers will experience. There are, however, other printing methods, for example: thermography, raised printing that gives an embossed or engraved look (and is cheaper than either); hot stamping, such as the letters and designs on the covers of books; electrostatic printing, where the plate never touches the surface of the material being printed; and more. These are printing methods usually reserved for special effects and are not mainstream procedures. Extremely interesting in themselves, they are not a concern for us here and are explained in detail in publications dealing with printing technology.

The designer's major skill in printing should be his or her ability to anticipate possible problems in print production *in advance,* and to eliminate those problems by the proper supervision of all people associated with the production of the job. This can be a minor miracle when it succeeds—and is the sure sign of a competent art director.

# THE PORTFOLIO
## Chapter 16

You will be getting—or have already gotten—enough opinions on the design, makeup, and presentation of your portfolio to make your head spin. There are as many variations on proper portfolio presentation as there are designers with ideas about them. Some believe a portfolio will make or break a job interview; others discount portfolio work completely as a regimented fabrication that tells nothing about an individual's capacity to function comfortably and creatively with either ideas or people.

The portfolio presentation can be as elaborate or as casual as you like, depending upon what type of person you are, but that portfolio had better do one thing very, very well ... *it had better present your personal strengths, your pluses, in as effective a manner as is humanly possible*. It is good here to reemphasize the importance of the word *personal*. All too often, student portfolios carry the stamp of the institution out of which the person came. No matter how good that institution is, this can be a disastrous consequence if *the style of the institution takes precedence over the character of the individual who is seeking the job*.

If an art director who is interviewing you can look at your portfolio and tell immediately—by the constant repetition of the same projects, or the repeated regimentation of comping procedures, or the constant usage of one or two type styles, or by the same predictable solution to every design problem—that you are a graduate of *X* university or school of design, your individuality is in jeopardy! Design firms are looking to hire *good people from good institutions* and not simply *people from good institutions* ... that may sound like splitting hairs, but there *is* a great difference. Ask any art director or designer who has seen a lot of designers looking for work. The portfolio that will stand out is the one that shows individuality as well as good design.

When the influence of a design department's philosophy is too evident in a portfolio, it is difficult to estimate the graduate's ability to reach an independent solution to a given problem. This is especially true when a designer's work is "buttoned up" in a rigid presentation *style* ... and the emphasis here is on the word *style*. Good, clear, attractive presentation is one thing, but uniform stylization of presentation is another. As cynical as it may sound to you, even the best professionals develop a set attitude when having to contend with this frequent phenomenon. This can work against you in more ways than one. The prospective employer may resent looking at "another portfolio from school *X* just like the last one." On the other hand, that employer may highly respect your particular school and its design practices and hire you on the strength of the *school's* reputation and its influence on your work, without delving too deeply into your own personal capabilities; you win the job briefly, but then get fired later when you don't live up to the image of your portfolio.

It is crucial that your portfolio reflect *you*. Often it is worthwhile to develop outside projects above and beyond what you do for your portfolio class, projects that may be closely aligned with the work done by the type of firm you wish employment with. For example, if you want an assistant art directorship with a large advertising agency, it may be good to sit down and sketch a concept storyboard that relates specifically to the clientele they service. How do you do this? Call up a few of the agencies you are interested in, talk to the art or creative directors, make appointments to see them and tell them what you have in mind, and ask them to recommend an account you can "show your stuff" on.

The real key to individuality in portfolio presentation is not tight presentation techniques, unless you have a format so blindingly original that it stands alone (and then you run the risk of the presentation style overshadowing the work itself). *The key lies in making effective use of concept roughs to show off your initial thinking and idea development.* Concept roughs—initial idea sketches, color variables, alternative solutions and notes on why you chose the direction you did, input from others—all these are important contributors to the final image you want everyone to appreciate. Ideally, your portfolio should say it all for you, right up front, so the interviewer will never have to ask you "why you did this," or "what was your thinking behind this." Words in an interview should be used to reveal your personality and never wasted on having to explain or justify your work. Your drawing style is a fairly individual skill. It should show your ability to get an idea across quickly—a very important asset. One question this author always hates to ask job-seekers is "Can you draw?" That question implies that the interviewer has not seen enough rough thinking to feel comfortable

with your abilities . . . comfortable enough to *hire* you if there is a job! Designers need people with adequate drawing skills, draw/think ability, and talented hands for rough comping techniques. A portfolio loaded with skillful, pertinent, and descriptive roughs tells potential employers right away if you are the person they need or if they will have to look further. Having a handsome presentation case and presenting your samples in some kind of uniform manner is important . . . but not as important as your ability to articulate, verbally and visually, the true scope of your individual talents.

Most probably instructors in your major will be delighted at your request to work up some individualized assignments, and you should not balk at the extra time it certainly will take. Those extra assignments may very well make the difference.

Judicious editing of portfolio material is also important. First, it is essential that you have enough to edit from! Second, it is important to get together the widest possible *range* of materials available for presentation (without sacrificing quality). Lastly, (once again!) support each piece of work in your portfolio with as much conceptual material as is necessary to reveal the extent of the assignment and your own artistic abilities. This is the surest way to set yourself apart from other applicants for the same position.

After you are working and developing as a designer, you will eagerly replace the schoolwork in your portfolio with printed samples of jobs you have done until you have a thoroughly professional sample case. It is important to *keep doing this* at periodic intervals throughout your entire design career. Nothing is sadder (or more suspicious) than a portfolio filled with obviously old work—the designer is clearly resting on the laurels of past work. No sample is sacred to a portfolio unless it is a hallmark design study, so obviously well-known that you will benefit from its biography. If you are a designer who has been around a while, it is helpful to show a few of your best older samples simply to give someone a perspective on your career; but the majority of the work should still be contemporary.

For the young designer emerging from school in search of his or her first professional job, there is one other thing: take the time and spend the money (perhaps a considerable expense from your standpoint) to design yourself a business card. It gives you an identity separate from the standard résumé left by every design applicant and is a much more professional way to present yourself to an employer.

# A BEGINNING . . .
## Chapter 17

So here you are, portfolio in hand, ready to go out and beat down the doors of the design world, land the job of your dreams, and live happily and productively afterwards creating award-winning designs for exciting and creative clients! Not an impossible dream . . . but how do you present yourself, where do you start looking to fulfill the dream, and who do you see?

Your talents may be there, your aspirations and your pluck may be nailed down tight, but what sense have you of what door to knock on and who to spread your "life's work" in front of? Some lucky students go to those very few institutions that offer an intern program, giving them the opportunity to gain valuable working knowledge in advance of graduation; others attend schools with some kind of placement organization that will, at the very least, get them in the door of a prospective employer. However, most of you who will be pounding the streets this spring will be state university graduates; the responsibility for finding employment rests entirely upon your own shoulders.

Designers tend to market themselves and their talents very poorly, especially as compared to other equally trained individuals in other fields. This fact is proven by the frequency with which designers change jobs and by the relative difficulty designers experience in advancing within any given organization. What specific ways can job seekers (other than showing a portfolio) present themselves to prospective employers that will increase the chances of getting that coveted, seemingly ideal position, after graduation?

## The Importance of a Design "Personality"

It is surely not news to you that personality plays a critical part in a job interview. What you may not understand is the subtlety of such situations. We have continually stressed the importance of a well-balanced education for the designer, and one of the payoffs of such an education is in competitive job-seeking. At the outset, we said that design requires individuals who are in touch with the contemporary world around them, individuals that have the capacity for interpretation based on education and experience and the ability for developing a sense of perspective on issues and ideas. The good design jobs and workplaces this author has been a part of have always exhibited an intellectually "charged" atmosphere. We are not a profession of dullards! Exhibiting a "whiz-kid" personality to a prospective employer is neither necessary nor recommended, but being able to use the English language well and discuss issues and ideas intelligently in an articulate fashion will definitely help to strengthen your presentation!

Well-developed interests are as important an ingredient of the design personality as is intellectual competence. This can work for you in other subtle ways. Many employers are keenly interested in their designers' outside interests and activities, and most designers seem to exhibit passionate devotion to all kinds of interesting and oddball avocations. As an example, the author knows a designer who is an intense and lorewise fisherman. He is lucky enough to work for a firm that has a fishing-gear manufacturer for an account. His firm considers him an invaluable asset to the running of the account because of his extensive knowledge of the sport and his ability to talk to the clients on *their* terms. The loving care he takes in the design and development of materials for the account is obvious to everyone involved, including the clients. Needless to say, the account would be very disturbed to lose his expertise and sense of perspective on this account.

Many times designers will become involved with an account, and an intense interest in that area or activity will develop out of their intellectual curiosity. Interplay between professional and recreational activities is quite common among designers.

The prospective employer understands the kind of personality that is *needed* to function well within his or her organization. The employer is looking, of course, for *potential* as well as immediate talent, and the way that potential is often gauged is by judging *your response to inquiry*.

Good response is essential, but it is no guarantee in the advancement of your case. You may respond enthusiastically and truthfully to a situation and still fall short of triggering a positive response in the interviewer. This is not your fault. The fact that the interviewer is looking for different responses to fit a specific need is totally beyond your control. Many designers have said many times, "I *know* my samples are good . . . *better* than others! Why didn't I get the job?" Just because you are a good, perhaps even a potentially great, designer does not mean others will see it. Even if they do, someone else may be preferred because of their *seeming* ability to mesh with other aspects of a job better than you. All you can hope to do is be as bright, articulate, and enthusiastic as you are capable of at the time and hope that the job you want *wants* someone like you!

The personality of the individual is so impor-

tant that the "superior" portfolio does not always win the day. In a critical evaluation of prospective employees, a design firm may choose to go for the potential they see, both personally *and* graphically, rather than take the immediately "superior" talent. This may sound counterproductive, but as we have mentioned before, some organizations prefer to take "raw" material and "bring it along" to their way of working. This certainly applies in the case of design "style." *You should not feel inferior because your work does not exhibit polish in the same manner as others'.* Remember, it is substance that counts.

Trying hard for a job is admirable up to a point, but beyond that point it can be harmful to both the design firm and you. It is virtually guaranteed that if that position you *really* want is in a design firm where the management philosophy is hard-charging, sophisticated, marketing-oriented, business-opportunity-minded—that fosters those kinds of aggressive qualities in their employees—and you are a soft-spoken, understated, work-at-your-own-pace person, you (no matter what your portfolio looks like) will not get the job! If you try to pass yourself off as something other than what you are, both you and the firm that makes the mistake of hiring you are going to be the poorer for it.

Take time and analyze the position you are after. Ask yourself what it is you want about it. If it is: (1) "a job," (2) the status of the job, (3) the money potential, (4) the seeming sophistication of the work, or (5) one, two, or all of the above, these are all the wrong reasons! The fact that you may not be right personally or potentially for the job will probably never enter your head unless you are honest with yourself and take the time to think it out. It is incredibly important to understand upfront that everything isn't right for you and you are not right for everything and that opportunism is a difficult diet to thrive on.

## *Finding Your Niche*

What do you want to do? Teach? Work in an advertising agency? For a large corporation? Do you want to make films? Do you want to be a packaging designer, specialize in the design of point-of-purchase materials and display, design magazine formats? Only you can know what you really want to do. But again, what you want and what you "think" you want can sometimes be hard to tell apart. Perhaps you are fooled by the impressive surface of certain organizations or people already? Don't kid yourself about glamourous occupations—this point cannot be stressed too much. In this profession *especially,* the glamour is in the eye of the observer and not in the eye of the involved worker! It may sound glamourous to work on big-name accounts critical to a firm's business interests. In truth, the related pressures can be killing unless your personality is up to it. Working for that well-known firm or individual can demoralize you very fast when you realize that everything you do will (out of business necessity) be sublimated to fit the public personality of that firm. You think traveling to service key accounts sounds important and glamourous? Try living out of a suitcase the majority of the time and you will change your opinion unless your lifestyle can accommodate such a schedule.

Before you even get to the point of analyzing a prospective position, you must ask yourself "Where do my real talents lie?" "What do I know *now* I do best?" Even given the fact that your talents and interests may change, it is important to approach the professional job market utilizing your best assets. If you approach it from this standpoint, you will *automatically* zero in on that part of it that is at least *applicable* to you.

The question arises, "Shouldn't I just concentrate on *getting* that first experience under my belt, no matter what area or personality environment it is in?" Certainly experience is an aid to you in every way, but the school of thought that says "get that *first* job . . . any job!" is no longer widely held, and indeed, as we have pointed out, that attitude has proven over the past to be one of the frustrations that contributes to the designer's career dilemma. Spending a little time "spinning your wheels" looking for something fresh out of college (as agonizing as it may be) is easier than marking time in an unhappy situation later, when your financial requirements are higher and your professional commitments more rigid.

In one very important sense, your *lack* of experience is a plus factor. A prospective employer can make less of a commitment to you as a beginner than as an established professional. He or she may be more willing, given the "rightness" of other factors, to give you a try; you don't expect the more permanent commitment the experienced professional would be seeking. While this sounds unfair, it is much *more* unfair from the employer's standpoint to take on a heavy responsibility for someone's life support (financial and otherwise) only to lose need for that person later on down the line. In other words, if hiring a beginner doesn't work out, there's less trauma for everyone. This consideration may give you an edge over a more experienced person if the employer is willing to accept your lesser experience. Many establishments have long-standing commitments to hiring young people; they give "good starts" to fledgling careers, and you should concentrate some of your efforts on seeking situations in your area of expertise that hold to such philosophies.

# Finding the Right Person to Talk to

Going to see your "uncle Bernie, the comptroller" may lend you a sympathetic ear in your quest for employment, but unless "uncle Bernie" has a tap on creative situations around town, you are wasting your time. To begin with, you may be in the *wrong* town.

There are design jobs around everywhere, from Oshkosh to the "Big Apple," but most *are* in certain areas, and those are the large metropolitan ones. Finding situations to your liking will be easier in New York, Chicago, and Los Angeles than in Pittsburgh, Dallas, and Seattle—and easier in Pittsburgh, Dallas, and Seattle than in Dayton, Lincoln, or Boise. Gravitate toward the larger metropolitan centers!

When you get to town, open up the Yellow Pages to the classification you are looking for and start calling. If you are looking for a job in one of the larger advertising agencies, contact the Director of Creative Employment (or equivalent title) unless you have been given specific names of creatives to approach. Large agencies, like companies, usually coordinate their hiring activities through personnel departments. The Director of Creative Placement will know exactly which creative groups within the agency are looking for talent. If you prefer to gain employment at one of the "boutique" shops (the smaller fashionable agencies), find out the name of the Executive Creative Director or Executive Art Director and make an appointment to see one (or both) of them.

If you are contacting design firms, ask to speak to the Design Director or one of the principals (owners). Because of their relatively small size, no one at a lesser level will have the authority to hire, and while you may have to interview with others within an organization, it is best to start at the top and then work your way down rather than the opposite. If there are names on the door, ask to speak to one of those "names." Even if that person is not a creative, it is almost certain that he or she will have some input in hiring and will probably direct you to the proper person if the "name" does not wish to see you personally.

In art studios of moderate to large size, seek out the Studio Director (or equivalent title). Like the personnel director of the large agency, he or she will know if there is a situation you might be qualified for. Smaller studios should be treated like design firms: go to the top whenever possible.

Major corporations usually departmentalize their creative services, and while you will ultimately have to go through a personnel department, the heads of departments you wish to be involved in are the first people you should contact, even if they send you along to someone else. Titles to look for at the corporate level are: Director of Creative Services, Marketing and/or Advertising Director, Director of Corporate Communications, Design Director, Corporate Art Director, Sales Promotion Director, Manager of Graphic Services, and in some cases even Art Director, depending on the company's area of design involvement.

By contacting the right people, you will find that even if they do not need your services, you will be passed along to others within their professional realm who might have a job opening. Once you start traveling through the "pass along" system, you will better understand the makeup of the professional group with whom you are seeking to associate. You will also come to understand the truth of that classic cliché, "it's a small world, isn't it!"

## The Professional Placement Specialist

If you can, you should try to find a position on your own or with the help of the "grapevine." If you are having no luck, however, it makes excellent sense to contact a professional placement specialist. Actually, you should do this in *any* event, because you never know when they might contact *you* with an interesting position!

By professional placement specialists we do not mean the standard employment agency. Unfortunately, most employment agencies, career management specialists, and so on, both large and small, do not handle creative art people and have little or no idea what to do with them if they do. Surprisingly, there are only a few placement firms of national scope that specialize in design people. This is both good and bad. It is good because between them they have established a large network of contacts in places that can be virtually inaccessible to you. Being few and small, they establish contacts on a personal level and usually sustain those contacts for future opportunities that are sure to arise. It is bad because everyone is funneled through these agencies and the competition for jobs can be fierce. It is also easy to become overexposed through such firms. This means that your résumé and portfolio may be sent around too often to too many people, and you become tagged as a constant "looker."

It is easy enough to find a professional placement specialist because they continually advertise in professional journals such as *Industrial Design* magazine. Registering with any of these long-standing firms

is advised for those of you needing aid in seeking design positions outside your current location—that is, places you might find too expensive to stay in for a sustained job-search period.

## Teaching Design

For those of you interested in teaching design, many opportunities are available for people with an undergraduate degree in design and professional work experience or with a graduate degree in design. Although the majority of positions available at institutions of higher learning require an M.F.A. in design or a related area, some positions can be applied for with just an undergraduate degree, work experience, and the intention of completing the graduate degree within a limited time period. A great many part-time positions are also available to professionals currently working in the field. The best sources for these and regular full-time faculty positions are through the professional placement agencies listed above and through a newspaper for the professional educator. For subscription information, write to:

THE CHRONICLE OF HIGHER EDUCATION
1333 New Hampshire Ave. N.W.,
Washington, D.C.        20036

It is recommended that most individuals seeking to teach design at the university level get at least three or four years experience in professional design before entering the education field.

## Starting Your Own Design Business

For those who wish to start your own design business, understand this: it is easy to *start,* but exceedingly difficult to *sustain,* such an effort. Talent is only one of many factors necessary to do this. Once again, it is advisable to get at least four or five years intensive experience under your belt before attempting such a herculean task! Contacts are the key to success in the design business. Contacts carefully developed from previous work experiences, from successful past associations with clients, and from recommendations because of the quality and effectiveness of your professional work. Luck helps . . .

8266 100

PRENTICE HALL, INC., Englewood Cliffs, New Jersey 07632

ISBN 0-13-363226-1